JOURNEY THROUGH
THE HOLY LAND

Betty Hartman Wolf

JOURNEY THROUGH
THE HOLY LAND

DOUBLEDAY & COMPANY, INC.
GARDEN CITY, NEW YORK 1967

Maps by Stephen Kraft

Library of Congress Catalog Card Number 65-19891
Copyright © 1967 by Betty Hartman Wolf
All Rights Reserved
Printed in the United States of America
First Edition

Preface

The Holy Land is decidedly different. It is a small land mysteriously selected to assume a gigantic role in providing an atmosphere wherein man matured in spiritual concepts. This land is so haunted by prophets, peasants, and kings that as the twentieth-century visitor wanders its hills inspecting its treasury of ancient civilizations, he senses that he intrudes upon the past and that the past is yearning to communicate with him. He senses further that if he could but peek over his shoulder quickly enough, he would see the ghosts who silently, sympathetically, but passively watch his efforts to unscramble puzzling aspects of history. While such ghosts are elusive, the illusion that the visitor has been able to step back into time is heightened by very real persons who live in the Holy Land and who in dress and daily customs could be specters—mirrors of the past.

Why have two great religions—Judaism and Christianity—germinated here? Why has a third—Islam—born in a neighboring land of similar climatic conditions flourished here? Those two questions pose conundrums that confound logic. But a third question may be more pertinent to the immediate needs of a potential Holy Land pilgrim. Can a man of the twentieth century gain deeper insights into religion by returning to the scene of such religious drama? The answer to that question, I believe, is yes.

Far more simple to answer are the many questions Americans habitually ask. What it is like to spend Christmas in Bethlehem, Easter in Jerusalem? Have the walls of Jericho ever been found? How authentic are the Christian shrines? Did a year in the Holy Land bolster or shake your faith? What are the people like in the Holy Land? Are there still desert tribes? How do they live? Is it safe to travel through the Holy Land on your own?

My husband and I had an unusual opportunity to become familiar with this ancient and fabulous country. We were able to give an entire year to the study and enjoyment of the Holy Land. My husband is a biblical scholar, an ordained minister and professor of Old Testament and archaeology. He had many years ago been given a scholarship for a year's study in Jerusalem. Later when he was given a sabbatical year, he chose to spend a second year at the American School for Oriental Research in Jerusalem, Jordan. The school is a residence maintained by many universities and seminaries for scholars who do field work in archaeology. The project that my husband undertook was a translation into English of the *Onomasticon* of Eusebius.

Eusebius (c. 260–c. 340) was one of the first church fathers to attempt to identify biblical sites. It was my husband's intention to check this old fourth-century "guidebook" against the evidence found by archaeologists on as many of the sites as possible. This assignment kept us quite busy scouring the landscape, reading reference books, and making notations in a card file for at least three hundred ancient sites. In company with the other scholars who stayed in Jerusalem for the full year and with many others who visited for periods of time, we toured the entire country. The tour was the more valuable because the scholars voluntarily rotated assignments to gather information for on-the-site lectures.

While my husband's project was most intriguing and educational, it is far beyond the scope and interest of the average person who wants to know more about the Holy Land. Consequently, he started compiling an archaeological guidebook for the Holy Land. My feeling was that in addition to so much technical information, the reader of a guidebook would enjoy knowing what the Holy Land was really like—he should not neglect to give to the reader the marvelous local flavor of the land. Jordan is fascinating—not only because of its religious history, but because of its Eastern culture, its exotic foods, its Muslim traditions.

My husband challenged me to sit at the typewriter and write

down samples of what I had in mind. I did. These samples were sent to an editor at Doubleday who encouraged me to continue. The result was this book—a project I had not even remotely considered undertaking!

It is hoped that this book will be enjoyed by the person unable to make a pilgrimage to Jerusalem as well as by the person about to make the trip and desiring an introduction to the Holy Land. In addition, it is hoped that the tourist who has visited the Holy Land will find in the book pleasure in shared experiences. If the tourist has made the usual three-day tour of the Holy Land, he may find this book helpful in reacquainting him with facts that have slipped his memory and in enabling him to gain better insight into the significance of the religious shrines so long preserved.

The kingdom of Jordan incorporates what was formerly Transjordan (to the east of the river Jordan) and part of what was formerly Palestine (to the west of the river). The country is bounded on the north by Syria, on the northeast by Iraq, on the east and south by Saudi Arabia, and on the west by Israel.

I must give thanks to my husband first for taking me along— in learning and understanding it was the most glorious adventure of my life—and second, for reading the manuscript to check its accuracy.

May I take you now to the marvels and joys of the Holy Land?

List of Tables

1 The Old City of Jerusalem and Environs 30–31

2 From Jerusalem to Bethlehem and Hebron 62

3 From Ramallah and Bethel to the Sea of Galilee 90

4 Jordan East and North of Jerusalem 152

5 Southern Jordan 232

Contents

Preface   v

List of Tables   ix

I   INTRODUCTION TO JERUSALEM   1

II   THE HISTORY OF JERUSALEM   11

First Mentioned in Genesis . . . David's Capital . . . Solomon's Temple . . . Isaiah and the Assyrians . . . Jeremiah and the Babylonians . . . Nehemiah's New Walls . . . The City Jesus Knew . . . After Christ . . . Muslims and Crusaders

III   THE HOLY CITY   25

The Via Dolorosa . . . The Pool of Bethesda . . . Where Pilate Tried Jesus . . . The Holy Sepulcher . . . Early Holy Week Services . . . The Service of the Holy Fire . . . The Foot-washing Ceremony . . . The Search for Christ's Body . . . The Mount of Olives . . . Garden of Gethsemane and the Church of All Nations . . . The Church of Mary Magdalene . . . The Eastern Church . . . The Dominus Flevit and the Pater Noster Church . . . The Mosque of the Ascension . . . The Dome of the Rock . . . The Aqsa Mosque . . . The Muslims . . . The Islamic Religion . . . Pictures and Cameras . . . Recreation . . . Precious Water . . . The Dew of Heaven . . . The Garden Tomb . . . The Palestine Museum

IV WHERE JESUS WAS BORN   63

The Road to Bethlehem . . . The Birthplace . . . The
Church of the Nativity . . . Tourist Guides . . . Souvenirs
. . . Christmas in Bethlehem . . . A Walk Through Beth-
lehem . . . Shepherds' Field . . . Christmas Eve Services
. . . Herod's Fortress . . . The Top of the Herodium . . .
Tequ'a, the Home of Amos . . . Cave-dwelling Bedouins
. . . The Women of Tequ'a . . . The Children . . . Goats
and Wells . . . Medicine, Hygiene, and Morals . . . The
Road to Hebron . . . The Tombs of Abraham, Isaac, and
Jacob . . . Is the Shrine Authentic? . . . Inside Haram al
Khalil . . . Cameras and Forbidden Images . . . The Hebron
Potter . . . The Glassworks . . . The Oak of Mamre . . .
Hospitality Plus

V "THE ARABIAN COUNTRYSIDE"   91

Ramallah . . . *Mousakhan* and Ice Cream . . . The Women's
Dress . . . Education . . . Bireh . . . The Biblical Bethel
. . . Its History . . . Beitin . . . Blond Children and Ameri-
can Jeans . . . A Modern David . . . Seeking the Real Em-
maus: el Qubeibeh . . . Amwas . . . The Hill Country . . .
Jordanian Homes . . . *Mansef* and Table Manners . . . Jor-
danian Women . . . *Madefah* . . . Spinners of Tales . . .
The Art of Drinking Coffee . . . An Invitation to Dinner
. . . The Blessings of Lamb—and Other Foods . . . Vendors
on the Street . . . Herbs Outside the Kitchen . . . To Visit
a Home . . . The Little Beggars . . . Health Hazards . . .
The Clinics . . . Precautions for the Tourist

VI SAMARIA   127

Jacob's Well . . . Jesus and the Samaritan Woman . . .
The City of Shechem . . . The Sweets of Nablus . . . Ref-
ugee Camps . . . Enforced Idleness . . . Refugees Outside
the Camps . . . The Home of Jezebel and Ahab . . . Jesus'
City of Samaria . . . Antiquities for Sale . . . Sebaste . . .
The Riddle of the Samaritans . . . Samaritan Passover . . .

Where Joseph Was Sold . . . The Miserable Border Towns
. . . Visit with the *Muktar* . . . Don't Go Overboard with
Praise!

VII   THE ROAD TO JERICHO   153

The Tomb of Lazarus . . . Entertainment on the Road
. . . Only *One* Wife? . . . The Good Samaritan Inn . . .
Racing Camels and Horses . . . The Dead Sea Scrolls . . .
The Qumran Monastery . . . The Essenes . . . Community
Life and Beliefs . . . To Get to Qumran— . . . Herod's
Splendor . . . The Old Roman Road . . . The Jordan River
. . . The Missing Walls of Jericho . . . "The Oldest Walled
City" . . . A Modern "Ancient" Town . . . Difficulties with
Education . . . The Spring of Elisha . . . The Oasis that
Is Jericho . . . The Vision of Musa Al Alami . . . The
Scarcity of Meat . . . A Caliph's Palace . . . Driving into
the Desert . . . The Alexandrium . . . Arabs Behind the
Wheel . . . The Evil Eye . . . Irrigation . . . Emotional
Men . . . The Status of Women . . . Succoth and Zaretan
. . . The Archaeologists' Search for Biblical Sites . . . How
Old Are the Finds? . . . The Significance of Archaeology
. . . The Bible and Its Authors . . . "The Other Peoples"
. . . Later Biblical History . . . The Scrolls and the New
Testament . . . Can the Bible Be Proved? . . . Will More
Information Be Found?

VIII   THE CAPITAL AND ITS
       SURROUNDINGS   197

Amman—Its History . . . The Modern City . . . The
Magnificent Flowers . . . The City Roads . . . Amman
Antiquities . . . The Museum . . . The Wealthier Part of
Town . . . The King's Palace . . . Shopping and Customs
. . . The Customs Office . . . Reconstruction of Jerash . . .
Gadara or Um Qeis . . . Ghost Town . . . Night in the
Desert . . . The Mosaic of Madaba . . . Mount Nebo . . .
The Moabite Stone . . . A Modern Arab Girl . . . Kerak
Crusader Castle . . . The Bedouins . . . Responsibilities of

the Sheiks . . . Hospitality . . . Traditions . . . Raiding and
Revenge . . . Marriage . . . Medical Practices . . . Modern
Help for the Bedouins . . . The Summing Up

IX BEYOND THE JORDAN   231

The Way to Petra . . . Tragedy at the *Siq* . . . The Wonders of Petra . . . The Nabateans . . . The Thousand-Yard
Plain . . . The Battle with the Sun . . . Hotel in Petra
. . . The Treacherous Arabah . . . Aqaba . . . Encounter
with Royalty . . . A Royal Incident . . . Solomon's Seaport

X FOR THOSE WHO HAVE EYES . . .   249

XI TIPS FOR THE TRAVELER   259

The Best Hotels . . . You Need a Visa . . . Driving Your
Own Car . . . Vaccination . . . Customs . . . Foreign and
Jordanian Currency . . . The U. S. Consulate . . . How
to Dress . . . Tourist Services . . . Museums . . . Repairs
and Services . . . Some Arabic Expressions

JOURNEY THROUGH
THE HOLY LAND

I Introduction to Jerusalem

Three of us went to the Holy Land—my husband and I and our youngest child, a teen-age daughter. We traveled across the ocean by ship, then in our own car from Copenhagen, Denmark, through Germany, Switzerland, Italy, Greece, Turkey, Syria, and Lebanon to Jerusalem, Jordan—a long and scenic route we heartily recommend. We know, however, that few tourists can manage so much spare time; almost all of them will take to the air and set down in Jerusalem about twenty-four hours after leaving the United States.

Our orientation to the changing cultures from Europe to the Middle East was quite gradual and smooth. The tourist who leaves New York, eats and catnaps on the plane, and then disembarks at the Jerusalem Kalandia Airport may be slightly overwhelmed by what he sees. The airplane was excellent, well appointed and new. The airport seems acceptably modern, but sipping coffee at a table in the lunchroom are men dressed in long robes, with white flowing kerchiefs held on their heads by a double row of braid. They are bronzed by the sun and their marvelously crevassed faces would look more at home in a drama of the Old Testament than in an airport. If the tourist looks around at the landscape, he will have his first glimpse of the drab, brown hills of the Holy Land. Where there is a patch of green there will probably be also a shepherd, lingering while his hungry flock denude the hill of its greenery. Riding off over the hills on burros will be husbands and sons returning to their family homes. They will be dressed exactly like the men in the airport.

The taxi that transports the tourist from the airplane to Jerusalem will be a new American car. If it is a typical taxi driven by a young man who is proud of his vehicle, it will have vials of artificial flowers both front and rear.

The taxi driver will quietly speed his passengers to a fine and comfortable hotel. Touring will start later. If the taxi driver decides to launch into a travel-tour talk on the trip to Jerusalem, all of a fifteen-minute ride, the tourist would hear something like this:

"On your left the small town on the height is Er Ram, where Jeremiah was imprisoned by King Zedekiah and later freed by the Babylonians.

"To the right the roadway leads a few miles to Gibeon where Joshua and his invading Israelites fought so long and hard that it seemed to them the sun stood still. You can still see at Gibeon the most spectacular ancient water system in the Holy Land. Cut entirely from solid rock, the system includes a pool eighty-two feet deep, thirty-seven feet in diameter, equipped with a circular stairway of seventy-nine steps; beyond the pool there is a tunnel, again carved from solid rock, a distance of one hundred sixty-seven feet, which leads to a spring outside the ancient city.

"Again on your right, an old Roman road, the same road on which Paul was walking toward Damascus as he left Jerusalem to carry out his threat to slaughter the disciples of Jesus.

"On your left, the promontory housed the birthplace, residence, and sometime fortress of King Saul, first king of Israel. Immediately below, the modern building of stone trimmed in red and gold is the Jerusalem guesthouse of the present king of Jordan, King Hussein.

"On your right, the spire rising toward the sky marks Nebi Samwil, Muslim shrine in memory of the prophet Samuel. It is one of the possible sites for Mizpah, a place of prayer and worship which may have been the seat of Samuel, the judge.

"On your left, Anatoth, the home of Jeremiah. From this height the prophet looked toward Jerusalem, shook his fist at that wicked town and retired to his home to write prophecies of doom for Jerusalem."

If by this time the tourist is not spellbound, trying frantically to sort out these famous biblical names, he is going to comprehend rather quickly at least one fact—that the Holy Land is a small country crowded with places of biblical significance. Today the kingdom of Jordan is only 37,000 square miles, smaller than the state of Ohio.

The tourist, while whipping his head to the right and left, has also seen some other interesting sights on the roadway. He has seen women in brightly colored medieval gowns, walking along the roadway with huge baskets of groceries balanced on their heads. He has seen shepherds shuttling a flock of sheep to the side of the road. The sheep don't really look much like the ones back home on the farm. These sheep have bony foreheads, long pointed noses, floppy "spaniel" ears, and a tail big as a beaver's that flaps up and down. These tails couldn't wag. They're heavy—up to twenty pounds. The sheep are not white, but a dingy beige and they are all splotched up with henna, a practice sometimes explained as a method of facilitating the counting of sheep who blend into a field of fleece, sometimes as a remedy to protect the sheep from the evil eye.

There are other strange sights on the road. There is a little cart, a metal frame pulled by a donkey. On the frame sits a familiarly shaped cylindrical oil container. The container is bright yellow and it has a large red scrawl of Arabic on its side. The Arabic says "Shell." The driver is the kerosene distributor who is making house calls to supply fuel for lamps and small stoves.

If the tourist were to hear a loud sustained blast of a horn, it would be a monstrous bus calling for clear passage so that it could plow by, spewing black diesel smoke over the taxi. The bus would be a dilapidated model, but chances are ninety-nine to one that it would be well furbished inside with tassels bouncing up and down at the top of the windshield, flower arrangements strewn across the dashboard, and outside, a graceful, gaily colored ostrich plume in the radiator cap.

The bus drivers seem to feel an urge to brighten up the corner where they are and each one tries to excel the other in creativity, though they are colorful enough as they are in their native dress. In summer their white headdresses flow behind them in a straight line in the breeze. In winter, the headdress is so closely wound around the head and face for warmth that only the eyes of the driver can be seen.

As the tourist looks around the landscape, he has a feeling that something is missing. What is it? There are no billboards to impede your view, but that is a very pleasant omission. The land is quite barren, it is not cultivated. Still something else is missing. There are small settlements of houses both on the roadway and scattered throughout the hills. In the distance there are towers that rise up into the sky that mark the city of Jerusalem—ah, yes, now he knows what is missing. There are no spires of smoke streaming skyward from chimneys of busy factories.

Jordan is almost entirely agricultural. Two decades ago this land was sparsely populated by tent dwellers and their sheep and goats and farmers. It was a part of a larger land that stretched to the Mediterranean coast. Now, because the Jews and Arabs found it difficult to live together without tensions that broke out into gunfire, the United Nations has partitioned the area into a Jewish nation and an Arab nation. The citizens of both countries are trying to build a more complete economy. But since the Arabs are working with a parcel of land almost without natural resources, progress is slow. There are only a handful of factories in all the Jordanian Holy Land.

That hostility still exists between Israel and Jordan is no secret to the tourist who sees the testimony of barbed wire and armed soldiers along the roadway.

If the driver wanted to give his passengers some insight into the circumstances that cause tensions in the Holy Land today, he would have the perfect opportunity as he nears the city of Jerusalem. On the east of the roadway there is a commanding hill that is the site of an impressive group of buildings. The hill is Mount Scopus. The buildings housed Hebrew University and the Hadassah Hospital. At the time of the separation of the two countries, this small island of land was given to Israel to own and maintain despite the fact that it is entirely surrounded by Jordan.

Every two weeks a convoy moves from Israel into Jordan to replace the garrison of Israeli soldiers stationed there. The United Nations supervises this convoy, but despite that fact the Arabs have misgivings about the purpose of a garrison of soldiers who are stationed inside Jordan. The Arabs remember that in A.D. 70 Titus, the Roman general, held Jerusalem under seige from this vantage point.

The Arab misgivings are not dispelled when they see the Israeli trucks that travel to and from Mount Scopus. The trucks are made of metal and completely sealed except for a slit of a few inches through which the driver can see the road. Why are the trucks so tightly sealed? One answer is that the United Nations must offer this protection to soldiers who might be subject to sniper fire.

Because there is secrecy involved in the operation of the convoy, it is not surprising that the Arabs wonder if it is possible for the Israelis to build an arsenal on Mount Scopus that would be ready to blast Old Jerusalem in the event the two countries again resorted to armed warfare. The resentments surrounding Mount Scopus present one major reason for tensions in Jerusalem today.

A second reason for tension in Jerusalem is that the city is now a divided city exactly as is Berlin. A high wall thrown up in the fifties runs north to south through Jerusalem. As the tourist approaches Jerusalem by taxi from the airport, he sees a wall on the west side of the street and west of the wall he sees streets filled with apartments and large buildings that look like hospitals or schools. This is rather an attractive view because the Israeli town is brightened by hundreds of red tiled roofs. The tourist to Jordan should take a good look. He won't see this section of town for a while. He is looking at Israel. For the time being the tourist must confine his interest to the east side of the town.

Passageway through the wall must be arranged at the consulate where the tourist will be given a time and a day to make his

crossing. There will be no return. The tourist should know that
when he has a stamp on his passport showing that he has passed
through the Mandelbaum Gate (the only entrance) into Israel
from Jordan, he will subsequently not be allowed to enter Syria,
Iraq, or Egypt. He will also not be able to return to Jordan.

There are some few persons who travel back and forth between
the two countries at will. These persons are United Nations
officials and priests who teach in Roman Catholic schools on both
sides.

At Christmas and Easter, Arab Christians are allowed to come
from Israel into Jordan to attend services and visit relatives. This
is the only contact between relatives who live on opposite sides.
There is no telephone or mail service between the two
countries.

At the time of the Samaritan Passover, Samaritans in Israel
are permitted to join their religious brothers in Jordan. These
religious visits are short, and when the pilgrims return to Israel,
the gates are closed to them for another year.

On the east side of the wall is the marvelous confusion that is
the Middle Eastern city of Old Jerusalem. It is loud and colorful
and fun. Even on this side of the divide, Jerusalem is building up
a very respectable suburban population. There are neighborhoods
with beautiful homes where the citizens maintain a standard of
living similar to your own. The men from these homes are well
educated. They hold responsible positions. Their wives and
daughters dress in the very latest fashions, often in clothing
bought in the marvelous Lebanese city of Beirut. Their sons and
daughters go to private schools and will go on to college, perhaps
in the United States. Almost all of this upper level of society
speak excellent English.

On the city streets in this newer section of Jerusalem are
dozens of modern offices for travel agents, the *major* Holy Land
business. The tourist is the most promising hope for an improved
Jordanian economy.

The travel agents offer plenty to entice the tourist—trips to the extremely interesting antiquities of the land and accommodations in a series of new, excellently appointed hotels.

Surrounding the hotels in newer Jerusalem are dozens of up-to-date shops selling a gigantic array of stunning fabrics imported from Germany, the United Kingdom, Italy, Egypt, and the Orient. Tailoring is a big business in Jerusalem. Beware, tourist! Jerusalem tailors have the most unshakable convictions of what comprises the latest fashion. They make clothing according to their own consciences, not the customer's. It is, unfortunately, also true that the tailor will agree to a price for the hours involved in making clothing, but when the customer arrives to pick up the finished product, he will find the tailor wrestling with problems of how difficult the job was and how much longer it took to complete it than he had figured. Translation? It is going to cost more than the agreed price.

The tourist may be pleasantly surprised to notice that Jerusalem is well supplied with clean pharmacies where he can find any cosmetics, sanitary supplies, toiletries, or antibiotics.

A walk down the streets, even in newer Jerusalem, is very exciting because the tourist is soon caught up in the atmosphere of the Middle East. The sidewalks are filled with pushcarts, vendors, shoeshine boys, newspaper boys, and candy salesmen. There is no need to feel lonely in Jerusalem. The tourist is always in the center of the stage, the beloved potential customer for the battalions of merchants.

The newsboys will tag along with the foreigner today, tomorrow and subsequent tomorrows, if it is allowed, offering their products, their services as guides, and their conversation. Most of these boys speak a smattering of several languages and they are clever enough to know that, even though they do not effect a sale, they are engaging in valuable practice in using languages.

The shopkeepers will cajole you from their doorways, "Come in, please. *Please*, come in. It costs nothing to look. My shop is your shop. *Please*, we have something for nothing."

If the tourist passes the shop five times a day, five times he will receive the same invitation. What does the shopkeeper have for nothing? He has a neat little business card imprinted with the name of his shop and decorated with a tiny arrangement of dried and pressed Holy Land flowers.

The entranceway into the Old City of Jerusalem via the Damascus Gate can best be described as "dramatic." Here is a handsome medieval fortress—a city secured on all sides by massive crenellated walls, a monument to the past when walls and gates guaranteed more than a modicum of safety to those who lived within.

Four gates enter the Old City at the present time. The Damascus Gate is the main entrance leading into the *souk*, "market." Herod's Gate, also on the north side of the city, opens into a residential area. St. Stephen's Gate on the east takes the tourist to the start of the Via Dolorosa. The Dung Gate on the south leads into the former Jewish quarter near the Haram, a Muslim mosque and school. Gates on the west have been closed because persons no longer enter the Old City from Israel.

For the beauty and design of present city walls, credit is given to Suleiman the Magnificent of Turkey. His excellent craftsmen rebuilt the fortress in the sixteenth century. Happily, these men did not disdain to use some solid sections of old walls, so that we can still identify huge stones that were quarried and shaped by the workmen of Herod.

The Jerusalem walls and gates are beautiful to see, but at no time are they more beautiful than in the late afternoon, when the setting sun tints them with an orange-yellow glow. Truly, this is a sight of Jerusalem, the golden. On many nights, this glowing golden city is seen against a purple haze in the sky at twilight. It is exquisite. Jerusalem is also striking to see at night when floodlights play on the walls.

Today camel caravans are no longer admitted inside the walled city. This is not to be regretted. The narrow streets are already filled beyond reasonable capacity. Shoppers stand on the street as they bargain at open-front shops. Farm women squat on the streets with their baskets of grape leaves, marrows, or eggs. (Women do not seem to sell their wares from a stand and a tray.

They are always seen squatting on the ground, and quite often their produce consists of eggs since it is considered beneath a man's dignity to sell eggs.)

Sitting cross-legged in niches in the walls are cobblers and tinsmiths. They are occupied with their trade, but are never too busy to engage in lively conversations with their neighbors. They will handle small repair jobs in a hurry while the customer waits and seem to be thoroughly enjoying the bustle of the market all the while.

Occasionally the tourist must press himself flat against the walls in the narrow streets to allow a burro to pass by. Farmers bring their grain to town by packing it in sacks and loading it onto the burro.

"Human" burros, too, rush through the narrow streets and the casual shopper is most hesitant to delay these men in their haste to dispose of their burdens. Many of the poor hire out their backs for a living. These porters support unbelievable loads on their backs, loads that are larger and heavier than the porters themselves. I have seen these men bent almost double, their hands clenching a rope that held a *refrigerator* on their backs.

These persons, plus the milling city traffic, plus guided tourists make up the mob in the *souk*. Together, the crowd makes for shoulder to shoulder traffic that slowly surges its way through the streets and alleys.

The Old City has not changed much in two thousand years. It still presents to the visitor the most enchanting intimate scenes of daily living that could date back to the time of Jesus. Memories of Jesus' last days are everywhere present. Old Jerusalem belongs still to Jesus, the Christ.

II The History of Jerusalem

Jerusalem is not one of the oldest cities in the world. It is not one of the most beautiful cities in the world. It has never spawned a great society, *avant-garde* of the world's learning and culture. It could never boast that it had nurtured a school of profound philosophers, great artists, sculptors, or craftsmen. Jerusalem has held its place as one of the world's most interesting cities because of its close association with events in history that have been interpreted as *sacred* by three religions.

The city still stands on almost the exact spot where it was when we first read about it in history. True, it has edged slightly north and west since its early occupation, but the move is so slight geographically as to be negligible. The earliest known occupied site at Jerusalem is immediately southeast of the present Old City walls.

Since the city has rather doggedly held to its firm ground, archaeologists cannot probe at will into its buried secrets. Nothing would be more welcome to them than the opportunity to explore this fabled city from top to bedrock. Because of the many destructions of Jerusalem, bedrock has been . well covered by a build-up of debris from ancient walls, houses, and buildings. In some areas of the city, the valleys and hills of ancient Jerusalem lie sixty to seventy feet below the surface of the modern town. Archaeological probing within the modern city has been accomplished in those areas that have become the property of the Christian religious groups. Otherwise excavations of ancient Jerusalem have been pretty well confined to the ridge, slope, and valley that lie southeast of the modern city, specifically just below the Dome of the Rock complex. In these areas archaeologists may work freely without disturbing the present occupants of the city.

Fortunately, these spotty excavations have produced many evidences of early walls and fortifications that confirm the biblical records of the various occupations, destructions, and rebuildings of Jerusalem. One question, however, remains unanswered. Where, exactly, were the city walls at the time of Christ? This question concerns Christian scholars particularly. If the Bible record is correct that Jesus was crucified and buried outside the city walls, we must know where this wall was, in order to be certain that the Holy Sepulcher can qualify as an authentic site.

Jerusalem has shifted its boundaries with almost every rebuilding of the city. Today, the Holy Sepulcher lies in the heart of the walled city. Where was the Holy Sepulcher in relationship to the city of Herod? We do not know. In the second century A.D. when Hadrian destroyed Herod's city and completely rebuilt Jerusalem, he destroyed the clear evidences archaeologists search for today. Clues do remain, however, and from these clues we can infer what we want to know. In an excavation very near the Holy Sepulcher, excavators dug through fifty feet of fill dirt to reach an old quarry bed. This quarry bed had been worked as early as the seventh century B.C. The fill dirt dated to the second century A.D., that is, the time of Hadrian. Apparently, the quarry was still a quarry until Hadrian built his new city. The quarry was certainly outside the city walls. If it was, we can feel quite secure that the site of the present-day Holy Sepulcher was also outside the city walls.

First Mentioned in Genesis

The earliest mention of Jerusalem as a city comes from the Book of Genesis. Jerusalem was at that time a Canaanite city, probably a city state, independent, yet co-operating in periods of distress with other Canaanite city states throughout the area. These city states were powerful enough to maintain peace along the great trade route from Damascus to Egypt. It is known that the Canaanites had a system of fire signals that could be relayed from high hills along the route. The protection of the trade route made it possible for great caravans to move securely, transporting their cargoes, and for tribes to migrate in search of better pasture land. It is believed that one great migrating tribe to take advantage of this peaceful period was that of Abraham, about 1800 B.C. Abraham apparently was able to roam the country almost at will, from Shechem to the Negev to Egypt and return as he pleased.

Abraham, in his migrations, at one time presented himself to the "king of Salem," Melchizedek. The biblical account relates that Abraham was wined and dined by the king and was further given the king's blessing. In return Abraham gave to the king a tenth of all he owned (Gen. 14:18–20). The biblical account does not tell us any more about the importance of Melchizedek, or *why* Abraham presented himself to this king. We only know that Abraham did. For our purposes at the moment, it is only cogent that Melchizedek was "king of Salem," a city which scholars identify with Jerusalem. There was a city on the Jerusalem site at that time. Excavators have uncovered Middle Bronze walls dating to 1800 B.C. on the west edge of the Kidron Valley and on the southeast spur of the hills coming down from the Dome of the Rock. The old city was then centered around the only immediate water supply, the Fountain of the Virgin. The old city remained by this water supply until at least the time of Nehemiah and the return from the Babylonian exile.

A second early mention of Jerusalem dates from approximately 1400 B.C. Egypt had by then extended its influence or protectorate over the trade routes, and apparently the Canaanite cities had become vassals of Egypt while retaining their own princes. The Canaanite princes had written hundreds of pleading letters to Amarna, capital of Egypt, registering complaints and seeking military aid against encroaching enemies. These letters, all clay tablets, were discovered by accident in Egypt late in the last century. Among this diplomatic correspondence there were letters from "Urusalim."

The reason we have found this treasury of correspondence may be that the pharaoh was too preoccupied with his own affairs to concern himself with his vassal cities. The Canaanite princes were forced to send repeated requests for help. This pharaoh would have been Akhenaton, famous for his beautiful wife, Nefertiti, and famous also for his preoccupation with religious philosophy and his neglect of the administration of his empire. It is possible that Joseph, by this time an influential man in Egypt, might have been Akhenaton's prime minister or secretary of agriculture.

At the time of the Israelite invasion of Canaan, Jerusalem is described as a Jebusite city. The Jebusites were close relatives of the Canaanites. Archaeological excavations have revealed the Jebusite walls as well as many platforms on which the Jebusite city was built. While the Israelites describe Jerusalem as a city unfriendly to them, Joshua apparently made no attempt to take it. Perhaps it was too securely fortified. During the period of the Judges, too, Jerusalem remained outside the influence of the Israelites.

David's Capital

It was David who brought the "plum," Jerusalem, into the hands of the Israelites. This was during the transitional period ending the Bronze Age and beginning the Iron Age about the year 1000 B.C. David was riding high with his record of military successes. He was living in Hebron. He had eyed Jerusalem and apparently found it well fortified because in II Samuel 5:8 he speculated that whoever would take Jerusalem would have to do it by infiltrating through the water shaft. (Excavations by Miss Kathleen Kenyon have shown that the Jebusite water supply was indeed inside their fortification walls.) If David used this method to enter the city, it was successful. He settled himself in a new home on Mount Ophel, the ridge on the southeast of present Jerusalem.

Traces of David's city are hard to find. It is possible that he used the Jebusite walls and platforms. References in the Bible to "repairs in the walls" and "reconstructions" during his reign might also point to the fact that David did not have to build new city walls. He was never called a great builder; his reputation rested more on his military abilities, his musical talents, and his political astuteness.

David brought the ark of the covenant to Jerusalem, placed it in a tent and announced that henceforth Jerusalem would be his new capital. Had David kept Hebron as his capital, the northern tribes would have been antagonized because of Hebron's close association with the southern tribal loyalties. Similarly, Shechem or Shiloh as Israel's capital might have been an offense to the southern tribes. Jerusalem, the city bordering the southern and northern territories, was the capital that united the kingdom.

Solomon's Temple

David had at least one dream for the future of Jerusalem. The fulfillment of that dream fell to his son Solomon. In the fourth year of his reign Solomon fulfilled a promise to his father by beginning the construction of a royal chapel to house the ark of the covenant. The chapel, completed in seven years, the famous Temple of the Jews, is believed to have been located on the present site of the Dome of the Rock. (This area cannot be excavated. Whether an excavation, if it were possible, would produce any information about the Temple is dubious. In 587 B.C., the Babylonians reported that they had destroyed the Temple completely and carried off to Babylon all the Temple treasures. Sections of the Dome of the Rock complex show clearly that some of the buildings stand on bedrock.)

Solomon's reign is known as a period of great prosperity not only for Jerusalem, but for the whole kingdom. Jerusalem grew northward. Many materials were brought into Jerusalem at this time not only to build the Temple but other shrines, to satisfy the wishes of Solomon's many foreign wives. The king imported wood of cedar and cyprus from Lebanon. He imported wood paneling for his palace and an ivory throne for himself. Solomon's ambitions for the country called for heavy taxation. Perhaps the burden of taxes, perhaps dissatisfaction with Solomon's "foreign shrines" alienated the people. When Solomon died, his son Rehoboam found himself fumbling with the responsibility of leading a disgruntled populace. The northern tribes deserted him, rallying instead around Jeroboam and making Shechem their new capital. Jerusalem became for most of the next five centuries the capital of the southern kingdom.

Isaiah and the Assyrians

In 701 B.C., the Assyrians, the great predators and plunderers, blazed a path of destruction through the Holy Land. They swept down to Jerusalem and surrounded it. Sennacherib was the invading king; Hezekiah, the defender. Hezekiah was not exactly unprepared for a seige. He had had the foresight to oversee a remarkable feat of engineering. He had channeled spring water into the midst of his city by carving a tunnel through 1749 feet of solid rock. This tunnel is the more remarkable because, we are told, two teams of workmen started on opposite sides and met in the middle! Hezekiah had thrown up fortification walls. He had also paid heavy tribute to the Assyrians to keep them at bay. In spite of his precautions, the Assyrians were breathing down his neck and doubtless presumed they could smash Jerusalem at any given moment. There was one man who was able to bolster the courage of Hezekiah. That man was Isaiah, confidant of the king, adviser to the king, who was living and prophesying in Jerusalem. Isaiah reminded the king that he had not called on his most reliable "fortification," the Lord. Why deliver the city into the hands of the Assyrians? Why quiver over the reports of the might of the

Assyrian army? There was one clear line of action. Lay the matter before the Lord in confidence—the Lord would not fail to save the city for the sake of his servant David.

The Scripture tells that Hezekiah did turn to the Lord. A miracle occurred. At night an angel of the Lord went out among the Assyrians. By morning Sennacherib arose to find 185,000 of his soldiers dead. Aghast, Sennacherib returned to Nineveh, and Jerusalem was spared the terrible destruction wrought by the Assyrians in cities of northern and southern Palestine during the last three decades of the eighth century. Sennacherib, a typical Assyrian in reporting exaggerated claims of mighty victories, could in this instance only report that he had had Hezekiah shut up like a bird in a cage.

Manasseh, the son of Hezekiah, was only twelve years old when he came to the throne. His reign during his earlier years was so filled with foul practices in religion that the Lord threatened to "wipe Jerusalem as a man wipeth a dish, wiping it and turning it upside down" (II Kings 21:13). Perhaps because of his youth, Manasseh was easily influenced by pagan religions. He burned his own son as a sacrifice. He was content to see Jerusalem run red with the blood of innocent victims. He indulged in witchcraft and communion with the dead. The Lord threatened to turn Jerusalem over to its enemies, and Jerusalem did fall to the Assyrians and remained a vassal for a period of seventy-five years, from 697 to 622.

Jeremiah and the Babylonians

Toward the end of this period of servitude, King Josiah made a strong effort to purify Jerusalem and the kingdom. A priest of the Temple brought to the king a "book of the law." Josiah had not before seen this section of Scripture. He was astonished at how corrupt were the religious practices of the children of the Lord when compared with the laws of God spelled out in the "newly found book." Josiah scoured not only Jerusalem of its idols and altars to Baal, but the whole kingdom—even to destroying the buried bones of false prophets.

Attempts at a complete reform of the kingdom were not long lived, however. After Josiah died, succeeding kings slipped back into corruption. Jeremiah, who had witnessed the evils within the kingdom, had repeatedly warned the people that they were inviting punishment from the Lord. When Nebuchadnezzar invaded the Holy Land after defeating the Assyrians, Jeremiah looked to the Babylonians as the fulfillment of his prophecies— they would be the "servant of the Lord" who would punish Jerusalem. Because of this belief, voiced on occasions to King Zedekiah, Jeremiah was thrown into prison as a traitor. The Babylonians did punish Jerusalem. In 597 and again in 586, the Babylonians sacked not only the capital city, but most of the cities in the kingdom. They killed many persons holding high office. Other officials were rounded up and along with many of their countrymen and the treasures of the land were carted off to Babylon.

During the Exile, Jerusalem was in pitiful shape. In the works of Ezekiel and in the stories of the return told by Ezra and Nehemiah, we can read a graphic description of a people wringing their hands in misery and poverty.

Happily for the Jews, the fortunes of the Babylonians did not run an endless sustained course. As the Babylonians had flattened the kingdom of the Jews, so were their cities to be subject to the humiliations of armies that invaded from Persia. The king of the accomplished Persian warriors was Cyrus the Great, worthy founder of the Achaemenid dynasty. On the strength of his previous successes, Cyrus entered Babylon without a battle in 539.

Cyrus was a new breed of conqueror. He did not subscribe to the usual practice of "stepping on the neck" of the vanquished, stripping them of their possessions and hitching them to the yoke. Cyrus treated his vassals with kindness. His interest was in consolidating an empire and giving to all its people good rule and just law. The new and enlightened policies of Cyrus

extended to the practice of religion. Cyrus himself was perhaps
a follower of Zoroaster but he allowed the people in his empire
to worship as they pleased. He gave to the Jews permission to
return to their homeland if they wished and further issued a
decree that they were to be allowed to rebuild their Temple in
Jerusalem.

Nehemiah's New Walls

Some of the Jews did return to Jerusalem but they did not
immediately rebuild the Temple. Jerusalem was in an economic
depression. The returned exiles found it most difficult to eke
out a living. The walls of Jerusalem remained in the battered
condition in which the Babylonians had left them. Defenseless,
Jerusalem was an easy prey for raiders. The Jews became apa-
thetic about undertaking a building program for a religious
shrine. It took the most forceful leadership and the repeated
proddings of Haggai and Zechariah to rally the people sufficiently
to comply with their spiritual responsibility, the rebuilding of
the Temple. It was finally dedicated in 516 B.C.

Apparently Jerusalem continued in its economic slump for
some time. Nehemiah, cupbearer to a succeeding Persian king,
was the recipient of some letters from Jerusalem. He felt such
deep concern for the safety of his fellow Jews in the Holy City
that he used his influence to get permission to rebuild the
walls of Jerusalem. He arrived in Palestine about 440 B.C. and
found the old walls in such a pitiful state that he decided not
to attempt to use them. Nehemiah claims to have built all new
walls within fifty-two days. Portions of these have been found
by archaeologists. They are smaller than the walls that enclosed
David's city and also enclose a smaller area.

The biblical record of Jerusalem in Old Testament times
comes to a close with the books of Ezra and Nehemiah. While
Ezra might not have been responsible for changing the physical
face of Jerusalem, he certainly exerted considerable moral influence on the inhabitants. It was Ezra who sought to re-establish

a religious state and who reminded the people of their covenant relationship with God. It was he, too, who reinstated the practice of reading the law, a practice dictated formerly by Joshua and Josiah in the covenant renewal.

According to Jewish tradition, it was through the influence of Ezra that the first five books of the Old Testament became valid Scripture.

Scholars have puzzled over ambiguities in the books of Ezra and Nehemiah that do not present a clear picture of which man preceded the other. There are elements in the books that seem to suggest that Ezra returned to Jerusalem before Nehemiah came to rebuild the walls. Other elements have led scholars to the conclusion that Ezra followed Nehemiah and that consequently Ezra should be dated about 397 B.C. Acceptance of this later date for Ezra is growing among scholars.

Another invader came through the Middle East. Having toppled the Persian Empire, Alexander the Great marched through the Holy Land on his way to Egypt and Jerusalem opened its gates to him (331 B.C.). When Alexander died in 323, Jerusalem came under the domination of Egypt and, later, the Seleucids of Syria.

Under the influence of the Seleucid dynasty Jerusalem became Hellenistic in culture to a degree that provoked the wrath of the Hasmoneans, a group of Jewish high priests and kings. Their persistent rebellions and battles to save Jerusalem from becoming a completely pagan city are recorded in the Book of Maccabees. This stormy period in Jerusalem's history began in 167 B.C. when a priest resisted the demand of a Seleucid king to sacrifice to a heathen god, and it ended in 141 B.C. when Simon, a Hasmonean, became ruler of Judea. Hasmonean walls and towers to protect Jerusalem have also been identified, usually as additions to Nehemiah's walls. Eighty years of peace ensued. In the first century B.C. rivalry broke out in the Hasmonean ruling family. Both John Hyrcanus and Aristobulos, struggling for the throne, appealed to the Romans garrisoned in Syria for help. The upshot was Pompey came in 63 B.C., took Jerusalem for Rome, and left John Hyrcanus in charge of the city under Roman guidance.

The City Jesus Knew

In 37 B.C. the Roman senate appointed Herod (a half Jew) to be king of the Jews. Herod refashioned Jerusalem after the pattern of a Roman city. His fortress, on the northwest side of the city, he called the Antonia in deference to Mark Anthony. His palace, a three-towered building, stood on the north of the city (a site presently marked by the Herodian foundation stones in the present so-called Tower of David or Citadel near the Jaffa Gate). He doubled the size of the temple area and built a shrine more magnificent than that of Solomon. (The present Wailing Wall was a part of this temple complex and is the southeast corner of the Dome of the Rock.) He constructed a theater, amphitheater, and a place for athletic games. He built aqueducts to bring water into the city; to enclose the city, he built a wall with sixty towers. Herod died in 4 B.C. and his city was Jerusalem as Jesus knew it.

This lovely city, perhaps the finest face Jerusalem ever owned, was the setting for the death of Jesus. It was at Herod's Antonia that Jesus was tried as an insurgent and it was through these streets that Jesus marched to Golgotha.

After Christ

After the death of Herod, his son Archelaus ruled. Archelaus was a poor leader of men and his subjects appealed successfully to Rome to replace him. Rome sent procurators to keep the peace. Some of these procurators were skilled administrators, some were poor, some lived in Jerusalem, some preferred to live and enjoy the climate in Caesarea on the Mediterranean coast.

Among these Roman officials was Pontius Pilate. Just as Pilate tried to turn back to the Jews their "criminal" Jesus, saying that the complaints against him were no affair of the Roman state but a Jewish matter, so later procurators found themselves in difficulty in dealing with the Jews. The Jews were split into factions among themselves. Their strong political views caused not only uprisings against the Romans, but frequently bitter battles among themselves. Efforts by authorities to mediate between the groups failed and finally Rome sent Vespasian to the Holy Land to settle the rebellions.

It was the plan of Vespasian to make a clean sweep of the land, stopping all rebels wherever he found them, but the efforts of the Roman army proved to be so time-consuming that finally it was left to Titus, son of Vespasian, to tame Jerusalem. This he did in A.D. 69–70 by encircling the city, starving it and finally besieging it—a battle of six months' duration.

Jerusalem was again in ruins. In 130 A.D. the Emperor Hadrian leveled all that was left of the troubled religious city and completely rebuilt it, giving it a new name, "Aelia Capitolina," and forbidding Jews to enter the city. Where Jewish shrines had stood now rose temples to Bacchus, Venus, and Jupiter.

Jerusalem remained a pagan city until the time of Constantine the Great (A.D. 325), the Roman emperor who was converted to Christianity. Constantine reopened Jerusalem to Jews and to Christian pilgrims. Foremost among the pilgrims was his mother Helena who toured the Holy Land in search of the important sites connected with the life and death of Jesus. On the more important sites, Constantine built Christian shrines, among them the church of the Holy Sepulcher. A succeeding Christian emperor, Justinian, also assumed responsibility for preserving Christian shrines, and rebuilding them more elaborately.

Muslims and Crusaders

In A.D. 614 the Persians successfully invaded the Holy Land but they were in turn routed by the more significant invasion of the Caliph Omar in 639—the beginning of the Muslim occupation of Palestine. Though we are apt to think of the encounter between Muslim and Christian in terms of violent skirmishes distinguished by excessive bloodletting, the fact is that Caliph Omar was very kind to the inhabitants of Jerusalem. He allowed Christians and Jews to stay on subject to the stipulation that they pay tax. Most inhabitants stayed. There was no religious oppression. Omar visited the Holy Sepulcher, but deliberately stepped outside and away from the church to pray, lest his Muslim brethren misinterpret a prayer within the church as a sign that the church should be turned into a Muslim shrine. Omar built his own temple of prayer located near the Aqsa Mosque. Even as late as the time of Charlemagne (768–814), there apparently was good will between the two religious groups since the keys of the Holy Sepulcher were sent to the western emperor.

Later, there were serious troubles. In 1099 the Crusaders marched on the Holy Land to restore it to the Christians. They took Jerusalem, but were ousted by the great leader of the Arabs, Saladin. Saladin had plans to fortify Jerusalem so that it could be the more easily defended. He was stopped by another Arab leader who reasoned that if the city were refortified, the Crusaders might be able to hold it should they retake it. The Crusaders were able to recapture Jerusalem two more times but held it for only short periods. Much later, in 1517, the Arabs fell before the invasion of other Muslims, the Ottoman Turks.

Between the Arabs and the Turks Jerusalem remained in possession of the Muslims from 639 to 1917. During World War I, the British and T. E. Lawrence with his Arab legions, wrested the Holy Lands from the Turks. Palestine was placed under British mandate, but the British had no greater success than any preceding conqueror in bringing real peace to the troubled land. After thirty years of occupation, the British in frustration handed the country over to the United Nations. After "The Troubles" the land was partitioned. Jerusalem, the ancient city, belongs to the Muslims and is in Jordan. Jerusalem, the modern city, belongs to the Jews and is in Israel.

III   The Holy City

The Via Dolorosa

Most Christian pilgrims who travel to Jerusalem have come to this city to fulfill a lifelong dream. They want to walk the Via Dolorosa, the traditional Way of the Cross. The tourist may walk the Way of the Cross at any time he chooses and any Jerusalem guide will be able to show him the way. However, the altars at each of the stations will not be open, except on Fridays when the Franciscans make their weekly pilgrimage. The pilgrimage starts around three o'clock on Friday afternoons and tourists who wish to join it may assemble at the First Station in the Umariyyah School, supposed site of Pilate's praetorium. The pilgrimage will end at the Tomb in the Holy Sepulcher.

If the tourist is so fortunate as to be available for this pilgrimage on a Friday when there are not too many other tourists in Jerusalem, he will find this a most meaningful and worshipful experience. At each Station of the Cross, he may step in to see the altar that has been erected in commemoration and join the priests in their prayers.

During the height of the tourist season, this group of pilgrims becomes so large that it is difficult to get close enough to the priests to hear their prayers, and if the tourist takes time to inspect the altars, he will soon find that he is tagging along one or two Stations behind the lead priests. For this reason, if the Via Dolorosa has special meaning for a pilgrim, it would be wise for him to walk it first alone to become familiar with each Station and then join the Friday group.

Good Friday is a very special day for Christians in Jerusalem. On this day, many groups of pilgrims walk the Via Dolorosa and it is usual for each group to carry a replica of the Cross. On this solemn anniversary, priests lecture to the pilgrims as well as pray at the Stations.

The Pool of Bethesda

Many pilgrims come to Jerusalem hoping to walk quite literally in the footsteps of Jesus. This may not be possible since the Jerusalem of Jesus' day lies far below the present street level of the city. A very graphic illustration of how much the city has raised its level in some areas over a period of two thousand years is pointed out to tourists who visit the Church of St. Anne, near St. Stephen's Gate.

The Church of St. Anne is an outstanding example of Crusader architecture. It was erected in honor of the mother of Mary and in memory of a long tradition that Mary was born near the Pool of Bethesda.

Near the church an excavation has been in progress for years to explore the remains of two earlier churches built over the Pool of Bethesda. This is the site where Jesus is believed to have healed a man with an infirmity of many years (John 5:1-9). It is a particularly satisfying excavation for the layman because the architectural remains are clear and easy to understand without any previous knowledge of archaeology. The tremendous supports for a church have been uncovered. On top of those supports, parts of the floor of the original church are still in place, and above *that* floor there are remains of another floor that belonged to a succeeding church. Columns, capitals, carved Christian symbols have been gathered together in a small museum on the site to testify that our forefathers thought this a site of sufficient importance to Christian history to perpetuate by the erection of a very fine church.

Far down at the bottom of the excavation, about sixty feet below the present street level, is water. Just above the water can be seen the *tops* of Roman arches and columns that date approximately to the time of Jesus.

What is known about the history of the Pool of Bethesda?

Actually there are two pools here, reservoirs that were used as a source of water for the old Jewish Temple (now the site of the Dome of the Rock). Archaeologists feel they confirmed the matter when they found canals that lead from the pools toward the Temple area.

Later, during the time of the Romans, these pools were believed to have healing powers and a temple to Aesculapius, the pagan god of medicine, was built here. Archaeologists have found such a temple represented on coins made in Jerusalem at about that time. The scholars know that if this temple followed the pattern of other excavated shrines, it would have contained a number of porches where the sick were privileged to sleep. Such a temple would certainly fit the story of the healing as related by St. John. You will recall that there were pools visited by the sick who waited until an angel had disturbed the waters in the belief that the first person lowered into the water at that time would be healed. It was here that Jesus encountered the man who complained that he had no one who could lower him into the water and he appealed to Jesus to help him. Jesus healed the man on the spot to show that the healer was not the water, but Christ.

Christian pilgrims in the fourth century mentioned visiting these pools. By the fifth century there was a Byzantine church here. This church was destroyed by the Persians in 614. The Crusaders (11–12th centuries) restored and rebuilt the church, which has subsequently fallen into ruin. The Crusaders also built another church east of the pools in memory of St. Anne, and it is this lovely church that still stands, preserved because Saladin, the great Arab conqueror, used the building as a school. It needed some restoration late in the nineteenth century, but St. Anne's remains an authentic Crusader church, almost as fresh as the day it was erected.

Thus, in a single shrine in Jerusalem, the tourist has the opportunity to learn something of the science of archaeology; he can learn some facts about the Byzantine churches; he can see a Crusader church intact. The site is the property of one of the Uniat Churches and it is administered by the White Fathers.

They maintain a seminary within the grounds and have added to the beauty of the site by planting an attractive garden. This is one of the few shrines in Jerusalem that lends itself to the type of quiet, undisturbed meditation that many pilgrims seek.

Where Pilate Tried Jesus

Near the Church of St. Anne there is a Roman Catholic girls' school, the Sisters of Zion. In the basement of the school building there is part of the old Roman road through Jerusalem, built during the reign of Hadrian, thought to be the Lithostrotos (pavement) where Pilate publicly tried Jesus. Nearby was the Antonia, the fortress castle built by King Herod, and the residence of Pilate at the time of the Crucifixion. It was to the Antonia that the people brought Jesus to Pilate. Pilate brought Jesus into the palace and interrogated him. The Roman procurator sent Jesus to Herod in the hope that Herod would judge the man. Herod sent Jesus back to Pilate, and it was on the Lithostrotos that Jesus was turned back to the crowd for crucifixion and was given the Cross.

The Sisters of Zion conduct tours in several languages at regular intervals throughout the day. They point out designs cut into the flagstones of the road that earlier had served as "gaming tables" for soldiers. Some of the flagstones are striated (it is believed the narrow grooves prevented horses' hooves from slipping). Gutters in the road channeled rain water into cisterns which can still be seen far beneath the roadway. Excavators have unearthed bedrock and some arches in the area beneath the school. The Sisters will explain what they believe to be the history of these Roman remains.

The Holy Sepulcher

If the pilgrim follows the Stations of the Cross, he will be led to the Holy Sepulcher. The old church is not hard to find. The pilgrim will hardly have set foot inside the Old City before guides, both professional and amateur, are besieging him with offers to take him to and through the old church. This is the most important Christian shrine in the world.

The Holy Sepulcher, believed by many to be the site of Jesus' Crucifixion and burial, has been until recently one of the most dismal-looking churches in Jerusalem. "Dismal" is a mild word in comparison to others that have been used to describe the church—"a horror," "a disgrace to Christendom." Some of the devout have advocated leveling the church to the ground and rebuilding it. My personal reaction to the church after the first visit was that I would never again set foot inside that hideous monstrosity. Despite that vow I spent more time in the Holy Sepulcher than in any other spot in the Holy Land. This old shrine cannot be ignored. Its ancient history includes a marvel beyond comprehension—the Resurrection of Christ—and its present history involves a marvel of twentieth century engineering.

The Holy Sepulcher when erected by Constantine some sixteen hundred years ago was a magnificent shrine. It was again a stately and impressive church when it was restored by the Crusaders in the eleventh and twelfth centuries. Unfortunately, it was not exempt from the fates and humiliations of Jerusalem— the armed conquests, the fires, and the earthquakes. The church has been patched, altered, added to, and hastily plastered for safety precautions. Most damaging to its appearance is the scaffolding erected throughout the interior and against the face over the entrance because of fear of loss of lives in an earthquake. The church has become a labyrinth with the scaffolding the most dominant structural feature. Discussions on "doing something" about the Holy Sepulcher had not been too fruitful because of the complicated problem of securing a consensus among the various branches of Christendom each of which had rights and privileges within the church.

There were and are five such groups: the Roman Catholics, the Armenian Orthodox, the Greek Orthodox, the Copts, and the Syrian Orthodox. A sixth, the Abyssinians, have rights to the roof of the church near the cupola of the Chapel of St. Helena.

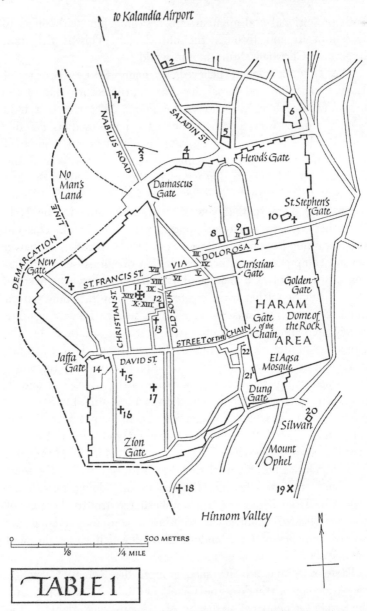

to Kalandia Airport

NABLUS ROAD

SALADIN ST.

No Man's Land

DEMARCATION LINE

Damascus Gate

Herod's Gate

St. Stephen's Gate

New Gate

VIA DOLOROSA

Christian Gate

Golden Gate

ST. FRANCIS ST.

CHRISTIAN ST.

OLD SOUK

HARAM

Gate of the Chain

Dome of the Rock

AREA

STREET OF THE CHAIN

Jaffa Gate

DAVID ST.

El Aqsa Mosque

Dung Gate

Silwan

Zion Gate

Mount Ophel

Hinnom Valley

N

0   500 METERS
    ⅛   ¼ MILE

TABLE 1

TABLE 1   The Old City of Jerusalem and Environs

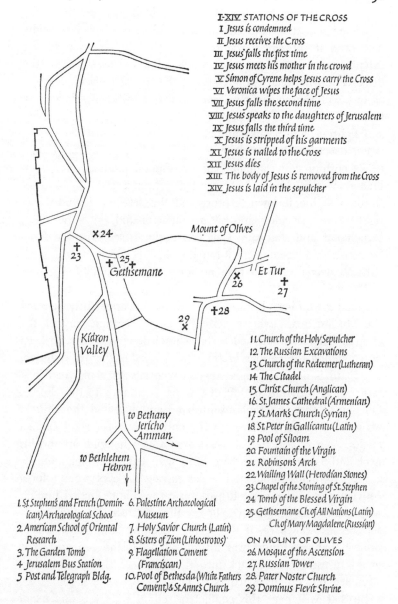

I-XIV STATIONS OF THE CROSS

I *Jesus is condemned*
II *Jesus receives the Cross*
III *Jesus falls the first time*
IV *Jesus meets his mother in the crowd*
V *Simon of Cyrene helps Jesus carry the Cross*
VI *Veronica wipes the face of Jesus*
VII *Jesus falls the second time*
VIII *Jesus speaks to the daughters of Jerusalem*
IX *Jesus falls the third time*
X *Jesus is stripped of his garments*
XI *Jesus is nailed to the Cross*
XII *Jesus dies*
XIII *The body of Jesus is removed from the Cross*
XIV *Jesus is laid in the sepulcher*

Mount of Olives

Et Tur

Kidron Valley

to Bethany
Jericho
Amman

to Bethlehem
Hebron

11. *Church of the Holy Sepulcher*
12. *The Russian Excavations*
13. *Church of the Redeemer (Lutheran)*
14. *The Citadel*
15. *Christ Church (Anglican)*
16. *St. James Cathedral (Armenian)*
17. *St. Mark's Church (Syrian)*
18. *St. Peter in Gallicantu (Latin)*
19. *Pool of Siloam*
20. *Fountain of the Virgin*
21. *Robinson's Arch*
22. *Wailing Wall (Herodian Stones)*
23. *Chapel of the Stoning of St. Stephen*
24. *Tomb of the Blessed Virgin*
25. *Gethsemane Ch. of All Nations (Latin)*
    Ch. of Mary Magdalene (Russian)

ON MOUNT OF OLIVES
26. *Mosque of the Ascension*
27. *Russian Tower*
28. *Pater Noster Church*
29. *Dominus Flevit Shrine*

1. *St. Stephen's and French (Dominican) Archaeological School*
2. *American School of Oriental Research*
3. *The Garden Tomb*
4. *Jerusalem Bus Station*
5. *Post and Telegraph Bldg.*
6. *Palestine Archaeological Museum*
7. *Holy Savior Church (Latin)*
8. *Sisters of Zion (Lithostrotos)*
9. *Flagellation Convent (Franciscan)*
10. *Pool of Bethesda (White Fathers Convent) & St. Anne's Church*

Each of these groups has traditions about use of the Holy Sepulcher that date back over a thousand years. Each has rigidly held onto its prescribed rights within the church, even to the extent that a line down the middle of a pillar spells out the demarcation between two chapels at the site of Calvary. Services of one sect that encroached on an area traditionally belonging to another sect have in past years been responsible for scuffles and fighting within the church.

Each sect has decorated its own area of "ownership" according to its custom with hanging lamps, candles, pictures, etc. Each branch of the church has operated with a certain amount of freedom within its own territory and this freedom included the right to add sleeping and eating quarters and, in some cases, extra floors and stairways. Can you begin to see how the Holy Sepulcher has become a cluttered conglomeration, overly used, with an over-all church plan no longer decipherable?

The zealous protection of "ownership" rights demonstrated by the monks who have lived within the area has apparently infected the Muslim guard who is stationed at the entranceway of the church. Originally assigned to the church long years ago to keep peace among the various brethren who worshiped in the church, the guard is now a vestigial remain who sits on a mattress in a rather large niche at the left of the main entrance to the church. On one of the days that my husband and I visited the church, we noticed a tourist sizing up the entranceway for good camera angles. As a typical tourist, he had a camera hanging around his neck and a heavy camera case filled with equipment hanging by a strap from his shoulder. He was casting his eyes around for a convenient and safe place to park his case while he busied himself with photography. His eyes lit on the mattress. He had hardly set the case down on it when the Muslim guard rushed up to protest that the tourist was intruding on Muslim property. The guard thrust the case back into the hands of the tourist, then stretched out on his mattress to rest.

Be that as it may, this conflict of self-interests was one major deterrent to headway for a new church on this most holy site.

A complete restoration is now under way, but the restrictions voluntarily assumed by the architect and his crew in attempting this task are all but unbelievable.

First, it was decided to reconstruct the Crusader church with its fine, clean, dignified lines while retaining every shred of earlier construction still in good enough condition to bear its weight. This means that every sound stone will be left exactly in place and that new stone (of the same kind) will be fitted around it so that repairs will be hidden. All additions to the church over the last eight hundred years will be tactfully and cautiously removed. Where a column shows damage calculated to date back to the Crusader church, the damage will be duplicated in new stone. Where mistakes or faults were made in the Crusader church, the mistakes will be incorporated into the new church provided they do not present a safety hazard. The present work crew in Jerusalem is literally reconstructing this church one stone at a time. Work is painstaking and extremely slow. The workmen cannot forge ahead too rapidly because they must hold to their promise to keep the church clear for all regularly held services and regular services are held daily. And the promise was also exacted of the architect that in the new church all the traditional rights of each sect will remain.

One of the first tasks of the restorers was to remove from the roof an accumulation of rubble. This debris totaled more than two thousand cubic yards. A second major task was to shore up areas of the church that would surely collapse if probed by workmen. This was accomplished by bolstering arches and walls with a generous network of steel girders. Inside the church, plaster was removed from the walls and columns to uncover the original building stones. This has been a rewarded effort. The frequent hasty plastering, an emergency measure to protect the columns from slow decay, has preserved the original designs of column capitals and these designs can now be copied with precision.

The workmen have been excited to find remains of the Holy Sepulcher that date just prior to the Crusader restoration and even more thrilled to find granite columns of Justinian (dated approximately A.D. 530) and some authentic remains of the Constantinian church (dated 335).

While the huge probe for the Crusader church continues, an archaeologist is using the opportunity to examine the foundations of the church and will, perhaps, have an interesting report of any significant details he can uncover at bedrock, which must date to the Crucifixion. The general shape of the bedrock formation on which the church was built is already known to conform to the description of the area at the time of the Crucifixion, and at the time of Constantine. A cistern, also supposed to be at the foot of the rock of Calvary, does exist there.

At the present time, tourists are led to a crypt in the Syrian area of the church to view a pre-Christian tomb, thought to be similar to the one offered by Joseph of Arimathea to hold the body of Jesus. The extent of the other tombs under the church may also be studied by archaeologists.

What type of shrine was erected on this spot from the earliest days following the Crucifixion is not known. During the reign of Hadrian, A.D. 135, a statue to Jupiter was built here and an altar to Venus. The purpose of the emperor in building on this spot was probably to discourage Christian pilgrims from visiting the site. In attempting to obliterate a Christian shrine, Hadrian helped to mark it for posterity. Some vestiges of Hadrian's structure remain in the Russian church adjacent to the Holy Sepulcher (and, possibly, in a baker's supply room in the old market).

After Constantine had proclaimed Christianity the religion of his empire, his mother, Helena, made a pilgrimage to the Holy Land. In the course of her tour, she is reputed to have found in this area associated with the Crucifixion, pieces of wood lying in a cistern. These pieces of wood Helena identified with the cross on which Jesus was crucified. At her instigation, Constantine built a church on this spot. It was a very large rectangular church, far more extended than the church today. Some of the columns and arches believed to belong to this church may be among the antiquities excavated in the Russian church, next door to the Holy Sepulcher.

The original Constantinian church was laid out east to west. There was an atrium, preceded by a great triple-door entranceway from the street. Inside was a colonnaded forecourt. Continuing west, the pilgrim entered a five-aisle basilica in which the floor was covered with varicolored marble slabs, and the ceiling paneled and decorated with gold. Included in the basilica was a chapel in honor of the discovery of pieces of the Cross. Above the chapel was a dome supported by twelve columns. Still more westerly there was a second colonnaded forecourt which housed the rock of Calvary, supposed site of the Crucifixion. Lastly, there was the room of the Tomb, the rotunda. The rotunda was a huge room with vaulted ceiling, with windows all around so that at any hour of the day the sun shone directly on the holy shrine, the Tomb of Jesus. This perfectly exquisite church must have been all light, all brightness, and all inspiration in contrast to its dull and depressing appearance today.

As with so many fine ancient structures, the church of Constantine did not stand for long. It was destroyed in 614 by the Persians and almost immediately restored. In the eleventh century, the Arabs destroyed the church, the Crusaders rebuilt it. Since that time, as previously reported, the church has suffered a thousand years of damage and decay. The present effort to restore the Crusader church is estimated to require a minimum of ten years. Some partially completed sections of the church are beginning to show the promise of a handsome new, yet old, church that will at last be in keeping with the significance of the event it commemorates.

Early Holy Week Services

It is believed that a regular schedule of services for the observance of Holy Week was instituted by Cyril, Bishop of Jerusalem between 382 and 386. Cyril, in filling the hours of that solemn week with services, was attempting to control the activities of pilgrims, who at best would have to be described as overly boistrous. In 379 Pope Gregory had made a pilgrimage to

Jerusalem and he minced no words in reporting that he found the conduct of the pilgrims unbecoming, to whit: "There is no form of uncleanness that is not perpetrated among them; rascality, adultery, theft, idolatry, poisoning, quarreling, murder are rife; and the last kind of evil is so excessively prevalent, that nowhere in the world are people so ready to kill each other as there; where kinsmen attack each other like wild beasts and spill each other's blood, merely for the sake of lifeless plunder."

After Holy Week observances were scheduled for hours of both day and night, the clergy of Jerusalem found they had to halt another misdemeanor among the pilgrims. During one of the services, the Cross was brought into the chancel in a casket. It was removed from the casket so that pilgrims might have the privilege of kissing it as they passed by the altar. The pilgrims, anxious to have a tiny personal holy relic, devised a ruse to ensure that they would have one. They bit into the Cross and carried a piece of it home in their mouths. When the clergy discovered that the Cross was slowly disappearing, they set a guard over it while it was in the chancel.

While we may find this latter antic of the pilgrims amusing, we must admit that the same sort of pilfering continues today. The Stone of Unction in the Holy Sepulcher has had to be replaced several times because pilgrims insist on chipping off bits of it to carry home.

The Service of the Holy Fire

On a normal day, it is possible to hear the singing and chanting of three to four services held at the same time of day in the Holy Sepulcher. Pilgrims are welcome to watch or participate in any one. The most spectacular of these services in the Holy Sepulcher at Easter time is held jointly by the Armenians, Greeks, Copts, and Syrians, with the Abyssinians invited as guests. This is the service of the Holy Fire. Listen to a description of the service in the Easter brochure distributed to pilgrims by the Jordanian Tourism Authority: "The Ceremony of the Holy

Fire is exciting and vociferous. People come dressed in all their best. Villagers come from the country in their colorful national attire. Banners wave, voices are raised in happy song; joy spreads about and an atmosphere of jubilance pervades. According to legend, fire is handed down from heaven to the Greek Orthodox Patriarch secluded in the Tomb, who then emerges with a lighted torch. The ceremony symbolizes the Resurrection of Jesus, the light of the world, out of the Tomb. The scene that follows the appearance of the Patriarch is indescribable. The acclaiming exultant crowd surges forward around the Tomb and the Patriarch to light their candles from the Holy Fire, and the church is instantly alight with candles, torches and lanterns, which are reverently carried away to bless homes and loved ones."

This description is substantially correct. Since this service is an important Easter celebration for so many of the faithful in so many branches of the church, the inside of the Holy Sepulcher and the courtyard are packed with people. Inside the rotunda, people plaster themselves against the walls and cling to the scaffolding. While the service itself does not take place until noon, the lay participant must present himself at the church before 10 A.M. Saturday if he wishes to view the ceremony from inside the church. By eleven o'clock, all space within the church is taken. (When I say all, I mean *all*. To illustrate: our daughter fainted, but was so well supported by neighboring bodies that she stood with her head slumped. Fortunately, in such an emergency, my husband was able to catch the eye of some of the tourist police who are provided and trained in great numbers by the tourism department to assist tourists in every manner possible. The tourist police helped my husband get our daughter out of the church. Unfortunately, however, as they were making their way through the crowd, a sympathetic worshiper gave our dazed child a little water from a pilgrim flask. This kind act only added to our problem because we had no idea where the water in the flask had come from. We spent an uneasy six weeks wondering if an illness would develop, but none did.)

In spite of the lack of elbowroom, it is true that the worshipers are in a most joyous mood and spontaneous demonstrations of religious fervor come from all areas of the church—usually in the form of women chanting and ululating. (Ululation sounds very much like an Indian war cry.) At the service I attended, a group of teen-age boys, with a boy atop their shoulders carrying a torch, banded together and pressed their way around the rotunda chanting at the top of their lungs. This demonstration was a bit alarming, and my first frantic thought was that we might be about to witness a political fracas within the church. An Egyptian gentleman next to me tapped my arm and said. "Do not be alarmed. The boys are shouting 'Jesus Christ has risen from the dead.'"

There are other, more orderly processions around the rotunda during the Holy Fire service. The participating branches of the church take turns parading. Priests carrying banners are led in these processions by their patriarchs. To be frank, the pilgrims attending the service find it hard to make out an orderly procession, but they can spot the banners moving slowly through the crowd and occasionally they may glimpse a headpiece that would be worn only by the clergy. But the *service* is hidden completely from the view of the worshipers. Sealed inside the edicule (the enclosed structure that holds the Tomb of Jesus) are representatives of the Greek and Armenian churches. When these gentlemen finish their service, they hand out, through a hole in the side of the edicule, the Holy Fire.

This is an ecstatic moment for the worshipers. Runners, who have been eagerly anticipating this moment, light torches from the Holy Fire and run with them as rapidly as they can to altars and chapels in other areas of the church. Some runners try to be the first to carry the Holy Fire to the very top of the church building. In the meantime small aisles through the worshipers have been partially cleared by tourist policemen for the runners. But before the runners can make a clean getaway from the edicule, worshipers have already started lighting candles from the torches. The faithful pass the fire from their candles to the candles of their neighbors.

Holy fire is as sacred to them as holy water to the Roman Catholic. As you can imagine, a church ablaze with thousands of candles can be a beautiful and moving sight and an unforgettable experience for the pilgrims. We saw many with tears streaming down their faces. However, it is also a highly dangerous ceremony. Thousands of lighted candles in this press of excited people is a most unnerving experience to a practical-minded worshiper. Tourist policemen, aware that this church has suffered fire damage from similar past services, try to enforce a regulation that candles be snuffed out soon after they are lighted. Many persons comply, but there are always those few, to whom the fire means so much, who will make every attempt to carry the fire back to their homes.

The Foot-washing Ceremony

The Holy Fire service is only one of many services dating back to Byzantine times that the tourist is able to witness in Jerusalem. Another ancient ritual, observed independently by the Copts, Greeks, Syrians, and Armenians, is the foot-washing ceremony. The patriarch, assuming the role of Jesus in the upper room on Maundy Thursday, washes and anoints the feet of twelve priests who represent the twelve disciples.

The Greek foot-washing service is held in the courtyard of the Holy Sepulcher and is extremely well attended. Pilgrims fill every inch of floor and roof space to see it. Women well beyond the age of such athletics climb ladders to perch on rooftops. Tourist policemen are again needed to control the crowd. Pilgrims jockeying for better position to view the ceremony engage in heated arguments that may erupt into explosive situations involving several families. Trying to photograph the ceremony, my husband raised his arms high over his head to avoid getting the heads of worshipers in his picture. Not until his neighbors allowed it by squeezing away from him was he able to drop his arms back to normal position.

The ceremony itself is brief, dignified, and impressive. Robed in stunning red and gold vestments, the twelve priests and the Patriarch proceed to a platform in the courtyard and re-enact the scene in the upper room (Luke 22:11–12), the foot washing (John 13:5), the announcement of the betrayal (John 13:21), and the Agony in the Garden of Gethsemane (Matthew 26:36). Appropriate scripture is read by a narrator and spoken by the clergy throughout the service.

Following the service, pilgrims vie for a few drops of the holy water with which the Patriarch has washed the feet of the twelve. If successful, they use the water to make the sign of the Cross on their foreheads. When the water in the basin has been exhausted, they look for water spots on the rug of the platform and press this moisture into a handkerchief, hug the handkerchief to their breasts and carry it home.

The Armenian foot-washing service is held inside the Church of St. James in the Armenian Quarter. This service has great solemnity, perhaps because it is held inside the church. The altar of the church is on a raised platform so that the pilgrim is the audience looking up at the service on the stage. A curtain hides the chancel before the ceremony begins. In front of the curtain is a pitcher of water, a basin and a receptacle holding a mound of fat. The Armenians use the fat to anoint the foot after washing it. When the curtain is drawn, the stage setting for this Christian service is absolutely magnificent.

The altar is handsome and in the candlelight shines like pure gold. Seated before the altar are the clergy and altar boys, dressed in the most beautiful robes. The altar boys wear light blue satin, the clergy cream satin robes, imprinted with floral designs. The Patriarch's robe is lavishly embroidered with gold thread. The clergy wear black hoods and have gold crosses hung round their necks; the Patriarch wears a gilt-decorated miter which he changes for a crown as he washes the feet of the twelve. Scripture readings and anthems by the choir complete this eye-filling and spiritual ceremony.

There are also burial services for Christ in Jerusalem. All take place in the Holy Sepulcher where either winding sheets or icons are carried from Calvary to the Stone of Unction, where it is believed the body of Christ was prepared for burial. There the winding sheets are incensed and spiced, the icons anointed; thus prepared for burial they are carried to the Tomb.

The Search for Christ's Body

The most unusual, unfamiliar, and perhaps most colorful ceremony held at Easter is that of the search for the body of Christ conducted by the Abyssinians. On Holy Saturday, they gather on the roof of the Chapel of St. Helena and hold the service under a tent. The meager treasure of the Abyssinian Church is displayed in the gold-braid robes and umbrellas used by the abuna (father of the church) and the jewel-studded miters and crosses. You may wonder about the "umbrella." It is the symbol of high office in the Abyssinian Church and was also so regarded in ancient Israel and Persia. (This symbolism is known in the Psalms where God is spoken of as "my shade" or "my parasol.")

After the service in the tent, the clergy and their attendants form a procession and they march four times around the dome of the chapel to the accompaniment of tom-tom drums beating African rhythms. Those among the marchers who are familiar with the rhythm shuffle their feet in imitation of an African dance. Following the march, the participants return to the tent for additional prayers and hymns.

*

In Jerusalem, literature is available that explains each of these services in detail. For a richer and fuller understanding of the ways in which others worship, the pilgrim needs English translations of the liturgies. Otherwise, the language problem will make attendance at the different services little more than a jumble and confusion.

A second way in which the tourist can increase his understanding of what he sees in the Holy Land is to talk with the tourist police. Most of these fine men speak English and they are usually well versed in what is going on. If they do not have all the answers the tourist seeks, they will direct him to where he can get the information he wants. Most Jerusalemites are delighted to give help when asked. They are very happy when tourists show an interest in or appreciation of any facet of their most fascinating city.

The Mount of Olives

The Mount of Olives is perhaps the most thrilling and satisfying area of Jerusalem for the pilgrim. The churches and monasteries here are lovely in design and beautifully kept. These are all newer buildings, many of them built over older shrines. Almost all of them have been rebuilt late in the last century or early in the present one.

Garden of Gethsemane and the Church of All Nations

The Roman Catholic Garden of Gethsemane Church is exquisite. The pilgrim can take special pride in it because funds to build the church probably came from his nation, as well as many others. The church is called the "Church of All Nations" and while this is an exaggeration, sixteen countries did contribute to it (the United States, Germany, Canada, Belgium, Britain, Spain, France, Italy, Mexico, Chile, Brazil, Argentina, Poland, Hungary, Ireland, and Australia).

The entranceway to the church is most impressive. Pillars and arches support a large mosaic that represents God the Father looking down from heaven as Jesus and the peoples of the world bow their heads in subjection to His will. Inside, the basilica has been designed to expose the bedrock that has been traditionally noted as the scene of the Agony of Jesus in Gethsemane.

To induce an atmosphere of solemnity and reverence, the basilica is lighted only to a minimal extent. The light in the church is so scant that for the first few moments the visitor cannot see any details. When his eyes have adjusted to the dimness, he is pleasantly surprised to see that the church architects have created a most unusual effect. The little light that enters the basilica through its translucent windows touches all of the interior with a soft purple glow. Since purple is the color associated with royalty, this lighting effect seems appropriate symbolism for a shrine dedicated to the Agony in the garden, where Jesus so well demonstrated his sovereignty by voluntarily drinking the bitter cup of the Crucifixion.

There the Franciscans maintain a garden that is a quiet, tasteful delight. It houses a number of old olive trees and beneath the trees native flowers are planted in each season. Bougainvillaea stretches the length and breadth of the garden walls. Visitors are welcome to take pictures (but not to pick the flowers—on almost every day enough tourists to denude the garden pass through it). The olive trees are claimed by many to date from the time of Christ. They look as if they might. All olive trees look as if they had lived too long, such is the physical appearance of the tree. If these are not the original trees from the garden, they are certainly worthy fledglings and probably in direct "blood" line.

The Church of Mary Magdalene

Another church dedicated to the Agony in the garden raises its beautiful onion-shaped spires into the sky, close by the Church of All Nations. This is the Church of Mary Magdalene, a breathtakingly beautiful shrine erected by the Russian Orthodox Church. Many sisters of that church live on the grounds and for that reason, the gate at the entranceway to the Russian property is usually locked. A pull on the chain near the gate will set off a clanging of bells that will alert the caretaker-gardener that there is a person without who wishes to enter. Pilgrims are welcomed. The Russian complex is another of the quiet, secluded sanctuaries in Jerusalem where visitors are privileged to wander or rest undisturbed.

The service on Sundays is open for visitors. It is a long service, starting at breakfast time. But there is much for the eye to see and much for the ear to hear. The robing of the clergy is magnificent and the same adjective can be used to describe the well-disciplined choir, all women, sisters of the church, who have trained themselves to assume tenor and bass assignments in addition to their usual female vocal range.

The Eastern services, so often seen in Jerusalem churches, date back to Byzantine times, perhaps to the time of Constantine. Liturgies of St. John Chrysostom, St. Basil, and St. James are used, the latter two only on special occasions. Detailed descriptions of the liturgies are available.

The Eastern Church

The tourist may be interested to know that there are many differences between the Eastern and Western Christian churches. Unlike the cathedrals of Europe and the churches in our own country, the Eastern churches attach no importance to windows. Perhaps this is because in the warmer climates it is better not to have windows so that the church will stay cooler in summer, warmer in winter.

The lack of windows gives the designer of the Eastern church great wall spaces to fill and this he is more than willing to do because the Eastern churches place great emphasis on the interior beauty of the building. The frescoes, the mosaics, and the symbols within the church building many times are dazzling.

This pervasive beauty serves a practical theological purpose— it reminds the Eastern worshiper at once that he has stepped from the material world *into heaven*, a bit of eternal life on this earth. He is, when he is in church, in communion with all of the saints who have passed on. For this reason, the Easterner who enters the church greets the saints with warmth and reverence. He kisses each icon in the church because each icon is the representation of a saint of the church.

The icons never look like flesh and blood people. They are

not supposed to. They are flat, two-dimensional pictorial representations, deliberately made so, to remind the worshiper again that the other world is not akin to this world. Mosaics and frescoes in the church also repeat the theme "we are not of this world."

The figures are usually flat, immobile, quiet, with eyes fixed to suggest a meditative attitude. Landscapes are usually distorted in perspective. Trees and buildings are used only to suggest a scene setting and are not represented in the same scale as the human figures beside them. The "feeling" of the art is that it reflects a well-ordered, stable, quiet scene. This is the message that the symbolism is supposed to portray—that the other world has none of the turbulence, the frustration, the sorrow of the present world.

In addition, mosaics are executed to enrich worship. As the worshiper tours the church, he is reminded of all the stories of the Bible. Thus, the mosaics serve as a teaching tool. Old and New Testament stories are usually portrayed in chronological succession on the walls and ceiling of the Eastern church.

As for the service itself, most of the action is limited to the officiating clergymen and his attendants. This body of celebrants moves from place to place within the church and behind the altar. At times, the chief celebrant appears with two candles that represent the dual nature of Christ and are pertinent to this moment within the service. At another time, the chief celebrant will appear carrying a three-branched candelabrum that represents the trinity.

At one point in the service, the entire group of celebrants proceeds with incense around the church. The incense is symbolic of the ascendance of our prayers to heaven. At other points during the service, altar boys light candles beneath icons. This ceremony tells the worshiper that the person represented on the icon has something to do with the service at this juncture.

Sections of the service are not heard by the lay worshipers. The chief celebrant prays inaudibly behind the altar screen.

Worshipers accustomed to this very old service have no difficulty in following it, even responding where a response is indicated. The service consists of preparation for Holy Communion, prayers and litanies, gospel reading, the Communion and the Thanksgiving.

Because of the length of the service, many tourists do not care to stay through its entirety. Since it is not in English, they tend to become restless and inattentive. One Russian church on the Mount of Olives—not the Mary Magdalene—found the coming and going and sometimes talking aloud of tourists too disturbing and closed its doors to outsiders. The Church of Mary Magdalene still opens its doors to all, so let us hope that all visitors will conduct themselves in such a way that it can continue to welcome visitors.

When we were there in 1964 a very large group of Protestant worshipers was granted the privilege of marching from the Old City to the Mary Magdalene church and holding a service in its garden sanctuary on Holy Thursday. Among the Protestants were Arabs, Swedes, Danes, Americans, and Germans. The Protestants do not own property in the Garden of Gethsemane area. What a fine gesture it is for the Russians to allow the use of theirs! An hour later the Anglicans held a service there also.

Since the Church of Mary Magdalene is on the side of the Mount of Olives, it is a good healthy climb from the entranceway to the church and the gardens behind the church. Those of us who engaged in the Holy Thursday night march were singing hymns quite gaily as we marched through the streets of Jerusalem but by the time we had climbed partway up the Mount of Olives our singing was punctuated by audible huffs and puffs.

The Dominus Flevit and the Pater Noster Church

Pilgrims enjoy visiting two other Christian monuments on the Mount of Olives. One is the Dominus Flevit, a small church erected to honor the memory of Jesus' crying over Jerusalem.

The second is the unusual Pater Noster Church, built on the traditional spot where Jesus first instructed his disciples how to pray. On the walls of the church are tiles inscribed with the Lord's Prayer in forty-four languages. The fathers who maintain the Pater Noster Church have recently excavated nearby a Constantinian basilica, which means that the tradition behind this site dates back at least to the early fourth century.

The Mosque of the Ascension

There is also a mosque on the Mount of Olives that is of interest to Christians. This is the Mosque of the Ascension, until 1187 a Christian shrine. Inside the mosque, guides point out the supposed last footstep of Jesus, imprinted on a rock, as he ascended to heaven. You may not know that the Muslims revere Jesus as a great prophet and believe in the doctrine of his ascension into heaven. The Muslims believe that Mohammed, to them the greatest and latest prophet of God, *did* die and that Jesus did not. On resurrection day, they further believe, Mohammed will be the first person to be raised from the dead by Jesus.

I noticed in the mosque a rather curious circumstance. The main souvenir for sale is an olive-wood rosary. Business, it would seem, is no respecter of differing religious creeds.

The roof of the mosque is usually filled with tourists busily engaged in snapping pictures. From this vantage point you can overlook all the area surrounding Jerusalem. The panorama includes the Dead Sea, the Hill of Evil Counsel (now ironically housing the UN office personnel), the Augusta Victoria Hospital (now used mainly for refugees), Mount Scopus (the Israeli enclave entirely within Jordanian territory), as well as the whole city of Jerusalem.

The Dome of the Rock

The view of the Old City of Jerusalem is quite forcefully dominated by the many minarets that rise above the houses and

markets. Most imposing is the huge Muslim complex that includes the Aqsa Mosque and the exquisite gilt-domed Dome
of the Rock. In all, the houses of worship, museum, and
school of the Muslim complex cover thirty-four acres.

Every tourist includes the Dome of the Rock in his tour of
Jerusalem, not only because it is such a work of art, recently
refurbished with new tiles on the outside and a gilt dome, but
also because the site of this mosque has meaning in Old Testament history. The Dome of the Rock is believed to be on
Mount Moriah, the place where Abraham took Isaac and was
relieved of the duty to sacrifice his first-born to God. Solomon's
Temple, a fulfillment of a promise of David, also probably
rested on this spot. Herod's Temple was here, more grand,
more spacious, more pretentious than that of Solomon. This
latter would have been the Temple where Jesus came, as a
boy and man. Archaeologists yearn for an opportunity to probe
beneath the present mosque, but this is, of course, impossible.

Ten gates lead into this area, called the Haram, but only
one gate is normally open to Christians and tourists. One
reason that there is only one gate for outsiders is that aimless
wandering by visitors might disturb students and worshipers.
A second reason is that an entrance fee is collected at this
gate. This fee is actually payment for a booklet that gives the
history of both the Dome of the Rock and the Aqsa Mosque.

Inside the Dome of the Rock, a head-high fence surrounds
a large piece of bedrock that Muslims believe was the spot of
the intended sacrifice of Isaac. Muslims also subscribe to the
tradition that Mohammed visited Mount Moriah during one
of his night flights. Mosaic work inside the dome is most beautiful.

The Aqsa Mosque

Nearby is the Aqsa Mosque, not nearly so stunning on the
outside as the smaller Dome of the Rock, but truly lovely inside. Oriental rugs cover the floor and visitors as usual are

asked to remove their shoes or rent a shoe-covering. They are also cautioned to enter the mosque quietly because in almost all areas of the building, the faithful are praying or reading the Koran.

Gorgeous Arabian-style windows, stucco latticework holding small bits of colored glass, send shafts of colored lights playing on the luxurious carpets. The ceiling of the mosque is exquisite woodwork—the gift of the late king of Egypt, Farouk.

The mosque is divided into seven aisles by columns of rose-colored limestone and marble. Many of these columns have Corinthian capitals—a reminder that Jerusalem properties have changed hands from time to time! (Underneath are remains of a Byzantine structure.) The pillars lead to the vaulted dome of the mosque, a piece of mosaic artwork, largely gold. Arabic writing covers the ceilings and walls with very graceful and pleasing designs. This is not *merely* design because the writing spells out beloved words from the Koran.

In the courtyard outside there is a large fountain and basin, a necessary part of every mosque. The faithful are required to wash hands, face, and feet before prayers.

Usually visitors are gently ushered out of the Haram before the formal prayer hours. If visitors present themselves at the gate just at the prayer hour, it is customary to ask them to wait a while before entering.

I happened to be showing a group of American friends through the Haram on a day when the whole area was filled with the most colorful group of pilgrims—Muslims from all over the Near East and Africa. I had left my friends in the courtyard while I sought out a tourist policeman who might give us a guided tour. The tourist policeman was busy and my waiting for him kept me and my party on the premises into the noon prayer hour. When the policeman was finally free to accompany me back to where I had left my friends, I saw to my horror that they were completely engrossed in snapping pictures of the Muslim pilgrims as they performed their ablutions at the fountain. Such photography is strictly taboo. I am sure I turned purple in embarrassment.

The tourist policeman, disarmed (I think) by the obvious naïveté of the Americans, did not say a word of rebuke but graciously led us out of the courtyard toward other areas of the Haram. Those Americans are the possessors of some very rare photographs.

The reason that I had needed the service of a tourist policeman was that he keeps the key to an area of the Haram that is locked. He must unlock the door to the stairway that leads to the substructures of the Haram, a simply amazing series of huge arches that are popularly called "Solomon's Stables," although they are not Solomon's Stables and do not date back nearly so far into history. Cut through the stone in some of the arches are holes that suggest that animals may have been tethered here at some time in history.

Here beneath the mosque are other architectural remains of an earlier Jerusalem. There is a small altar believed by the Muslims to have been part of a church that was built on a spot where the Holy Family rested on its flight to Egypt. Also beneath the mosque are remnants of what must have been a sizable Byzantine church.

The Muslims

Who are the people who flock to the mosques on Fridays, who have erected the mosques and minarets, sometimes over Christian shrines, and what is their faith? It is important that tourists know the Muslims because visitors to the Jordanian Holy Land are guests of the Muslims. You might in a sense call the Muslims the preservers of the Christian shrines because this land that you and I hold so dear and that we like to feel "ours" is, in bald fact, "theirs."

Jordan is almost completely a Muslim country. It is through the courtesy of the government that we as tourists are allowed to make pilgrimages. The figure given for religious affiliation in Jordan is over 90 per cent Muslim. The Christians consist of *a*. those monks and sisters allowed to live on in the shrines and monasteries that have been theirs traditionally from the early days of the Christian church, *b*. those few Arab and Armenian Christians living in Jordan, and *c*. United Nations personnel, personnel from various churches doing welfare work in Jordan, a handful of archaeologists, and the tourists.

My husband and I worshiped in many Protestant churches with congregations no larger than twenty-five to fifty persons, except on festival days. At the Greek foot-washing ceremony, we witnessed the service along with perhaps a thousand other people, most of them pilgrims. At the joint Holy Fire service, perhaps two thousand were present, again largely pilgrims.

The Protestant churches are the smallest in number in Jordan and sad to report, increases in the size of their congregations are effected by proselyting from the Orthodox Christian churches. Evangelism as such, an effort by Christians to convert Muslims, would not be tolerated by the government. So, let's look more closely at the Muslims and find out who these people are who live among the scenes of Jesus' great triumph and yet are not sufficiently affected by it to deny a first allegiance to Mohammed.

The people of Jordan are a small part of the great Muslim world comprised of Turkey, Syria, Egypt, Saudi Arabia, Lebanon (½), Yemen, Kuwait, Iran, Iraq, Sudan, Libya, Tunisia, Algeria, Morocco, Afghanistan, Pakistan, and Indonesia. Notice that Islam, the Muslim religion, now predominates in some countries not populated by Arabs.

The Islamic Religion

Mohammed, the founder of Islam, was an Arab, a leader of caravans through Saudi Arabia and Syria. He lived in the sixth and seventh centuries A.D. He believed that he had received a revelation from God and the truths so learned he wrote down in a book called the Koran. Mohammed was strongly influenced by the culture of the Bedouin and by the religion of the Jews, but he was adversely disposed to Byzantine Christianity with its orientation toward Mary, the saints and their images, and the doctrine of the Trinity. This Christianity, Mohammed saw as a form of polytheism. He preached that there is only one God (in Arabic, God is called "Allah") and the proper way of life for a person was to bow in submission to Allah and the will of Allah. Thus, the doctrines of Islam consist of *a.* a belief in one God, *b.* a duty to pray five times daily, *c.* the observance of a month of fasting (Ramadan), *d.* a pilgrimage to Mecca, the most sacred sanctuary, and *e.* the giving of alms.

Later, Mohammed thought it wise to hand down decisions on civil matters to clarify further the proper way to live. He prohibited the eating of pork, gambling, and drinking alcohol. Man should not realize a profit on money lent to another and interest was not to be charged. As a precaution against idolatry, Muslims should not make representations of animals or human beings. Polygamy was acceptable, but to the limit of four wives.

How conscientiously do the Muslims in Jordan live up to the rules prescribed by Mohammed? While it is impossible to look into the heart of any man, one can observe the influence of the Muslim religion on the daily lives of the people.

The belief that there is but one God and that this premise leaves no room for granting to Christ equality with the Father is strongly held by the Muslims. They no longer draw a sword to cut down the "Christian dog" in their midst, and most are courteously tolerant of the Christian's right to believe as he wishes. It is possible to see a few bemused smiles or hear a few scoffs from the Muslims when they watch Christian observances at Christmas, but this is not the rule.

The duty to pray five times daily, traditionally by prostrating yourself and facing Mecca, seems to be practiced only by the most devout. The call to prayer is regularly broadcast in stentorian tones from every minaret (sometimes by a recording). It is rare to see a man stop in his tracks and heed the call.

The fasting during Ramadan is quite rigidly observed. This month can occur any season of the year since Mohammed followed the uncorrected lunar calendar for fasts and feasts. For the entire month, Muslims are not allowed to eat, drink water, smoke, or have sexual intercourse during daylight hours. Rather, they are to devote themselves to prayer, meditation, and the giving of alms. If Ramadan occurs during the winter when the days are shorter, the fast is not nearly so taxing as it is during the hot, dry summer. In Jerusalem during Ramadan, the boom of a cannon in the very early morning hours wakens Christians and Muslims alike, but to the Muslim the cannon announces that it is time to rise, pray, and eat before the sun comes up. Again in the evening, the cannon announces that the sun has descended and it is time to pray and have an evening meal.

Muslims become their brother's keeper during this fast. It is not easy to take food or drink unobserved. At one of the archaeological digs, one of the Muslim workers thoughtlessly lit a cigarette and he was immediately fallen upon by an angry group of Muslim brethren. So ended his brief smoke. The restriction against smoking during daylight hours must work a great hardship on many persons, because the Arabs, both men and women, smoke heavily—almost fiercely. One young girl confessed to me that her father would arise at night and smoke until he was sated to help him to get through the day.

Exceptions from the restrictions of the fast are sometimes made for the ill or for men who must engage in heavy labor. Men who work on archaeological digs are not given an exemption. Out of consideration for these men, some dig supervisors adjust the day's working hours so that work starts earlier in the morning and stops at noon.

At the end of the month of fasting, all Muslims are supposed to wash, clothe themselves in clean garments, and partake of a most happy feast. We found it amusing that the shopkeepers in closing for several days for the feast announced that "they would be closed for their Christmas."

The rule against the eating of pork still applies. In fact, I did not see a pig in the Middle East from Turkey to Iran. However, pork is occasionally served in the hotels to tourists.

Whether or not people gamble is difficult to say. Most of the people do not have enough money to gamble. In the coffee houses, men play cards, backgammon, dominoes quite spiritedly but there is no money passing across the tables. At a track near the Dead Sea that offers horse and camel racing there is gambling for certain. Spectators rush to place bets before each race.

If alcohol is drunk by the Muslims, it is sub rosa. There are few, very few, bars in Jordan and the patrons are usually tourists. Never did I see a Muslim under the influence of alcohol, nor did I personally ever see a Muslim take a drink. The wines of the country are made by Christian monks and, along with their cheeses, provide the monasteries with some income. Wines and spirits are sold everywhere in Jordan. The groceries have huge stocks of all liquors, mild and potent. They are moderately priced and purchased by Westerners. It is possible to see very poor people begging for money on the streets but none will be drunk. Lest that statement give the impression that beggars are common in Jordan, it must quickly be added that beggars in Jordan seem to be seasonal imports when the tourist trade is at its height. Otherwise only the young children tease for gifts of money.

The obligation to give alms is taken seriously by the devout. Perhaps for that reason it is common to see some of the poor spending their days inside the mosques where the more faithful worshipers will not pass them by without handing them some coins.

The lifetime goal of every Muslim is to make the pilgrimage to Mecca. How many Muslims from Jordan make the trip, I do not know. I did, however, see many Muslim pilgrims from all over the Middle East and northern Africa who stopped in Jerusalem on their way to or from Mecca. Most of these pilgrims were in modest circumstances, we assumed, since they were traveling the distance in ramshackle buses.

Pictures and Cameras

Mosques do not have images or pictures of any kind. Some Muslims do have family pictures in their homes and the most westernized Muslims see no contradiction in patronizing the movies. In some Muslim villages and tent communities, however, there is such a strong feeling against images of any kind that the tourist who raises his camera for a shot may have his camera taken from him and smashed. The commandment against images includes photos as well as representation of human forms in mosques. Some Muslims feel quite sincerely that the image carried away on the camera may take with it a part of a man's immortality. Pictures of animals are taboo for the same reason. Some Muslims are superstitious about the "evil eye" that can curse a man, and they see the camera as a possible "evil eye." This latter belief does not come from Islam, but rather from the nomads who, while nominally Muslim, have not forgotten desert traditions.

My own experience with a camera was that persons who did not know me and my purpose refused to allow pictures. If the people involved were acquainted with me and my husband, they were usually very gracious about posing for us asking only that we send them a developed copy of the picture.

Recreation

As stated earlier, when we tour Jordan, we are guests of a Muslim society. Muslims do not work all day and then live it up at night. The Muslims go to bed. If they are true believers, they will be up before dawn to pray. Consequently, there is very little night life in Jordan, although a few night clubs have been opened for the tourists.

The theaters in Jordan are very well attended. Movie houses may show as many as three double features during a week. Movies supply an escape outlet for Arab males, but there is little other recreation offered in Jordan. Except for a few persons, Jordanians have no opportunity to swim, play tennis, or play ball, and there is almost no way for them to "let off steam" through wholesome activities. It is no wonder the Arabs tend to be restless and possessed of unused nervous energy. This expends itself in the movie houses where the men, well fortified with nuts and seeds and soda pop, settle down to take in the show.

Films from all countries are presented. European films have English and Arabic subtitles, American films Arabic and French subtitles.

Incidentally, if a woman tourist attends the theater in Jordan, she and her escort are ushered into the balcony. Men only on the first floor! In the balcony there would be other women with their escorts, all in Western dress. Never did I see a woman dressed in native clothing in the theater. The theater is for the men folk.

To repeat, there is very little night life in Jerusalem. All shops have their metal doors down and locked by eight o'clock and there are very few people out on the streets after that time. The only interruption in the quiet of the evening will come at about eleven o'clock when the theaters close and the men make their way home.

Precious Water

Since the purpose of this book is to acquaint you with the way of life in the Holy Land, you may as well learn about one of the sad facts of life in the country. Jordan is short on water. Tourists may feel that a brief three-day stay in the Holy Land can have no effect on this problem. The hotels, so anxious to appear modern and Western, may not impose water restrictions and thousands of three-day tourists will innocently use up or waste one of the most precious Jordanian necessities. How? Tourists take *long* refreshing showers or relax in a *full* tub of water. They will probably use the toilet at times in lieu of a wastebasket for cleansing tissues, cigarettes, etc. Most Americans have no idea of what it means to conserve water. And *American* tourists are the worst offenders in wasting water. One new Jerusalem hotel, catering mainly to Americans, uses as much water per day as the rest of the city. Only three springs supply the Jerusalem public water system.

Otherwise Jordan is almost entirely dependent on the mercy of the skies for water. In years when the skies do not bountifully supply, the people thirst. Yes, *thirst*. The few affluent citizens of Jordan can always buy a tank of water to refill their cisterns when droughts come, but the majority of the people must rely on filling their cisterns with winter rains and when that supply is used, the water is gone until rain comes again. When winter rains are scant, Jordanians must impose severe rationing on themselves. Think if you can what this may mean.

One of our friends in Jordan told us how difficult it is for parents to comfort a thirsty child. During one summer when the cisterns had been drained except for a bit of stagnant residue, it was necessary not only to train the children to do without water but to warn them not to touch the little remaining in the cistern because it might be contaminated. To distract the children when they awakened thirsty in the night, the parents took turns telling them stories to coax them to fall asleep. In spite of the warnings of the parents, one little fellow got up during the night and helped himself to a few swallows from the cistern. Result? Typhoid.

As far as baths are concerned, it is easy to notice that the ordinary Jordanian does not fret about keeping himself scrubbed. The Jordanians may "offend," as we phrase it, but there is good reason for it. How many Jordanians do you think have running water in their homes? Very few. If you were to ride through the country between eight and nine in the morning or between five and five-thirty in the afternoon, you would see the Jordanian "running water." It would be carried in jugs or cans on the heads of women and girls from a spring or well back to their homes. They use this supply sparingly.

When you prepare dinner at home, you wash rice and

vegetables under a spigot and let the water run down the drain. Water used for this purpose in Jordan is saved, and if usable for no other purpose, it is sprinkled on the garden.

If you should visit the Holy Land, remember to exercise conscience and judgment in using water lest you inadvertently cause suffering to others.

The Dew of Heaven

Nature has a unique method of partially compensating Jordan for its lack of rainfall. During many nights of the year, there is an extraordinarily heavy dew. (The Bible often speaks of this dew as a blessing: Gen. 27:28, "God give thee of the dew of heaven and the fatness of the earth"; Ex. 16:13 and Num. 11:9 speak of manna coming with the dew, etc.) This dew will drain off the rooftops into welcoming barrels. It will also drip off the trees on passers-by. This dew is the lifesaver of many shrubs, trees, flowers, and vegetables. It is probably also a godsend to the sheep and goats. When I was up early in the morning, I often saw taxi drivers washing their cars with no other moisture than dew and finding that sufficient to clean away all the dust of the previous day's journey.

The Garden Tomb

Thus far, in taking you on a tour of the town of Jerusalem, I have followed a logical itinerary through the Christian shrines and I have mentioned a few things about Jordanian life that might interest you. Before we leave Jerusalem, I must mention that there are two places that hold interest for tourists although they are apart from the usual tourist's pathway.

On the Nablus Road, not too far from the Damascus Gate, there is a sign "This way to the Garden Tomb." The Garden Tomb? You and I have already been told that the Tomb lies within the Old City, now covered by the Church of the Holy Sepulcher. But, nevertheless, if we took the pathway suggested, stopped at the doorway, rang the bell, we would be admitted to a pleasing little sanctuary around a beautiful ancient tomb. It looks just like the pictures in your Bible. You can almost see Mary coming here on Easter morning looking for her Lord. You can imagine an angel of the Lord sitting inside the tomb announcing that her Lord was no longer here but had risen from the dead.

As I looked at the tomb, I saw above its opening a tremendous solid arch of stone, twice as tall as a man. At one time, a monumental stone disc fitted up against it to seal the tomb. It rolled into position in a carved stone track. This sealing stone also fits the Easter story. It would have been impossible for one or two women to have moved this huge stone aside so that they could enter the tomb. They would have needed help.

There is one other coincidence that appears to confirm this tomb site as genuine. Just to the right of the tomb there is a small hill that might have served as Calvary. When this hill is seen from the front, holes and depressions in it give it the uncanny appearance of a gigantic skull—Golgotha means "the place of the skull." This site is called "Gordon's Calvary" after General Charles Gordon of Chinese and, later, Khartoum fame who after a year spent in studying Holy Land antiquities in 1883, proposed it as the genuine site for the Crucifixion. On the type of evidence outlined above, many Protestant pilgrims have confirmed in their own minds that the Garden Tomb is indeed here.

Pilgrims are not alone in clinging to the hope that this is the original tomb. Some scholars of the last century wrote books to persuade other scholars that this was the original tomb. Their writings have not been taken seriously, however, by cautious and meticulous scholars.

One of the arguments put forth by protagonists of the Gordon site is that the tomb of the Holy Sepulcher lies within the city walls of Jerusalem whereas the Bible clearly states that the Crucifixion took place *outside* the city walls. This argument is not convincing because while it is not definitely known where the

city walls were in the time of Jesus, it is positively known that
the present city walls were built later than the Middle Ages.

Cautious scholars also point out that the long continuous
tradition of the tomb beneath the Holy Sepulcher cannot be
thrown to the winds as meaningless. It is possible that eye
witnesses to the Crucifixion were still living in Jerusalem when
the earliest pilgrims came to seek the Tomb. And another argument against Gordon's Calvary as the true tomb site seems to be
irrefutable—archaeologists have dated the tomb as early Christian,
no earlier than the second century A.D.

In any case, the Garden Tomb is an interesting historical find.
It provides the setting for many an Easter sunrise service; how
glorious it was to be in Jerusalem at Easter, to sit in a garden
before an open tomb as the sun came up and to join with other
pilgrims in singing hymns of praise and honor to Jesus, the
Christ. I mentioned previously that it is possible to see a first-
century tomb in the Syrian crypt at the Holy Sepulcher. The
tourist may also see a large Jewish tomb complex dating from
the first century at the so-called "Tomb of the Kings" just
opposite St. George's Cathedral on Saladin Street. Here a small
rolling stone still in its tracks sits beside the entrance to the
tomb. Such a stone would have sealed the tomb of Jesus. This
tomb has a deceivingly small entrance, a hole a person can
just get through, which opens into large chambers filled with
niches for burials. It belonged to one Helen from Mesopotamia,
who was a convert to Judaism about 50 A.D.

The Palestine Museum

Before tourists leave Jerusalem, they should allow plenty of time
for the Palestine Museum. Around the country, there are many
ancient archaeological remains, but the artifacts coming out of
the archaeological excavations are all safely stored in museums.
In years past, archaeologists have in a sense "plundered" the
Holy Land, excavating and carrying back to their native lands
whatever treasures they could find. More recently Jordan has

become aware of the value of ancient artifacts so that all antiquities unearthed become the property of the government and thus find their permanent home in local museums.

The splendid Palestine Museum was built, and endowed, thanks to a generous $2,000,000 gift of the late John D. Rockefeller. The exhibits, a panorama of the prehistory and history of the Holy Land, are arranged chronologically and are well lighted and displayed. Even a beginning student can see the evolution of that most important archaeological dating tool, the pottery. This is a teaching museum; to aid the student or tourist further, the museum has provided catalogs in several languages in each room. The catalogs give excellent, succinct information about the important art pieces displayed, from the Stone Age through sixteenth-century Arab craft.

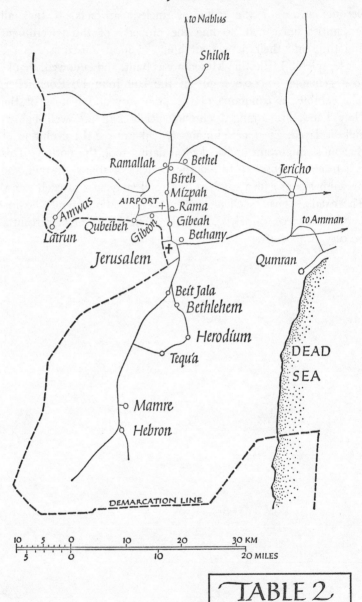

TABLE 2   From Jerusalem to Bethlehem and Hebron

IV   Where Jesus Was Born

The Road to Bethlehem

The ride from Jerusalem to Bethlehem is so picturesque in both directions that the tourist is torn to know whether to look forward or backward. The panorama of Jerusalem and the Mount of Olives is a pretty sight and it is almost always viewed against a brilliantly blue sky. Ahead, the roadway twists sharply and steeply down into a valley. To those uninitiated to driving in the Holy Land, all eyes will be on the road, all eyes on the hairpin turns, or the frightening abrupt descent from the side of the road into the valley. What a pity! The journey only takes thirty minutes, and those minutes could be put to better use watching the many cave dwellers in the area.

Some families have farmed patches of land in the immediate vicinity of their caves. A few have a handful of goats or sheep corralled by a bramble fence. Some of the caves are sealed by doors and the living area has been extended by a front porch. Some of the doorways of the caves are partially sealed by bramble bushes. Christian hermits lived so in the caves in the early days of the Christian era.

How large are the caves? We did investigate some uninhabited caves that proved to be part of a series of small caverns, sometimes side by side, sometimes front to back. An inside cave to the rear or to the side of the entrance cave room will provide a real shelter from the weather—cool in summer, warm in winter.

Archaeologists, using caves for sleeping quarters in wintertime, found the inside temperature a pleasant 72–74° F. Blackened ceilings give evidence that shepherds light fires in caves and that housewives cook in them. It is conceivable that some families might prefer the solid shelter of a cave to that of a tent. In some areas of Jordan, there are caves that could provide a hiding place for hundreds of persons—caves larger than a football field. But it was in the vicinity of Bethlehem that a small cave was used as a stable, a shelter for Mary and Joseph as they awaited the birth of a child.

Why is it believed a cave would have been used as a stable? It is rare even today in the Holy Land to shelter animals in a specially constructed enclosure. There are many caves available, to serve as shelters for shepherds' flocks. In early Holy Land history, caravansaries were usually built near caves that could house animals.

Justin Martyr, an early Church Father (150 A.D.), mentions Jesus' birthplace as a "cave." Later, Constantine sought the proper "cave" on which to build the Bethlehem Church.

The Birthplace

The road to Bethlehem today descends into tilled fields and orchards along a valley covered in spring with wild flowers and fruit trees in bloom. Beyond the valley at the top of a hill sits the quiet, charming town of Bethlehem.

Bethlehem had some Old Testament fame. Rachel died nearby shortly after giving birth to Benjamin (Gen. 35:19, 20). A small shrine in her honor is at the fork in the road where you turn off to Bethlehem from the main road south to Hebron.

Bethlehem was also mentioned in the Bible as the town where Ruth returned with her mother-in-law, and later married Boaz (Ruth 1:19 and 4:13). Since Joseph traced his lineage through Boaz (Luke 3:32), the story in the Book of Ruth accounts for Joseph's having to return to the family village on the occasion of the census (Luke 2:1–5).

Where was the cave in which Jesus was born? When Queen Helena, mother of Constantine the Great, made her pilgrimage in the early years of the fourth century, she felt that the evidence was quite clear. The Christians in Bethlehem said the grotto was in a grove of trees planted by Hadrian as a sanctuary for worshiping Venus and Adonis. Queen Helena found the grotto. Constantine built an elegant church above it, a church decorated with frescoed columns and mosaic covered walls. The grotto was not allowed to remain in its natural state (more is the pity!) but was enlarged to accommodate more pilgrims and rebuilt of marble and silver. When his mother died, Constantine sent to Bethlehem gifts of gold, silver, and embroidered curtains as a memorial. This church stood for two hundred years.

When the Emperor Justinian (527–565) came to Bethlehem he found that the church had been destroyed. There is no clear record to tell us how disaster came to the church, but some scholars suspect that the Samaritans may have had a hand in it. There was a Samaritan revolt early in the sixth century and the revolt was accompanied by much destruction in other parts of the land. The Emperor Justinian must have felt that there was not enough of the church left to bother about for he leveled the site and built a completely new church.

Archaeologists discovered in 1934 that Justinian had covered with dirt the mosaic floor of the Constantinian church and had laid a new floor of marble. Enough of the floor of the early Constantinian church remained so that archaeologists could at least determine the floor plan of the first Church of the Nativity. The mosaics can now be seen beneath trap doors in the floor of the present church.

How much of the Justinian church remains could only be ascertained from accurate records of the many restorations that have been necessary since the sixth century. The church as it stands is Justinian's church in plan. The red limestone pillars and Corinthian columns were shaped by Justinian's workmen. It is also possible that some of the roof beams date back that far. Less than a hundred years after the church was erected the Arab invasion overcame the Middle East. Apparently the Arabs made no attempt to destroy the church, but when the Crusaders came to the Holy Land they found the church in need of much restoration. The wall mosaics inside the church were the work of the Crusaders; it is possible that they simply repaired mosaics that belonged to the Justinian church.

The Church of the Nativity

The Church of the Nativity as it stands today appears from the outside to be quite substantial. Inside, the church has rather a drab appearance. The long basilica would look like nothing more than a huge hall were it not for the Justinian pillars and the few remaining mosaics high on the walls. Huge lamps suspended from the ceiling give a hint that at times the church may be gaily lighted, but the lamps are dark and covered with cloth except on festival days.

In the apse of the church there are altars belonging to the Greek and Armenian Orthodox churches. These two denominations share the Church of the Nativity.

The Grotto of the Nativity is beneath the altar of the church and the silver star in the center of the grotto supposedly marks the very spot of the Nativity. The decorations in the shrine are of the Eastern type—hanging lamps, lighted candles, and wall hangings. This holy place is usually well filled with pilgrims who stand quietly, waiting their turn to approach the "manger," kneel before it, and place a kiss on the star, or, cameras cocked and held in position, to photograph the "manger" at an opportune moment.

The Armenian and Greek priests, who are responsible for the preservation of this church, hold services daily, and visitors are invited to watch or participate. The Armenian service is quite colorful since the priests wear purple and cream-colored robes and there is some pageantry involved in the service as the priests move from altar to lectern to grotto in celebration of the mass.

The daily Greek service is not colorful to watch since these priests are dressed entirely in black—black robes and black pill-box hats. The Greek priests do not cut their hair—all have beards and a bun of hair at the back of the neck.

The beauty of the Greek service lies in the singing. The soloists employed at intervals during the service have well-trained, selected voices and it is doubtless an honor to be chosen and give one's talent to enrich the beauty of the service. During the Greek mass, Holy Communion is celebrated, at which time many loaves of native bread are consecrated and incensed. At the conclusion of the service, this bread is distributed among the priests and any other persons in attendance. Tourists such as ourselves were offered portions of bread to eat in a modest fellowship meal, but the poor folks who attended the service were given whole loaves to take home. This is a gesture of the church to provide alms for the needy.

Tourist Guides

While Bethlehem is not nearly so commercial a city as Jerusalem, the tourist will find it difficult to get near the Church of the Nativity without a guide. Several men make it their career to serve tourists at this church. They plant themselves daily at Manger Square, the large parking lot immediately in front of the church, and a visitor will hardly alight from his car before one of them has him by the elbow.

My husband and I visited the Bethlehem church at least a dozen times and we were greeted each time by the same persistent guide. A tour of the church was offered to us free—no charge for the guiding. However, the guide urged us to tip the tourist policeman who lifted the trap door to expose to view the floor mosaics of the Constantinian church and he asked us to "put a little something" in the box to help the brothers of the church to maintain the shrine.

At the end of the guided tour of the church, we found that we were back on the Bethlehem street and, conveniently, just a few doors away from what the guide described as his "brother's shop." Of course, we would want to take just a few moments to browse in his "brother's shop." The guide receives from the shop owner a percentage of the price of any purchases made.

Souvenirs

Many pilgrims like to take home souvenirs from Bethlehem. There are many little shops on the narrow streets behind the Bethlehem church. Near the shops are the "factories" that produce the souvenirs you will see. It is well worth the time to stop in one or two of these factories. The workmen will be seated on the floor, five to ten men in a small room, amid a clutter of materials and tools. They are most genial and will not be annoyed if visitors pick their way around the factory for closer inspection of the craft work with which they are occupied.

Particularly interesting is the sawing and drilling of mother-of-pearl. This iridescent shell is made into necklaces, earrings, pins, and detailed reproductions of biblical scenes (the scene in the manger, the Lord's supper, etc.). Since mother-of-pearl is fragile, you can well imagine that even a skilled craftsman can make a few slips with the drill or the saw. Tourists purchasing articles made from mother-of-pearl would be wise to ask permission to take the article out into the daylight so that it can be scrutinized. Chips and imperfections do not show up in the dimly lighted shops, and since the shopkeeper will charge the same price for each item of like kind, it is sensible to pick out the one most nearly perfect. Olive-wood souvenirs are also produced in Bethlehem. The price of souvenirs is likely to be a little less in Bethlehem than in Jerusalem.

Christmas in Bethlehem

What is it like to be in Bethlehem on Christmas? This is a question that my husband and I have been asked perhaps as often as any other. From a distance of thousands of miles, American Christians can picture in their minds that this tiny town must come alive and glow with joy on this most happy occasion, the celebration of the birth of Jesus.

It was amusing to read in our American newspapers that the

town of Bethlehem was alight with Christmas trees for the season. This was not true. The Christmas tree is a custom that has come from Western civilization. Where the West has infiltrated the East, in churches and schools maintained in Jordan by Germans, Englishmen, Americans, there will be a Christmas tree. In sum, we saw no more than a half-dozen trees decorated for Christmas.

Christmas does not make a big "splash" in the Holy Land. Remember, first, that the Christians in Jordan, even including pilgrims, make up a small minority. Second, the Christians in Jordan do not all celebrate the holiday on the same day. The Western Christians observe the celebration as we do on December 25. The Greek Orthodox, the Syrian Orthodox, the Copts, and Abyssinians also observe December 25 as Christmas, but since they follow the Julian calendar, *their* December 24–25 falls on *our* January 6–7. The Armenian Orthodox Church does not place the season's doctrinal emphasis on the *birth* of Christ, but on the *baptism* of Christ. Thus, they celebrate Christmas (the ancient Eastern Feast of the Incarnation) on January 18–19. (By the Western calendar, the Feast of the Baptism of Christ, Epiphany, falls on January 6.)

If this discussion of dates has thoroughly confused you, just remember that there are three different days that are selected as Christmas by branches of the Christian church within Jordan. There is no single Christmas day. For this reason, each group gathers with its adherents on its own day and the Christmas celebration does not take on the proportion of the Easter festivities.

My husband and I celebrated Christmas with the Western Christians on December 24–25. The schedule of events was: *a.* at noon on the twenty-fourth the Latin Patriarch arrived at the Church of the Nativity; *b.* at four-thirty in the afternoon, there was a service at Shepherds' Field; *c.* in the evening, there were church services in the various Bethlehem churches, some as early as eight o'clock and others as late as midnight.

Along with many tourists, we arrived at Bethlehem at noon

to witness the entrance of the Latin Patriarch. The ceremony is interesting, but short, and without any public worship involved. The Patriarch drives from Jerusalem to Bethlehem, alights from his car on the main street of Bethlehem about three city blocks from the church. On the streets the priests have arranged themselves in two orderly lines, waiting to greet the Patriarch and walk with him, in procession, to the church. The priests and the Patriarch wear festive robes, but the short walk to the church completes the ceremony.

A Walk Through Bethlehem

As there are no other Christmas services scheduled until late in the afternoon, the tourist is left to his own resources for four hours. We decided to tour the town. This can easily be done because it is small. Bethlehem is not exactly set up for tourist comfort. There are no cozy little lunchrooms where you can slip inside and warm up with a hot drink. There are no comfortable hotel lobbies where you can idle away an hour or so reading magazines. There are only streets and open-air shops, and houses and churches; and while the churches do offer a place to sit for a moment, they are unheated, and the damp, penetrating chill temperature inside is more uncomfortable than the outside air. So—in Bethlehem you *walk* and learn what you can about the way the people live.

We wandered through the market, watched the cobblers shaping shoes, walked past the court house and observed the scribes out front writing letters for persons unable to do so. We poked our noses into the many churches that were unlocked. We walked through the residential areas and enjoyed seeing a few women who still wore the old Bethlehem headdress, the conical cap covered with a white veil. This traditional headdress is not indigenous but came from Europe with the Crusaders, who also introduced the embroidered and lavishly trimmed bolero jacket occasionally worn by Jordanian women with their robes.

On our excursion we passed a funeral procession. The small

band of marchers was preceded by two young men carrying palm branches. In the midst of the male mourners were the pallbearers and the coffin. As the coffin passed by, we were able to view the deceased. Coffins in Jordan are sometimes covered with a rug but more often are open on top. The deceased was a middle-aged gentleman, neatly laid out in clean clothing. Round his head was a *kaffia* (much as if we were to lay out the dead in a hat). The women mourners tagged along at the end of the procession. This led us to believe that the procession was on its way to a church, for women in the Middle East do not usually accompany the body of the deceased to the graveyard for interment. This is the job of the men. There are no morticians in Jordan, and the cleaning and laying out of the dead devolves upon the women relatives. Nor are there embalmers in Jordan; the dead are buried before sundown, or as quickly as possible. Sometimes the body is buried in a coffin. To the poor who cannot afford this luxury, a coffin is made available by the church; after interment, it is brought back to the church for future use. The coffins are not decorated, but plain wooden boxes. This was a Christian funeral, but Muslim customs are similar.

Shepherds' Field

In the late afternoon hours of Christmas Eve, we drove a short way out of Bethlehem to Shepherds' Field. We should say "fields" (plural) because the exact location of the shepherds when the angels sang out the news to them can hardly be pinpointed. Three denominations have land in this area so that pilgrims can visit the general site and participate in services.

At the Protestant field, maintained by the YMCA, we were privileged to attend a carol sing and service held at dusk. We stood for about an hour for this service in the company of many other Christian tourists. The tourists stand on high ground. The service is held in a depression that leads into a cave. Following the service, the whole crowd presses down through the depression and into the cave. Why? Your ticket of admission to the

Shepherds' Field entitles you to a sandwich, half a loaf of round native bread with cooked lamb and its juices tucked into the pocket of the bread. Inside the cave, men dressed as shepherds hand you a sandwich as you file by and on out an exit that takes you back up to the field. Numbers of children, aware that this Christmas service ends with a small meal are on hand to wheedle the sandwich away from you. Since many tourists are squeamish about eating except in first-class hotels, it is likely that the children have found the occasion easy pickings.

Just before the service in Shepherds' Field began, we were treated to a fitting but unplanned event. Just a few feet from the assembled worshipers were a shepherd and his flock. One of the ewes picked this moment to deliver a lamb. The birth was easy. Before our eyes, this baby lamb came into the world. It stood rather uncertainly on its feet. The shepherd picked up the lamb and led the mother to a secluded spot where the ewe occupied herself with licking her baby clean. Very dramatic! And for those not raised on a farm, very educational.

Christmas Eve Services

On Christmas Eve in Bethlehem, there are services in the Protestant and Roman Catholic churches. We attended two Protestant services. The first was an Arabic service and was attended by about thirty persons. It was unusual to hear the old familiar Christmas tunes sung in Arabic. The Arabs love to sing and don't hold back an ounce of their full volume; the thirty persons almost made the rafters ring. As a special treat for the Arabs, the choir had selected "Silent Night" for their anthem and sang it in English. A later service in the same church brought together pilgrims and tourists who understood English or German. Short sermons in both languages were delivered to the congregation of about two hundred and fifty persons.

The most popular Christmas service among pilgrims is the Roman Catholic midnight mass. St. Catherine's Church, adjacent to the Church of the Nativity, is the setting for this mass, which is also broadcast.

The church is quite beautiful and both the altar and the medieval cloister in the front of the church are worth inspecting.

Beneath St. Catherine's, a subterranean passageway leads to the Grotto of the Nativity. This passageway was hollowed out by the Franciscans in 1470 to ensure their access to the shrine. The arrangement apparently grew out of a conflict lasting many years between the Roman Catholic and Greek Orthodox churches over "rights" to the important shrine.

Herod's Fortress

Just southeast of Bethlehem are two sites of great historical interest. One is the Herodium, a gigantic pile of dirt that was once a glorious palatial retreat and fortress for King Herod. The pile of dirt did not just happen of itself. There had long been a mound here but Herod, in a colossal dirt-moving operation, extended it higher and higher into the sky until his "mountain" seemed to dominate all the surrounding landscape. This sounds as if he was trying to erect another Tower of Babel, but he was not. Herod had two far more earthly and practical purposes in mind.

First, he had won a victory over Antigonus on this site. This fortress would be a monument to his superiority in battle and it would serve as a strong link in a chain of fortresses protecting all of his domain. King Herod was not a man to skimp his defense budget. He had numerous fortresses like this one. He used the Alexandrium in the Jordan Valley as a fortress. Masada, in Israel, was still another of his vast chain of defense outposts. (Masada has been the scene of recent extensive excavations.) It is thought that because of the height of these citadels, it was possible for Herod's soldier-guards to send signals to the nearest neighboring fortresses, then on to the next, etc. If Herod did use the citadels for signaling, one to another, he was not an innovator. For years, Jews had signaled with fire from high peaks to Jews waiting on other high peaks to announce, for example, that the new moon had risen.

Second, Herod did not erect these fortresses merely as bastions for defense. He maintained on these sites "little retreat" centers for himself. At the foot of the Herodium there were palaces, terraced gardens, and pools. Two hundred white marble steps led to the top of the hill and to the towers of the citadel. An aqueduct brought in fresh water in good supply.

The Herodium was chosen by the king as a proper setting for his tomb. When he died in his summer palace in Jericho in 4 B.C., a solemn procession carried his body on the long march south to this fortress near Bethlehem.

The Top of the Herodium

The glory of the Herodium is gone. Today it looks exactly like a defunct volcano. Herod's marble steps are gone, but if the tourist chooses to climb to the top, he may follow a mud pathway that leads to the remains of the fortress. This climb is a bit steep. It takes about twenty minutes if you keep at it. I tried it, and I admired Herod's soldiers for their ability to perform this feat daily. This much exercise alone must have kept them in great physical shape, but it rather quickly puts the tourist out of shape! I exulted in the view from the top of the Herodium—miles in all directions. A further reward of this strenuous climb was that I was able to view the remains of Herod's citadel, to look over a monastery built out of Herod's ruined buildings, to see Herod's Roman bath and the aqueduct which brought water to his palace.

Tequ'a, the Home of Amos

Southwest of the Herodium is a site of quite a different type. This is a "tell," an Arabic word that means "mound." Here in ruins scattered over four to five acres is what is believed to

have been the old city of Tequ'a, the town called in the Bible
Tekoa, the home of Amos the prophet.

If you are a Bible student you would look immediately for
sycamore trees at Tequ'a, for the Bible says that the Lord
called Amos from his occupation as herdsman and dresser
of sycamore trees. But no tree of any description now stands
at Tequ'a. There is only a two-humped mound divided by a
road; the ancient living quarters and churches of Tequ'a lying
to the south, the former citadel or monastery to the north. Not
much remains on the surface of the mound to suggest the
former importance of the city: a few wall formations, some
huge cisterns, and if a tourist searched diligently, perhaps a
baptismal font, a few remains of a church, and some evidence
of old tombs.

A "living" city from approximately 1700 B.C. to A.D. 1200,
it now lies beneath the ground. One day, it will be excavated.
Why, then, waste time visiting a site that offers so little to see?
Archaeologists, both professional and amateur, delight in roaming around on tells in search of surface evidence of old civilizations. What might they find? Nothing spectacular. Just bits of
old pottery, old glass, or perhaps metal. As you might suspect,
on the top of tells such nits and lice of evidence should point
to the dates of occupation. On the slopes and bottom edges
of tells, it is sometimes possible to find small clues to far
earlier occupations. Rain and erosion sometimes expose to view
bits of pottery previously buried. This type of scavenger hunting
may sound like nonsense to you, but to the archaeologist is a
most absorbing pastime. Bits of the past can be recognized as
dating to definite periods of history and, when found, can
help to confirm the authenticity of any given site. This is reason
enough for people to visit Tequ'a or any similar tell in Jordan.

Cave-dwelling Bedouins

Another reason for visiting Tequ'a is that the tourist has an
opportunity to get a very close look at some of the most in-

teresting people in the land, the Arab Bedouins. When my husband and I approached the mound at Tequ'a, the entire area appeared to be completely deserted. We parked our car and started walking around the mound. People materialized, it seemed, out of thin air. In a very few moments we wondered where *all* these people came from—out of the ground? No one had been in sight and now here they all were as if we had inadvertently disturbed an anthill.

Where did they come from? They live here. Seeing us long before we arrived, they had run to gather up their small collection of ancient coins and now were ready to make a sale—to us! These Bedouins are part of the Ta'amira tribe who unearthed the Dead Sea Scrolls in 1947 and have scrambled all over the hills ever since looking for graves or any antiquities that could bring them more money. Probably the coins offered will first have been offered to a coin dealer and rejected. Byzantine age coins are common at Tequ'a, however, and for a *dinar* ($2.80) one may buy a small handful of coins that, authentic or not, make good souvenirs of ancient Jordan. The people can use the money! These Bedouins look very poor and they may be. They also may not be poor. We were shocked to see a brand new American car at the doorway of a cave dwelling. (Around the countryside there are quite respectable homes of stone, a big step up in the standard of living of the Ta'amira tribe—one due largely to the money realized from the sale of Dead Sea Scrolls.)

The Women of Tequ'a

We visited Tequ'a one sunshiny day that followed a spell of rain. The women of the cave family were sitting at their "front door," sewing and preparing a few things for dinner. All their material possessions (sleeping mats) were strewn over the rocks, drying in the sun. Bedouin women are not so colorful in dress as other Jordanian women. They usually wear a simple long black robe and headdress; when we were close to them, we noticed that many of them have tattoo marks on their faces and hands—perhaps on their feet. These are tribe markings and the tattooing is done exactly in the same pattern for all women of one tribe. The tattooing is usually blue in color and is anything but a beauty treatment. Offhand it seems like an effective method of making your wife so unattractive that no other man would ever look at her. Also as a matter of custom, although I have not tried to prove it at firsthand, I have read that the tattooing is done not only on the face, hands, and feet but also on parts of the body kept covered. Bedouin women use henna on their skin and not infrequently on their hair.

It is apparent that the Bedouin woman has a freedom that is denied the Western woman. The long flowing robe frees her from wearing what we think are necessary undergarments. If she is a young woman, she will very likely be pregnant and unconcerned about her figure. If she is old, her shape will have been ruined by her childbearing (one a year) and she is unconcerned about her figure. She is also unconcerned about the neatness of her hair or the softness of her skin. The hot sun, the winds, and the blowing sands have taken a toll of her beauty. It isn't important to her. She just lives and endures "in sha'Allah" (God willing).

The Children

If the tourist can avoid it, he should not go to visit Tequ'a or any tell on Fridays. This is the Muslim holy day and all the children are at home. At Tequ'a we found the most disconcerting group of children in Jordan. They were bored, I guess, and consequently happy to have someone to look at. Believe me, they do look at you and from a distance of about one foot. They are very curious and fit the word "uninhibited." Great touchers, they find it very interesting to touch your hands, your clothes, and your hair, particularly if it is blond. *And*, it is always the children with runny noses and skin infections that push themselves closest to you. They will not steal from you nor harm you but they will cling to you like glue. I carried a rather large shoulder bag, and when I unzipped it to reach for my light meter, three little heads popped down into the bag. There was nothing to do but wait until their curiosity was satisfied and I could reach into the bag and take out what I wanted.

If the children take the notion, they will set up a chorus, chanting over and over, "Hello, *baksheesh*." They feel, perhaps, that since they know one American word this automatically entitles them to a gift of money. If you try to take a picture, these children are a terrific nuisance. They will have their hands all over your camera. They will try to block your lens with their palms. They will yell at you that it is forbidden to take pictures but some will *ask* you to "take mine for *baksheesh*." You can tell them to scat, but they find your annoyance amusing. If you would particularly like a picture of some of the archaeological remains, the children may make a very firm stand in front of it. You could "swat" them, but you grit your teeth and remind yourself that you are sight-seeing on land that is their home and playground. If the tourist does not go "tell climbing" on Friday, he will not have more "guests" than he can handle.

On the other hand, after a day of really distressing nonsense from the children, a group from our school sat down on the mound at Tequ'a to eat a picnic lunch. In a wink, the native children retired to a respectful distance and did not come near the sightseers until they had completely finished their meal. The reason for their respectful behavior at this point may have been that it has been a tradition in Bedouin culture that the male of the household and his guests eat first. Women and children eat only after the father has satisfied his appetite.

We found the families that live at Tequ'a to be very polite. One of the women approached us with coins. When we showed no interest, she did not persist nor ask for money. She had two small children, very nice youngsters, who saw us picking up

bits of pottery. They scurried around bringing back to us hand-
fuls of pottery pieces and never once asked for money. We
were delighted to tip them.

Goats and Wells

Tequ'a is an elevated site and thus offers a fine view on all
sides. We could see great distances and we could observe both
far and near tent dwellers and shepherds tending their flocks.
We listened carefully. The shepherds often pipe to their flocks,
and it is charming. We looked to see if the shepherd had a
young lamb in his arms. It is usual for these fellows to make
a pet of one of the flock. It is fascinating to see how adept
the goats are at getting little bites of nourishment off bramble
bushes that are a mass of thorns. It has been strongly recommended to Jordan that if the economy is to improve, the natives must get rid of their goats. Pasture land is sparse in
Jordan and the little goats eat tender young trees and shrubs
and kill them. All over the land young trees are protected by
circular fences. As of the present time, the goat population of
Jordan is high.

One word of caution to tourists about Tequ'a. You remember
that Jesus once made a reference to pulling an animal out of a
cistern (Matt. 12:11). You'd think it a pretty dumb animal
that would stumble into a well. *However,* Tequ'a is *loaded*
with cisterns that have not been filled in. You could quite
suddenly come upon yard-wide holes in the ground, and if
you were to peek into those holes you would see that these
cisterns are *deep.* This is not a safe place for children.

Medicine, Hygiene, and Morals

Often, a white hospital truck sits beside the road in the Tequ'a
area. This is the mobile hospital clinic of the Lutheran World
Federation that visits and ministers to the Bedouins on a regular weekly schedule. The clinic is open for business by nine

o'clock in the morning and shortly after that time the Bedouins will gather, sitting on the ground in the open sun waiting to see the doctor. In this gathering will be lovely young dark-eyed mothers with their babies and elderly Bedouin men, weathered almost as much as the hills they live in. If the people are from a distance, they will have come to the clinic riding on donkeys. They will be courteous to the tourist so long as he does not take their pictures.

Inside the mobile unit, immaculate doctors and nurses maintain a complete health clinic. The quality of professional personnel and equipment given to help the Jordanians with their health problems is excellent.

If you were visiting in the Holy Land, it will surely not escape your notice that the Bedouins are not very clean. This is an understatement. If you could look at the territory where they are living, you would see there is apparently no supply of water. They do the best they can. What little water they have, they must use for drinking. Do not equate dirt on the skin with morals. We learned in Jordan to respect the Bedouins. They have a moral code developed over the years that is based on the practical needs of staying alive in the desert and also developed from their interpretation of the Koran. A good part of this code deals with man's duty to respect the rights of his fellow man. The tourist may be startled to discover that most Bedouin men carry a curved dagger at the waist. Never fear. They won't use it on people. The Bedouins are kind and helpful. They may be unkempt, but they are good men. They deserve respect.

The Road to Hebron

The scenery between Bethlehem and Hebron is quite pretty because it is in this area that some reforestation is being done. There are huge vineyards just south of Bethlehem and nearer Hebron there are many fruit and olive orchards.

In this attractive hill country, there are two old sites of interest. The first is a series of three pools, popularly called "Solomon's Pools." This title has been conferred on them because of one interpretation of Ecclesiastes 2:6: "I made me pools of water, to water therewith the wood that bringeth forth trees." The pools do not date back to the time of Solomon. Herod the Great brought water from here by aqueduct to the Herodium, and Pontius Pilate constructed a great aqueduct from the pools to carry water into Jerusalem. The three reservoirs are fed by water from a nearby wadi and from spring waters in Hebron. The pools are lined with pine trees and altogether the site makes a delightful picnic spot. Farther south on the road to Hebron is Philip's well, where Philip baptized the Ethiopian eunuch, Acts 8:38. The spring is used as much today as in earlier history.

These towns, Bethlehem and Hebron, for many years were at loggerheads because they were settled by tribes with enmity between them. The tourist will notice that there is a difference in the inhabitants today. Bethlehem is a friendly, warm town to tourists. Hebron is actually hostile to them, and those tourists who walk through the town to see the markets and houses will feel easier if a tourist policeman accompanies them. New facilities in the area, a rest and refreshment house and new souvenir shops, will probably bring more visitors into the town. As the people of Hebron become accustomed to seeing more tourists, and as they understand that tourists buy Hebron products, the hostility may fade away.

The Tombs of Abraham, Isaac, and Jacob

In biblical history, the town of Hebron is most closely associated with Abraham, the great tribal leader who is venerated by Muslims, Jews, and Christians. Some other Old Testament persons were acquainted with Hebron. Moses sent out spies from his wilderness camp to scout the area of Hebron (Num. 13:22). Some years later Joshua conquered Hebron, destroyed the city

and killed the king (Josh. 10:36-37, 11:21-22). David knew
Hebron intimately. He made it his first capital and raised some
of his children, including Absalom, there. It was to Hebron that
Absalom went to gather strength and forces for his unsuccessful
attempt to unseat his father (II Sam. 15:7-10).

Long before any of these men was born, Abraham had dwelt
for periods of time at Hebron, had selected the nearby cave
of Machpelah for a family burial plot, and was buried there
(Gen. 13:18, 23:4ff, 25:9). The site for this burial ground
for the family of Abraham is believed to be beneath the present
mosque, the Haram al Khalil. Abraham and Sarah, Isaac and
Rebekah, Jacob and Leah are buried here.

Is the Shrine Authentic?

How confident can the pilgrim be that Abraham's bones truly
rest beneath the mosque? Quite confident, really. Scholars
have not been able to study and date the remains that rest
in the tombs. Permission to excavate the area would have to
come from Muslim authorities who are guardians of the mosque.
It has been the practice of the Muslims since the Middle Ages
to forbid anyone to enter the area of the tomb, even those
persons of Muslim conviction. However, even if archaeological
confirmation is not possible, there are other good indications
that the shrine has a claim to authenticity.

First, in order for the shrine to be authentic, it would be a
prerequisite that the town of Hebron mentioned in Genesis
must have existed on this spot at the time of Abraham. The
Bible is helpful in supplying one good clue as to whether or
not Hebron could meet that qualification. Numbers 13:22 states
that Hebron was built seven years before Zoan. Scholars are
familiar with the town of Zoan in Egypt; it was famed as a
capital of the Hyksos and destroyed by its enemies in 1560 B.C.
Since Zoan was a capital city, it is not unreasonbale to assume
that it had existed for some time before it was so honored.

Thus, the founding of Zoan far prior to 1560 B.C. and the still earlier founding of Hebron would seem to confirm that Hebron was already an important city in the Middle Bronze Age when Abraham first journeyed there.

Second, samplings of old pottery found in the Hebron area date from the Middle Bronze Age and testify that this site was occupied at the time of the patriarchs.

At the time that Abraham was living, the town of Hebron lay just west of the modern city and the cave of Machpelah would have been on the outskirts. This ancient site of the town has been scheduled to be excavated and, when it is, much more will be known of old Hebron. As time went by, the town seemed to edge closer toward the tomb area, so that by the Middle Ages it was, as it is today, centered around the mosque. The ancient town lies on the outskirts.

That the Jews had maintained a reverence for the burial site through the years is not mentioned in the Old Testament. But it is most important that King Herod shortly before the Christian era erected a most impressive structure (197 feet long, 111 feet wide, and 49 feet high) over the cave of Machpelah. Some of the original building stones still support one section of the mosque.

When the Arabs overcame the Middle East, they assumed possession of this shrine to the patriarch. Later, the Crusaders took advantage of military successes to transform the mosque into a church. During the brief period that they had access to the tomb the Crusaders apparently did a very thorough job of checking the contents of the caves. In 1119 they reported that they had removed paving stones from the floor of the church and had penetrated the burial chambers.

Beneath the church, the Crusaders found a small room, an entranceway, from which a hallway led to two burial chambers. In the first chamber, they found remains which they attributed to Jacob. In the second chamber, the Crusaders felt the bones would be logically those of Isaac. They discovered there also a sealed sarcophagus which they assumed would most likely hold the bones of Abraham. In addition, they reported that in both chambers there were jars filled with bones—fifteen jars in all.

After the Crusaders had satisfied their curiosity concerning the contents of the cave beneath the sanctuary at Hebron, they secured them by replacing the flagstone pavement which had been removed from the floor of the church and sealing the flagstones.

Inside Haram al Khalil

Today in the mosque, pilgrims may peer through a small opening in the floor into the inky darkness below to assure themselves that there is a cave beneath the mosque. On the ground surface of the shrine, the Muslims have placed memorial tombs over the supposed burial site of each of the honored dead. These tombs (cenotaphs) are covered with richly embroidered tapestries.

The interior of the mosque is richly and tastefully decorated with marble and inlaid wood, and graceful Arabic inscriptions (parts of the Koran) remind the faithful of the commands of their prophet. Mosaics of sparkling gold tessera line the walls and ceiling of the prayer niche facing Mecca. These mosaics, like all Muslim art, do not outline human or animal figures. They are all abstract designs.

There are always many persons at prayer. The men will usually be gathered in the easternmost corner where there is also a beautifully decorated "pulpit." The women have their own side of the mosque for prayers and meditation. It is most necessary here at Hebron for the tourist to be fully aware that he must be very quiet as he inspects the mosque. The persons at prayer expect that visitors maintain a respectful distance and that they walk as silently as possible.

There are also persons who spend hours in the mosque reading the Koran. They may read silently, or aloud to those persons who are not able to read it for themselves. And in every mosque there are a few poverty-stricken people who sit in corners to warm themselves in winter, to seek relief from the sun in the summer.

Cameras and Forbidden Images

Many tourists find pleasure in photography. In Hebron, the photographer is confronted on all sides by the most gorgeous scenes of Middle Easterners in their daily life. What a frustration! It really is not wise to take pictures in Hebron unless a tourist policeman gives permission and help. Naturally, cameras are not allowed inside the mosque unless such photography has been sanctioned by the government. But even outside on the streets the tourist who takes pictures may be risking his camera. The natives will not be concerned that the camera may have cost hundreds of dollars. They know only that the instrument makes images and that images have been forbidden by Mohammed. They may take the camera and throw it on the ground. Many of the tourist policemen are not too happy to assist photographers. They are not exactly wild about standing between the tourist and a few irate citizens. And after all they are Muslims, too.

The *souk* in Hebron is one of the prettiest in the Holy Land. The streets in this *souk* are not so narrow as in the old market in Jerusalem. Enough sun comes in to light up the color and beauty of the costumes and the produce. Many of the natives engage in tanning and their boards of drying goatskins or sheepskins would make a beautiful color slide to illustrate an industry still conducted by the methods of antiquity. Some of the Muslim women in Hebron wear a painted veil that is most striking. They pull the veil tightly over the face like a mask. My first sight of one of these women at close range caused me to gasp, almost in fright. The painted veil is a very effective disguise—it would be difficult to recognize a relative hidden behind one. It is unattractive, truly spooky.

Surprisingly, Hebron has a swimming pool. This is an old reservoir just off the main street now used for the pleasure of the children. The few youngsters that we saw taking advantage of the cooling waters did not wear bathing suits, but simply swam with a minimum of their regular clothing. Muslims are not very much in favor of exhibiting the body.

The Hebron Potter

In Hebron, there are two delightfully educational factories where we were welcomed and where we could take as many pictures as we wished. The Hebron potter is a genial young man who is most generous in giving his time to show how he works. We had noticed as we toured the Holy Land that the clay pot is no longer the popular vessel to take to the well to draw water. Pots break and the archaeologists rejoice. The old-style goatskins leak and become slimy. The more modern tin containers, discarded by the merchants who have drained their contents, are most useful for carrying water and sit level on the head. For this reason, the potter no longer has a pressing need to turn out hundreds of the large water jars. The gentleman at Hebron turns out the pottery for the whole southern area of the Holy Land and even that task does not keep him too busy to demonstrate leisurely to the visitor the art of working on the old-style wheel. The shop is not a pretentious place of business. It has four walls and a mud brick floor on which are dozens of finished pots slowly drying.

The potter sits on the floor but his feet drop down into a well that holds the wheel. When the wheel is going at a speed that pleases the potter, he works swiftly with a glob of clay, shaping and molding it with his hands and fingers. When the model is finished to his satisfaction, he pulls a string through the clay at the base of the pot, thus freeing it from the wheel.

The potter is so accustomed to working by touch that he is able to sneak glances at his guests while he works. What he hopes to read on their faces is the compliment of admiration and respect for his art. He has found that while visitors do not buy his ordinary stock items, they are charmed and delighted to take home with them a series of miniature pots and jars, identical in detail to the regular line of pottery. As a good host, the potter will try to waive aside the tourist's attempts to pay for the "samples" but a generous donation will be appreciated and it will have been deserved.

The Glassworks

Hebron also has a glass factory. Glassmaking is not new to the town; indeed, it started before the Middle Ages. The glass windows in the mosque were made in Hebron seven hundred years ago. More important today is the opportunity for the tourist to see what usually comprises a factory in Jordan. The factory is composed of a few men gathered in a small building. These men work by hand methods since automation is far away from Jordan. Here in one of these small factories sit three or four men around a hearth, skillfully blowing or shaping glass that will more than supply the entire country. Fortunately, Jordan has found that the beautifully tinted small cylinders of glass, colored green, blue, and amethyst, can be massed together to make a stunning lamp. The new YMCA in Jerusalem has used Hebron glass for ceiling and wall lights that spread sparkles of color throughout the beautiful lobby, a stunning modern Middle-Eastern lounge. Very attractive desk lamps of Hebron glass are on sale in the gift shops. Glass necklaces have always been popular with tourists and are in good supply as are the graceful vases blown in the small factory in Hebron.

In the glass factory, as in the potter's shop, the spectator can become hypnotized by the rhythm and grace with which the men perform their skill. Even more heartwarming is the attitude of the men as they work. They are proud of their trade and they are still more proud to perform for an appreciative spectator.

The Oak of Mamre

Just two miles north of Hebron is the famous "oak of Mamre." This very old tree, reputedly the tree of Gen. 18:4, is just barely living. It is propped up by dozens of poles and looks as if it waits agonizingly and patiently to be allowed to die. Scholars tell us that this old tree is not Abraham's oak. This word from the scholars must be a keen disappointment to the Russian Orthodox Church, who erected here in the nineteenth century a monastery, church, and hospice in memory of the appearance of the three angels to Abraham.

The "oak of Mamre" beneath which the angels of the Lord rested and enjoyed the hospitality of their host Abraham, has a long history as a sanctuary. Abraham had built an altar here. David was anointed king here. The Jews revered the spot. Herod the Great built an enclosure around the area, and when the enclosure was destroyed, Hadrian rebuilt and enlarged the buildings at Mamre. According to Eusebius (4th-century church father), the mother-in-law of Constantine, Eutropia, was distressed by what she felt were pagan practices at Mamre. To put an end to them, Constantine built a new sanctuary dedicated to the Holy Trinity.

With this long continuous history of buildings marking a shrine, it is hard to imagine that nothing would remain to indicate where the "oak of Mamre" had been. Apparently, after the Arab invasion, the shrine was forgotten, unused. In the twentieth century, an archaeologist probing some ruins north of Hebron became interested in a couple of well-built walls that still met to form a corner. An ensuing excavation of this site disclosed that there had been on this spot a Constantinian basilica. Further diggings turned up construction work known to date to Hadrian, stones of the Herodian type, pavement dating back to the days of the Israelites, and terra cotta artifacts believed to belong to the days of Abraham. In addition, there was a break in the Israelite pavement that could have been the location of a tree. This rather definitive chain of evidence seems to confirm the historical record and to mark the ruins two miles north of Hebron as the true site of Mamre.

Hospitality Plus

I had read this story in Genesis 18 many times, but it was not until I had been in the Holy Land and had become acquainted with Middle Eastern culture that I realized that the story incidentally tells us that the customs of hospitality among the tent dwellers have not changed in three thousand years.

Among present-day Bedouins, the tent dwellers consider it a great honor to have guests. While they are in his tent, the host is obligated to prepare a feast for them and provide them with complete protection from harm. In Genesis, Abraham quite clearly fulfills the first obligation of a good host. He was sitting in his tent when he saw three men approach. He ran to greet them, bowed down on the ground before them, and invited them to wash and refresh themselves. Then he hurried to rouse Sarah so that she might start to prepare a feast while he, Abraham, fetched a calf from his herd to be roasted for his guests.

Similarly, in the next chapter of Genesis, Lot fulfills both of the duties of the host when two strangers come to his home at Sodom. Lot has a feast prepared for his guests, and in addition when the men of Sodom hear that Lot has guests, he begs them to leave his guests unharmed: "unto these men do nothing, for therefore came they under the shadow of my roof."

While these references to Genesis 18–19 may not add to a reader's basic understanding of the patriarchal narrative, they may add a bit of human warmth and flavor to the persons we encounter in the Bible. Greater insight into the customs and behavior of the people of the Bible is one of the significant rewards of a trip to the Holy Land.

TABLE 3

SEA OF GALILEE

YARMUK RIVER

Um Qeis

Irbíd

Taanach
Ya'bad   Jenín

Pella

Dothan   WADI YABIS

Tulkarm   Tubas   to Jerash

Samaria
Sebaste   Tírzah   Sa'ídiyah

Nablus   Shechem   Deir'alla   RIVER JABBOK

Qalqílíya   WADI ZERQA

Alexandrium

Salfit   Shiloh   Damíye
                                       es Salt   to Amman

JORDAN RIVER

Qasr
Hisham
Ramallah Bethel   Nimrín
          Bireh   Tell es
                    Sultan
Amwas   MT. TEMPTATION   to Amman
Latrun   Jericho   PLACE OF
                    ROMAN   BAPTISM
                    ROAD
Jerusalem   Bethany   Rama
                  Qumran   DEAD
       to Bethlehem   SEA

DEMARCATION LINE

TABLE 3   From Ramallah and Bethel to the Sea of Galilee

V "The Arabian Countryside"

If the tourist had the time, he would enjoy seeing all of Jordan. There, when you have seen one village, you most definitely have *not* seen them all. There is not a village in Jordan that does not have a character of its own. If you were versed on the subject of women's dresses, you could point out any woman on the streets of Jerusalem and tell exactly which area of Jordan was her home just by the manner in which her dress was made and trimmed. Each town has its own customs and traditions not only about women's dresses, but often about special ways to prepare foods, homemade remedies for the sick, and the manner in which families should live.

Ramallah

Several villages within easy reach of Jerusalem hold more than moderate interest for tourists. Ramallah, about fifteen miles north of Jerusalem, is usually advertised as the "Switzerland of Jordan." Since no spot in Jordan, Ramallah included, can claim snow-peaked mountains, lakes, and chalets, this "Switzerland" label is somewhat misleading. The town of Ramallah *is* situated on high ground, a little higher than Jerusalem, and as a result cool in summer. This superior climate is the basis for Ramallah's claim to be the finest summer resort in Jordan.

Ramallah is a comparatively clean town. It has many pine trees; stunning homes give it the appearance of a modern town. The visitor has a sense of orderliness and composure, the "busy, touristy" feeling of Jerusalem is entirely lacking: no shopkeepers entice you in nor do guides coax you to "step into my brother's shop." There are no antiquities in Ramallah.

Ramallah has tried to cater to vacationers by developing hotels, parks, and outdoor cafes. The parks in the town and in nearby Bireh, though small, are truly beautiful. Fountains and pools have been tastefully placed among lavish rose gardens (cannas and native flowers are also planted throughout) and here beneath gaily decorated umbrellas the tourist can thoroughly relax in comfort and enjoy a bite to eat or something to drink. In winter, the refreshment buildings are closed, but visitors are welcomed to the parks where they may sit and eat a picnic lunch. (Incidentally, almost all hotels in Jerusalem include meals in the price of the room. When you tour the country, your hotel will pack a lunch for you.) During the warm months, these parks are crowded. The large Ramallah park has a small play area for children with a few swings, slides, and teeter-totters—the *only* such equipment for public use in the country. The play area is no larger than a similar setup that you might have in your backyard for your growing family. Consequently, children must wait their turn to play and must pay a small fee which entitles them to a fixed amount of time to play.

For the adult, the parks offer relaxation and a chance to indulge in that fascinating pastime, observing the people. When you have selected a table, you may sit at that table until you are ready to leave. No one will pressure you to leave to make way for the next customer.

Mousakhan *and Ice Cream*

Ramallah restaurants are famous for their *mousakhan,* a unique chicken dish flavored with a tart purple powder called *summak.* This herb bears a name that suggests a relationship to our sumac but whether the two are one and the same, I could not positively determine. Many of us who delighted in eating *mousakhan* can testify that the Jordanian *summak* is not toxic and the chicken flavored with it is superb. The chicken is even more tasty because *mousakhan* is eaten the way we all yearn to eat chicken—with the fingers. When our order was set before us, my husband and I assuredly had a bad moment wondering how to manage with no utensils. There before us was a large circle of Jordanian bread topped by a whole chicken, split in two, covered with minced onions, *summak*, and olive oil. The dish had been charcoal-broiled until the chicken was tender and the juice from the chicken plus the olive oil had dripped down into the bread. To eat it, the diner just goes to it, tearing off bites of chicken and bread. With the meal, we were served a dry Jordanian wine. After eating, we retired to a washroom to clean up, then returned to the table for a cup of Turkish coffee.

Since the old recipe for *mousakhan* belongs to the women of Ramallah, the whole town takes pride in this Jordanian dish. But now there is a newer recipe that has come to the town via America. A former American, now living in Ramallah, has started an ice-cream business. This gentleman has originated a superb blend of sweet and tart flavors that turns out to be as fine an ice cream as you have ever tasted. Ice cream is considered a summer treat, and is not made in the winter. If spring is late in coming, the ice-cream man may lose a month of business because the natives will not buy it until the weather is warm.

The Women's Dress

The women of Ramallah vie with those of Bethlehem for the title of best-dressed in Jordan. The gowns of both places boast finer needlework and design than any in the country. The most striking Ramallah gown is the cream-colored robe with embroidery on the blouse and down the sides of the skirt. The embroidery is done with black and red silk thread, and all the designs are symbolic.

The girls and women of Ramallah use a simple but large white veil to cover their heads. The veil is draped around the head and falls softly over the shoulders and down the back. The older and traditional headdress of Ramallah, however, calls for an additional fitted cap which hugs the head and frames the face with a solid semicircle of gold or silver coins. This coin-holding cap was at one time the wearer's fortune. It was her dowry and her source of material security, so if her husband divorced her, she still had some money of her own to live on. How far these coins would go today in supporting a woman in a modern economy is discouraging to contemplate; prices in grocery stores in Jordan are on a par with prices in markets in America. However, some ladies still wear the coin caps, showing the world they have bank accounts sitting heavily on their heads.

Education

Ramallah has some fine schools. The newest of these schools is the UNRWA (United Nations Relief and Works Agency for Palestine Refugees in the Near East) school, a beautiful new complex of buildings that house approximately five hundred refugee girls. The school gives vocational training, thus preparing the girls to support themselves. Training and housing are offered free and some pocket money provided.

The American Quakers operate two schools in Ramallah, the Friends School for Boys and the Friends School for Girls. (In Jordan, the sexes are separated in school not later than the fourth grade on.) Young people attending these Quaker schools are offered the regular American curriculum with all classes in English, except for the Arabic language class. This course of study will ultimately qualify the youngsters to enter universities.

Since our daughter attended the Friends School for Girls she will be disappointed if I do not tell you a few details of her experience there. First, you will be surprised to know that while almost all the girls are Arabic and studying in a second language, the textbooks are identical to those our daughter would have used in her American high school. School starts at 7:30 A.M. and finishes at 2:30 P.M., with a fifteen minute recess at 10:20 and the lunch break.

Lunch was a rather traumatic experience for our daughter who, like most Americans, treasures the hamburger. Arabic foods were served, but they were of the ordinary variety, not the luscious festive dishes described later in this book. A large part of the diet is rice and greens and yoghurt—perfectly nourishing, but the sour taste of yoghurt may be unpleasant to people until they become accustomed to it.

More difficult to accept was the temperature in the classrooms. Most Jordanian buildings are not heated. Small space heaters are used, but rarely, to take off the chill. As Ramallah is cooler in the summer, it is colder in the winter. Children sit in classrooms fully clothed for winter—with coats, slacks, and sometimes boots. Many have mastered the art of writing while wearing gloves or mittens. The schoolrooms are very damp from the winter rains and this makes the cold more penetrating. When the sun comes out, the windows are opened to let in the warmer air from outside. On a good crisp day, you can see your breath inside. The girls school is a boarding school, and upstairs in the dormitory rooms, each girl has her own little hot water bottle to help her through the cold nights.

Bireh

Ramallah has a sister town that joins it to form one community. The sister town is called Bireh. Bireh is known traditionally as the first caravan stop on the way north from Jerusalem. If this label is correct, it could have been at Bireh that Mary and Joseph realized that the boy Jesus had not accompanied them on the journey home from a visit to the temple (Luke 2:41–51). Before 1948, Ramallah was predominantly a Christian town, Bireh was Muslim. In this community Christians and Muslims mingle in daily activities, shopping for their needs in stores that cater only to local needs.

The Biblical Bethel

About three miles northeast of Ramallah is the Beitin (Bethel) of the Bible. This is a small, quiet village, a completely unsophisticated town. If you are familiar with its history in the

Bible, you have every right to expect that marvelous remains of antiquity will almost overwhelm you in this town. Unfortunately, this is not true. Unless you know what to look for, you may see nothing old in Beitin. The excavations that took place here have been filled in so that the living may have use of the land. That excavations be filled in after a dig is often required of archaeologists by the Jordanian Department of Antiquities. Since the dig will have been thoroughly documented and photographed during the excavation, archaeologists willingly comply with this request. Still further, possibly very fertile hunting grounds for archaeological treasures are buried beneath the houses and buildings of present-day Beitin and must wait, perhaps indefinitely, to tell their story.

Its History

What is the biblical history of Bethel? Abraham, moving from Haran following the call of the Lord, came to the land of Canaan and pitched his tent in the mountain east of Bethel and there built an altar (Gen. 12:1–8). Then he journeyed south to the Negev, during a famine moved on to Egypt, and later returned to Bethel (Gen. 12:9, 13:3–4). The Bible tells us that when the tribe returned to Bethel the flocks and herds of Abraham and Lot were so great that the land could not support them all. Lot looked down from Bethel onto the valley of the Jordan River and decided to move his flocks into that "garden of the Lord" (Gen. 13:10). It was in this "garden of the Lord" that he came into contact with the wicked men of Sodom.

Jacob also was closely connected with Bethel. Genesis 31:13 tells of a message he received, in a dream, from God: "I am the God of Bethel, where thou anointedst the pillar, and, where thou vowedst a vow unto me." In the area southeast of Bethel, there is a horizontal outcropping of rock that seems to have distributed itself in layers from the bottom to the top of the high hill. This hill is popularly called Jacob's ladder and it does look as if the hill was a wide stairway—the stairway to heaven. This traditionally is the spot where Jacob received an earlier vision as he was fleeing Esau's wrath (Gen. 28:12).

At one time, the ark of the covenant was in Bethel (Judg. 20:26-27). At the time of Jeroboam I, the first king of northern Israel after Solomon's death, Bethel became a rival to Jerusalem. After the split of Israel and Judah into the northern and southern kingdoms, it became the important shrine to Israel. Jeroboam made a fortress of the city since it was so close to the border of Judah.

Today in Beitin there is a mosque, one of the few Jordanian mosques without a minaret, that is built partially from an old Byzantine church. It is possible that the church was built following a tradition that the shrine of Jeroboam was on this site.

There are some ruins of an old gate and walls in Beitin, and the community's threshing floor is the site of an ancient reservoir. The road east through town to Deir Dibwan is thought to be the same path continuously used since ancient times. These are the few scraps of history to be seen today in Beitin.

Beitin

Near the mosque there is a spring, the source of Beitin water. In the mornings between eight and nine o'clock and again in the evening between five and six o'clock, the women of Beitin parade to the well and carry home a can of water on their heads. Tourists have a fine view of the women at their chores because many of the houses in Beitin are right on the road.

The homes are very modest, most of them one- or two-room stone buildings with a courtyard where animals are kept. Some are surrounded by stone walls with a few layers of bramble bush on top (as effective for its purpose as barbed wire). On a bright day when there is no chance of rain, the ladies air their bedding in the courtyard. This is a colorful sight, for Jordanians love color. Their cushions and coverlets are bright reds, yellows, and blues. Tourists will wish they had their cameras.

Beitin is a friendly village. If the women are sitting in the courtyard sewing or cooking, they will wave to visitors and smile. How I wished that I could speak their language and talk with them about their homes and what they were preparing for supper!

Blond Children and American Jeans

I did have one good chance to communicate in Beitin. There are a few American families living there. I didn't recognize women of the family as American if they were wearing long Jordanian robes with the embroidered bodice but I did recognize blond children and American jeans. These children are bilingual and they love to talk with visitors.

What are Americans doing here? They prefer to live here. Born Jordanians, they have lived and worked for some years in the United States. Now they have returned home and have an opportunity to live on their U. S. Social Security. Other Americans are brides of university exchange students who have returned to Jordan with their husbands. But, to repeat, if you visit Beitin, look around for American children because you will find yourself a most willing and excellent guide to the antiquities in Beitin. You will also learn a lot about how children survive in Jordan without a playground or television. I noticed all over Jordan that *the* toy is a wheel hooked onto a piece of board. Children run up and down the streets pushing this toy ahead of them.

I do not recall any recreational facility in Beitin except for the post office: it doubles as a coffee house where the men assemble for a bit of adult conversation. Beitin is also short of shopping facilities; probably most marketing is done in Jerusalem or Ramallah.

On the road east of Beitin toward Deir Dibwan and Tayibeh there are some very attractive homes. The native stone, grillwork on windows and doors, brightly colored shutters combine beautifully to make a stunning home that still fits the Jordanian landscape.

A Modern David

There are some unexcavated ruins in this area and, since my husband has an insatiable curiosity, he had to investigate each one. My curiosity *is* satiable on a warm day, so car sitting appealed to me. During one of my waiting sessions I was rewarded by a re-enactment of history.

A young boy came up the road, but he paid no attention to me. He was busying himself with an ancient art in which he was not too proficient. He had a slingshot. No, it was not a forked stick with a rubber band attached. It was like a miniature hammock woven of some pliable material. One end of this implement was attached to the boy's hand. When the other end was held in the same hand, the hammock cradled a stone. Round and round, faster and faster the boy swung the weapon, then he let go the loose end to speed the stone to its target. This was the kind of weapon that killed the giant Goliath. For sure, I had seen a young king David. This boy was using pebbles to sail toward his target. The ancients when they were out for blood used round stones three inches in diameter. Ouch!

The same day, I tired of waiting for my husband so I left the car and walked up the road a bit, examining the flora. When I returned, beside the car stood a young Arab boy who had quite a story to tell me. As he was sitting on the hill, he saw a group of boys come down the road. The boys looked into the car and there they saw my hat lying unattended on the seat. They were going to steal it. My Arab friend had rushed down the hill, fought the whole group away and had stood guard by the car lest the bandits return. Translation—"baksheesh, anyone?"

Seeking the Real Emmaus: el Qubeibeh

In Luke (24:13–32) Jesus, after the Resurrection, encountered Cleopas and a companion as they walk sadly along the road to Emmaus. Jesus accepted the invitation of Cleopas to dine with him at his home. As Jesus broke bread for the meal, the two recognized him, whereupon Jesus disappeared.

Luke says that Emmaus was about seven miles from Jerusalem. Today four towns are claimed as Emmaus, but two of them are given the nod by scholars as having equal claims to being the authentic site.

The first town, the one closest to Jerusalem (seven miles west) is el Qubeibeh. When the Crusaders first found this town and labeled it as ancient Emmaus, they were basing their decision on the fact that an old Roman fort, significantly named Castellum Emmaus, was here.

Today the property is owned by one of the religious orders of the Roman Catholic church.There is a monastery, school, and church on the grounds. Preserved in the present sanctuary are the remains of an earlier church, including thick walls that are believed to be the only remaining traces of the house of Cleopas. To the west of the church a town has been excavated. Houses, shops, grinding stones, and cisterns give ample evidence that this was certainly *a* town of ancient history. Archaeological evidence supports the premise that people lived here at the time of Jesus.

As a modern site to visit, el Qubeibeh is charming. Many conifer trees have been planted on the property. The monks have planted a garden of native flowers as well, and they maintain a small zoo where the tourist can examine the lovely, delicate little native antelopes, Jordanian song and game birds, and pea-cocks. El Qubeibeh sits on a hill overlooking the plains that lead down to the Mediterranean. The tourist can look down from this vantage point into Israel, a beautiful view, and on a clear day see the water breaking on the Mediterranean shore.

Amwas

Amwas, the other possible site for Emmaus in Jordan, is twenty miles west of Jerusalem. Obviously, the distance does not fit the story in Luke. The claim of this site to be Emmaus rests on the fact that the Bordeaux pilgrims, St. Jerome, and Eusebius all claimed this was the town of Jesus' post-Resurrection appearance. Certainly Amwas was an important Christian site; the ruins of a very impressive church are here.

When the tourist visits Amwas, he is very close to the Jordan-Israel truce line. The tourist is allowed to travel the road one mile farther (barbed wire lines the road) to see the monastery of Latrun. (In the grocery stores in Jerusalem, several shelves will be filled with the many varieties of Latrun wine; this is where it is made.) Within the monastery the monks have taken a vow of silence. Only one of their number is allowed to speak and he is the host who greets visitors to the monastery. He offers visitors a glass of wine and the excellent cheese also made at the monastery. (The cheese is for sale.) The land formerly owned by the monastery is now in No Man's Land. The monks are allowed to work the land, provided they apply monthly for permission to do so. Through this stretch of land runs the old, once well-traveled road between Jerusalem and Joppa now in disrepair.

The Hill Country

Going north from Jerusalem to Samaria, the tourist is driven through a very attractive section of Jordan, rich in opportunities for photography and rich, too, in orchards, fields of grain, and village life. In the most picturesque part of the journey the narrow road winds through a pass in the hill country, a pass formerly known as the "valley of the robbers." The hills rise directly from the roadway, and it is a creepy sensation to let your imagination transport you back into history and see yourself in a camel caravan, silently and cautiously proceeding into the pass. Every few hundred yards, the road turns and each of these turns ushered the caravans into neat little traps where the robbers watched from the hill tops, waiting for the moment to swoop down and carry off supplies and animals. The pass is no longer a danger. The robbers no longer wait on the hill above although many people, remembering the former frightening reputation of the pass, will refuse to drive through it at night.

In this hill country, the Jordanians have terraced the hills to accommodate fruit and olive trees. This terracing is an artistic production, pleasing to the eye, with stark white limestone precisely set in semicircles on the red-brown earth and, above, the silver green foliage of the olive trees against the blue sky.

Between these hills lie some of the most fertile valleys in Jordan, and here the farmers of Jordan toil in the purest sense of the word. They work the land with their hands on the plow. A burro usually pulls the plow. Winter wheat is the large Jordanian grain crop. It is sown by hand, harvested in June. Large, flat outcroppings of rock will serve as community threshing floors. In June, the farmers will gather here to drive their burros 'round and 'round in their monotonous task of circling the threshing floor day in and day out until the grain is ready to be winnowed —as it was in biblical times—the wheat and chaff pitchforked into the air, the chaff driven off by the wind.

This manner of gathering and harvesting grain may be perfectly adequate for the future use of wheat as nourishment for the body, but often the bread made from this wheat will scour your teeth, thanks to a generous supply of grit. After the harvest, wheat is stored on rooftops (there will be no rain until at least late October) and the farmers can draw from their "bank" on the roof as the need arises.

To protect produce from possible theft just prior to harvesting, farmers often erect small watchtowers in the fields. Usually they are picturesque, flimsy, thatched-roof shelters, but occasionally you will also see old stone watchtowers standing as sentinels on the hills.

The Arabs use *burghul* (crushed wheat) in many of their dishes. Bread makes up a large portion of the daily diet although rice is also a popular grain food. Yoghurt is a staple in the diet and cheese, fresh fruits, marrows or eggplants, olives, and olive oil round out the menu. Breakfast in most Arab countries consists of bread, dried yoghurt, and olive oil.

Jordanian Homes

As my husband and I drove through this country, we noticed
that many Jordanians have taken advantage of their major "crop,"
stone, to build substantial homes. Mud brick is on its way out,
many times washed away in the torrential rains of January. The
new stone homes are sturdy and attractive, but the superior
exterior hides an inferior interior by American standards. Many
Jordanians will have little inside their homes save mats for sleeping. The home will be without kitchen or plumbing. The function
of the kitchen is served by a primus stove or an outdoor oven.
Most homes will not have electricity and will rely on kerosene
lamps for light at night. These homes are also not heated.
The rare *fellahin* (peasant) that can afford it may have a small
space heater. The average home will have one room or two and
it will probably also have a courtyard where animals are kept; for
safety, animals are sometimes brought into the house at night.

Since the family is the strong unit in the culture of Jordan,
it is common for the sons of a family, when they marry, to add
another room onto their father's house. This room will house
the new couple. The son will also join the father in the latter's
chosen occupation. In this way, the larger the family, the larger
the economic unit of the family and certainly the stronger the
economy of the family. Jordanian families are very close. The
father has great pride in his family and the children are trained to
have respect for the authority of the father. As the economic
unity of the family binds the group together, so the emotional
tie keeps family members genuinely concerned one for another.

If there is enough money in the family to build a marrying
son a new house, the entire community will take an interest in
the erection of the home and they will all be on hand to help the
builder complete it when the time comes to put on the roof.
This will be a grand festive occasion, a roof-raising, the equivalent
of an American housewarming. All the townspeople or villagers
or neighbors will pitch in with a hard day's labor to complete
this important step in finishing the home. The neighbors will

bring gifts of sheep, rice, and oil. Their host, the future owner of the home, is obligated to feed all of these people a noonday meal and he will use the supplies they have brought to prepare a mammoth *mansef*.

Mansef *and Table Manners*

Mansef is the national dish of Jordan. It is far from being the best-tasting of their extraordinary culinary art, but it is well suited to feeding a crowd. Mounds of saffron rice are placed on large circles of Jordanian bread spread with a thick layer of yoghurt. Boiled lamb is broken into chunks and placed on top of the rice. This dish is eaten by hand. The natives are very skilled at this operation. They use, as in all Muslim eating, the right hand only. Taking a small portion of rice, they press it into a compact ball by making a fist. Then pop it into their mouths.

My husband and I had the great pleasure of attending a roof-raising and were expected to join in the eating of *mansef* in the native manner. The meal was not a complete disaster, but we Westerners did disgrace ourselves with our awkward manipulations and we left a considerable sprinkling of rice on the floor. Our host kindly overlooked this obvious breach of etiquette. After the meal, he provided a towel and warm water so that we could clean our hands. He had served around two hundred persons at the noon meal, no small task since the sheep come in on the hoof. He was a well-pleased but extremely weary man— and six sheep to the good.

Jordanian Women

Throughout Jordan, the patriarchal organization of the family is the accepted way of life. The eldest male in the family is consulted on all matters and he makes the decisions. To illustrate by a homely example: we were driving to an archaeological site in a taxi and our driver became disturbed when our son who was briefly visiting us (a man of twenty-four) lit a cigarette. He asked us, "How is it that the son may smoke before the father?" My husband explained that he himself had never smoked. The driver shook his head in disapproval, "First, the *father* smokes and when the father offers a cigarette to the son, the son is allowed to smoke." Wives and daughters must seek this same nod of approval from the father for all of their activities.

Activities seems rather an inappropriate word for the women's limited sphere of social contact. The average Jordanian village woman's activities fall entirely within the category of housekeeping, animal tending, water drawing, and working in the fields. The women of Jordan catch up on the community gossip as they linger at the well, or they may snatch a few moments of lighthearted conversation as they wait at the community baking oven. On Fridays, the Muslim holy day, some families go to the mosque and fraternize in the courtyard. These few contacts make up the woman's social life. Unknown is the socializing between families in the evenings or at afternoon meetings or teas that makes up such a large part of Western living.

The Jordanian woman and girl have one foremost task and that is to cater to the taste, wishes, and dictates of the man, husband or son. The son's wife must even change her loyalty to her own family to that of her husband and his father. The Jordanian mother does have a minor authoritative role: she outranks her daughters and daughters-in-law. It is necessary for the daughter-in-law to learn to submit to her mother-in-law. If the new daughter-in-law cannot keep peace with her husband's mother, the mother may prevail on her son to find himself a new woman. This would be particularly true if the new daughter is not able to give proof of fertility after a reasonable interval of time.

Children are considered proof of the blessing of God. The converse also applies: women who do not bear are considered under the chastisement of God, and the son might feel that it would indeed be a proper step to rid himself of this woman whom God has not favored. (You are familiar with the demand of Eastern monarchs that their wives produce sons as heirs. Both King Hussein of Jordan and the Shah of Iran divorced wives who did not bear them sons.) Children abound in all Muslim

countries, including Jordan. Most mothers have one babe clinging to Mama's skirt, one babe in arms, and another on the way.
If you can trust statistics, the average Jordanian woman has
nine to ten children. The women of Jordan consider child-bearing
a proof of their continued youth and a guarantee of a husband's
love. Birth control is a mute subject.

In practice, many Jordanians are not so overjoyed at each
new conception. Such child-bearing takes a toll of the wife's
vitality and a large family imposes a financial burden on the
breadwinner. Yet, when we asked one doctor what medical
problem he dealt with most frequently, the surprising answer
was the administration of medicine to increase the fertility of
the woman. Apparently, if more than a year goes by without
conception, the woman runs to the doctor in a panic. One reason
for insistence on pregnancy is certainly that divorce is still too
easy in Jordan. The man of the house has only to tell his wife to
"scat" and she must return to her parents or brothers. Her chance
for remarriage would be very slim. There are not enough men in
Jordan to go around. The divorced wife may take her children
until they are, perhaps, five or six. After that age, the father
may have his children back. Particularly, the father will want his
boys.

I have heard it said that because a man may have more than
one wife, a divorced woman can easily find a new husband. In
practice, this is not necessarily true. The women whom we knew
to be without husbands and beyond the age of youth had
resigned themselves to living under the care and protection of
their brothers or fathers.

In some families it is still the custom that the eldest daughter
must find a husband before the younger daughters may marry.
In the book of Genesis (29:26) Jacob ran into this problem.
Thousands of years earlier Jacob was tricked into marrying the
elder daughter, Leah, before he was able to marry the younger
Rachel (Gen. 29:26–27). One of our American friends of Jordanian descent met with this same stumbling block within recent
years. He fell in love with a young Jordanian girl and asked

for her hand in marriage. The girl's father refused to consider the proposal until the elder sister was married. By the time the elder sister married, the younger sister had found another love and our American friend was left without a bride.

The divorced husband has every chance for remarriage. He has a choice of hundreds of lovely women younger than his former wife. The Muslim husband may keep two wives if he wishes, or more if his financial position can support several families at once. Polygamy (even though sanctioned under Muslim law to the extent of four wives) is not widely practiced. Having more than one wife under one roof turns out to be just as troublesome for Jordanians as you would imagine that it would be for you.

If a man does choose to have more than one wife, he is duty bound to spend his time equally with each one. He may have a favorite wife. In this case, the *quality* of the time spent with various wives may differ. Since the emotional makeup of women does not vary too much the world over, it is easy to imagine the jealousies and bickering that might emerge under one roof, or tent.

I remember seeing one Muslim man come into Jerusalem with three wives and about five young children. All eight of his charges were coaxing him to buy things for them and the man looked thoroughly burdened by the whole brood. Many Jordanian men are loyal to one wife for a lifetime, and in a country where the cards are stacked so completely for the male, this seems most commendable.

Madefah

Muslim men do have social life. They will gather at the coffee houses where they sit around small tables and play games and talk, or they will gather in the mosque and talk, or they will frequent a village *madefah* (community room) where they squat on the floor and converse over cup after cup of coffee.

Arabs have a full appreciation of the meaning of the adjective "leisurely." To an Arab there is no sense in being in a rush. The clock, as a taskmaster, has no place in their lives. Even conversation is quite deliberately paced. To the Arabs, conversing is an art that demands graciousness, mental dexterity and imagination and a soupçon of cunning. To sit down and engage your friends abruptly in a discussion would be considered rude. First you must observe all the niceties of language by exchanging greetings around the room, you must inquire after the health of community members, you must wish them God's blessing, commiserate with them over their sorrows, and exult with them in their joys.

There is a rather pat formula for this elaborate exchange of introductory remarks. A specific greeting calls for a specific response. It is a source of pride for an Arab to be able to use his language in its finest form. This finest form calls for expressing oneself in words and phrases considered to be the utmost in courtesy and graciousness. The finest conversation is also liberally filled with such phrases as "If the Lord is willing," "May God be with you." Most salutations invoke the Name of God: "God grant you a good morning. God vouchsafe you a good evening."

After the formal greetings have been completed, there is still no necessity to plunge into the heart of the matters to be discussed. It is preferable to turn the conversation slowly to a specific matter. It is also possible to drop a subtle hint that one has startling news and needs only slight encouragement to share it. It is possible to toy with the audience, tantalize it, until the curiosity of each man in the room is captured. Perhaps the speaker will have nothing to say that would warrant such a build-up, but whatever he had to say will be said with such flourish that it sounds very important indeed. The speaker may have heard a rumor. In the politically unsettled Middle East rumors are rife—about a dozen per day, always with the most ominous undertones. Arabs thrive on mulling over rumors and grumbling over their probable meaning. In truth, they rather enjoy harboring imagined grievances deep within their hearts.

Spinners of Tales

In the evening when pressing matters are not presented at the *madefah* there is still no shortage of conversation. Scheherazade was not the only person with a thousand stories. Arabs love to recount legends and have plenty to recount. There are superstitious legends of the past, many involving supernatural powers of animals, in particular, the hyena. There are marvelous and satisfying stories about clever sultans who with great wisdom and cunning outwitted every adversary. And there are wonderful little nonsense stories—this tale is one often told as an example of Arab logic:

A thief wandering through the city streets at night spied an open window in a merchant's home. The thief climbed to the second-story window but as he was about to swing his body through the window into the room, the window sill gave way and the thief plunged to the ground. The thief was enraged and he called to the merchant, demanding satisfaction for this injury to his body. The merchant appeared at the window, offered his apology for the offense perpetrated by the window sill, but suggested, "This was not my fault, but the fault of the builder of my home." Together the thief and the merchant sought out the builder of the house to demand satisfaction. The builder of the house apologized for the offense but denied responsibility, reasoning, "This was not my fault, but the fault of the stonecutter who fashioned the sill." Together the three sought out the stonecutter and demanded satisfaction. The stonecutter apologized for the offense, but added, "This was not my fault. As I was fashioning the sill a beautiful woman walked by and she distracted me in my work." Together the four sought out the beautiful woman. The beautiful woman apologized for the offense, but pleaded, "Oh sirs, this was not my fault, but rather the fault of the beautiful dress that I was wearing." Together the five set out to seek the maker of the dress that the woman had been wearing. The dressmaker apologized for the offense, but added, "This was not my fault, but the fault of the maker of such a beautiful fabric." Together the six sought out the

maker of such a beautiful fabric to demand satisfaction. The maker
of the beautiful fabric apologized for the offense, but continued,
"This was not my fault, but rather the fault of the maker of the
lovely dyes for the fabric." Together the seven sought out the maker
of the lovely dyes to demand satisfaction. The dyemaker apologized for the fault, and threw up his hands in despair. He knew no
one on whom he could cast the blame. The dyemaker was hanged
for the offense and the seven returned home, satisfied that the
crime was properly punished.

This is, of course, a foolish story. But retelling it, I am reminded that we were treated to a bit of the same philosophy.
While we were in Jordan, we took our car to a garage for lubri-
cation and general check-up in the course of which the car was
accidentally set on fire. Since the garage did not have adequate
fire-fighting equipment and the Jerusalem fire department was
at least five miles away, our car burned almost to an ash. The
garage owner did not have insurance. This was sad enough in
itself. But the surprise was this: a small bus that had been
standing next to our car when it caught on fire, got scorched.
The bus company *sued us* because it was *our car burning that
did damage to their bus*. Perhaps the Arabs have been sitting
around the *madefah* listening to stories for too long.

At any rate, at such an evening gathering, the older generation educates the young through oral tradition. The young hear
these same stories, told in the same form, hundreds of times
throughout the years. These young men will in turn so educate
their sons in years to come. By such oral tradition, great literature, like our Bible, was passed from generation to generation
until it was finally put in written form.

The Art of Drinking Coffee

In their homes, all Jordanians are most hospitable. For the
fellahin, hospitality means that he offers his guests coffee, cigarettes, and candy. These three items are expensive. They are
the luxuries in the home and they are in short supply. It is

particularly a compliment to be offered coffee because that cup of coffee is always made "to order" for guests. It is never brewed ahead of time. It must be freshly made and immediately served, to demonstrate to the guest that he is most welcome and warmly received.

Arabic coffee is a beverage laden with powdered coffee. It is served in tiny cups about two inches high with no handles. About one third of the cup of coffee will be thick coffee paste and when you reach this mixture of settled grounds, you cease drinking. True Arabic coffee is made only with coffee and water. It is very bitter. Coffee to which sugar and sometimes cardamom seed have been added is called Turkish coffee. Turkish coffee is more commonly served by the *fellahin*. The bitter coffee is usually served by the Bedouins. Whether Arabic or Turkish, the coffee is very strong—in fact, so strong that it seems capable of making its way through the alimentary canal by a brand new and utterly direct channel.

Properly the coffee is not drunk, but instead taken into the mouth by a rapid, strong (and noisy) sucking motion that skims off the surface of the coffee. Americans believe that coffee keeps a person awake, but the Arabs assured us that a cup of coffee before bedtime ensures a good night's sleep. Arabs are addicted to coffee and since they do not drink alcohol, they use as a substitute this strongly caffeinic liquid. If you are a guest in Jordan, you will drink plenty of it. It is an insult to refuse a cup of coffee.

An Invitation to Dinner

If the tourist is fortunate enough to receive a dinner invitation from a family in the Holy Land, he should accept graciously and joyfully. An invitation to dinner means you are invited to partake of a feast. The hostess does not prepare the stereotyped meal that we too often call dinner—meat, potatoes, vegetable, salad, and dessert. She prepares a variety of dishes all featuring meat, a variety of salads, yoghurt and purées that are

tart dips for Arabic-style bread. Garlic, onions, pepper, cinnamon, nutmeg are the flavoring agents commonly used and used
so skillfully that it is no hardship for the guest to flatter the
hostess by polishing off several platefuls at a sitting.

Arab living teems with tradition and legend and their foods
are sometimes selected to fit a tradition or occasion. There are
foods that are served only on happy occasions—foods that are
served traditionally at the end of a job well done—foods that
are served at funerals. Even coffee is varied in taste according
to the occasion. It is bitter for serious or unhappy affairs, sweet
to very sweet on joyous occasions.

Eating a meal in Arab lands is almost a ritual during which
you are completely occupied with tasting and savoring. The
salads and purées are blends that sharpen the appetite and
perfectly complement the delicacies made of meats. The sheer
delight of taste keeps the partaker eating long after the stomach
is comfortably and sensibly filled. Perhaps for this reason dessert
is superfluous, although fresh fruit in season is usually served
after the meal. Then for the perfect finishing touch—the tiny
cup of strong Arabic coffee.

The Blessings of Lamb—and Other Foods

What are their foods and how are they different from ours?
Considering that most of the meat in Jordan is lamb, it is a
tribute to the people that they have found so many ways to
serve it attractively. *Kibbeh* is perhaps the most popular dish,
and is always served on a happy occasion. It is a mixture of
ground lamb, crushed wheat, onions, salt, plus a second mixture
of meat that is used as a filling. The filling is also mainly
lamb, but it is seasoned differently with onions, pine nuts, salt,
plenty of pepper and cinnamon. To prepare *kibbeh*, you divide
the basic meat mixture in half. Press half firmly into the bottom
of a pan, place the filling on top of it and cover the filling
with the other half of the basic mixture. The *kibbeh* is again

pressed down firmly, then attractively scored in diagonal lines. Butter is spread on top and the *kibbeh* either baked or broiled. *Kibbeh* can also be made into patties in the shape of a large egg, with a pocket in the middle to hold the filling. *Kibbeh* in this shape can be fried or simmered in yoghurt. It is delicious made by any one of these methods.

Kafta is another "happy" meat dish made of ground lamb. It is a combination of lamb with lots of parsley, onions, and tomato paste plus salt and pepper. *Kafta* is usually shaped into finger-length cylinders. It can be broiled, baked, or fried.

There are endless varieties of meat balls prepared by using selected spices and each meat dish has a different name. Cinnamon, nutmeg, coriander, bay leaves, and vinegar are used to spice lamb.

Stuffed lamb is a special treat and while the Arabs do prepare the whole animal and stuff it for feasts, most Americans will have to content themselves with stuffing a leg or shoulder of lamb. If you have always felt that rice was somewhat useless in the flavor department, try adding to it salt, pepper, cinnamon, parsley, pistachio nuts, pine nuts, and almonds. Stuff a lamb with the rice mixture and roast it. DE-licious!

Pastries are filled with ground meat that has been seasoned with onions, lemon, nuts, pomegranate seeds, and spice.

Vegetables are stuffed with meat mixtures. Vine leaves stuffed with meat and seasonings and simmered in a small amount of liquid plus eight or ten garlic buds are served not only in Arab countries but in Greece and Turkey. Eggplants and marrows are similarly stuffed. Poor people eat many stuffed vegetables, but even among the better off meat is usually not included except for special occasions.

The salads and purées are a complete puzzle to Westerners whose palates cannot single out the ingredients. Small wonder! Some of the ingredients we never use. Some are used in combinations that we have not thought of. *Tabbouleh* is a great favorite among the salads. It is tart, crisp, and refreshing—an unusually fine complement for meat. To make *tabbouleh*, softened crushed wheat is well worked by the fingers along with mint, parsley, and onions. When the juices of the latter have mixed with the wheat, olive oil, lemon juice, salt, and pepper are stirred in. The salad is garnished with tomatoes.

Cucumbers are prevalent in Jordan—my favorite cucumber salad calls for marinating slices in yoghurt flavored with salt, garlic, and mint.

Chick peas and eggplant are the base for two very delicious purées and in each case the base ingredient is cooked, mashed, and stirred until smooth. It is then mixed with *tahini*, a solid sesame oil that tastes a little like peanut butter, and lemon juice. Crushed garlic is also added. When the purées are placed on the table, they are garnished with parsley, pine nuts, and pomegranate seeds.

These dishes by no means comprise a complete description of Arabic delicacies, but they are the most commonly requested. Now, think of this: if you were invited to an Arabic meal, it is more than likely that *every one* of the dishes here mentioned would be served. When you are a guest in an Arab home, your hostess has *worked* to please you.

Arab cookery is being discovered in the United States and it is now possible to buy cookbooks giving exact measurement of ingredients. Former cookbooks, obviously direct translations from the heart of the Middle East, abounded in such directions as: take a piece of meat from the shoulder of a sheep, pound it well in the mortar with salt, mix an onion with the meat and pound for an hour; *or:* soak a sheep's head overnight in cold water to get rid of the blood; *or:* boil milk and allow it to cool enough so that you can allow your finger to remain in the milk without pain while you count to ten. These directions may sound ludicrous, but the woman who knows what she is doing, although she be seated cross-legged outside her tent with a bowl and pounder, is turning out some mighty fine-tasting food. Arab children who are sent to Europe or America for college are understandably repelled by the flat, flavorless, monotonous diet endured by the West.

Vendors on the Street

The Holy Land hostess does not serve to her guests the type of foods that are sold by vendors on the streets. The street foods are just snacks—so many Jordanians walk the streets, eating as they go, one would think no meals were prepared in the home. The best seller at the street stands is the Jordanian "hamburger." It is a mixture of mashed chick peas and spices (mainly pepper) rolled into a ball, dipped in sesame seeds, and fried in the deep fat. Sandwich carts on the streets hold all the ingredients and equipment to serve as short-order kitchens for hot lamb sandwiches garnished with plenty of juice, tomatoes, and onions. That is, all of the equipment save one necessity—refrigeration.

Another version of the lamb sandwich is cooked lamb sliced very thin, stacked and pressed into a foot-long cylinder and placed on a vertical spit. When the customer orders this sandwich, the vendor broils the meat, slices off the browned bits of meat from the sides of the cylinder, and places the meat in the pocket of round bread. The sandwich smells marvelous but I was never tempted to buy one. I had an opportunity to observe that the same cylinder of meat, very slowly dwindling in diameter, was set up anew each day for a period of many weeks.

In the spring, Jordanians consume great quantities of fresh fruit while they walk and shop. When romaine lettuce first comes on the market, the natives are so hungry for it that they buy it from the vendors and eat it as they walk down the street.

One "delicacy" that tourists are almost certain to be served in any home in the spring is the almond. Much as most persons enjoy nuts, they may find these nuts a little hard to swallow. They are not ripe. Before the shell of the nuts has hardened, the pods are picked from the trees. Jordanians relish these nuts,

eat them pod and all after dipping them in salt. What do they
taste like? Like an underripe nut, green, flavorless and also as
though a good stomach ache might follow. The English, they
say, eat the walnut in this condition and the Jordanian, remembering the Holy Land under British mandate, so eats the
almond.

Nuts and seeds, ripened and toasted, constitute an everyday
necessity for most Jordanians. Perhaps the nuts supply protein
which is lacking in the diet. As for seeds, Jordanians are addicted
to them, particularly squash seeds, which they crack with their
teeth to suck out the meat inside. Squash seeds are good—to
eat only one is as difficult as it is to eat one peanut. The streets
of Jerusalem are littered with shells from seeds, the floors of
movie houses covered with them.

Herbs Outside the Kitchen

Many of the women of the Holy Land are doctors as well as
cooks in the kitchen. The spices of Arabia, so well used to en-
hance the flavor of meat and all their foods, are widely believed also to be helpful as medicines. If you meet a *fellahin*
woman in Jordan, she might tell you that she relies on ginger
to help ailing stomachs. Anise is also used for this purpose
and in addition thought to be an aid in liver ailments. Cumin
is used to settle gas on the stomach (as, I note, it is often
recommended as an addition to our chili recipes). Sage is supposed to soothe the nerves and relieve external itching. Mustard, as we all know, is a good agent for a poultice. Cloves
stimulate gastric juices. Yarrow tea is helpful for severe colds
while inhalation of cinnamon may prevent colds. Garlic is sometimes burned in the home so that the fumes penetrate the
lungs and reduce danger of infectious diseases. Nutmeg is an
aid for insomnia, bay leaf recommended for pimples and colic.
Tarragon and basil sweeten the breath; cinnamon inspires love.
Such legendary uses for spices are based on long and satisfactory
experience.

To Visit a Home

It is now possible in Jordan to visit the home of a native family by an arrangement with the tourist department. Most of the families that co-operate in this way with the department of tourism will probably be quite Western in their dress and in their thinking. They will be able to converse with you and will take an active interest in learning more about your country.

In the more conservative Muslim home, when guests are entertained, the guests may not see the women who have provided the hospitality. The host will offer refreshment, then partake himself while his wife peeks from the doorway. On one occasion when I specifically asked for the privilege of thanking the wife, she entered the room and sat with us but was obviously in such misery at this social sentence that she looked at her hands and at the floor the whole time, while acknowledging her husband's translation of the thanks by a nod of her head. I never precipitated this uncomfortable situation again.

When women are outside their homes and busy at their chores they seem more relaxed with strangers. They are never too busy to smile. They scrutinize your clothing and make pointed and obviously humorous remarks about it to their companions. Very, very sensitive as the Arabs are, the tourist seldom dares to suggest that he found any of their customs humorous—the natives would be humiliated and genuinely offended. On the other hand, the natives are quite ready to break into laughter over the tourists' shoes or hats and even to call tourists "fish muk"; they think the tourist won't understand, but it means "without a brain in the head."

We did find one custom of the *fellahin* amusing. The women do not carry handbags. They carry baskets, water cans, and sacks of food on their heads, but like to have their arms swing free. Their money, papers, etc., they carry not in a purse but inside the bodice of their dresses. I noticed that the women usually have a belt tied quite tightly at the waist. I assume this belt sometimes keeps valuables from slipping out. To a Westerner, it is absolutely hysterical—the natives are used to it—to see a woman in the street fishing into her bodice for loose change. The women are quite refreshingly honest about the whole operation.

The Little Beggars

One of our friends who was pestered and pestered by a little beggar boy finally opened her purse to him to show him that she really did not have a cent of money with her. After satisfying himself that she did not have any money there, he pointed to her bosom and asked, "Nothing there, either?"

This same friend, who seemed to have an attraction for the unfortunate, went shopping one afternoon and on the way picked up a little boy who tagged along at her heels, chatting incessantly. In shop after shop, she stayed overlong, hoping each time that the child would tire of waiting and run along his way. No such luck. He was always waiting. Finally at dinnertime, she was so thoroughly annoyed by the youngster that she told him, firmly, that she was now going home to dinner, that he could not accompany her but was to leave her immediately. The youngster held out his hand. She said, "You want money? Why should I give you money?" The child started to cry. "Lady," he said, "because I have stayed with you *all day*, and you are rich."

She gave the child money.

Health Hazards

What is the state of health of the villagers and townspeople? It is far from excellent. In 1912 Baedeker wrote in his guidebook to the Holy Land,

The chief dangers to travellers in Palestine are fevers (malaria, typhoid), diarrhoea (sometimes passing into dysentery), and opthalmia. These may however be avoided by the observance of a few simple precautions . . . the traveller's medicine chest should . . . contain gentle aperients, such as Cascara Sagrada or castor oil . . . which will be found especially valuable in the earliest stage of dysentery. Light cases of diarrhoea may generally be cured by rest in a horizontal position and a diet of rice or arrowroot and milk.

This advice from early in the century could still be heeded by tourists in the Holy Land. There are still some fevers in Jordan. Diarrhea is very common although the remedial diet has changed slightly to rice, yoghurt, and tea. Rest in a horizontal position is not only recommended—it is dictated by the complaint.

Let's look at the encouraging side of the health story first. If any single disease has long been associated with the Holy Land, it is leprosy. You might expect that there would still be lepers begging outside the city walls. Not so. There is one hospital in Jordan, maintained by German church funds, that is a home for all lepers in the country. In all, there are seventeen patients in the hospital and two of the seventeen are children with an incurable skin condition. Of the lepers, almost all are arrested cases and none is a new case. My memory is that the adults in this hospital have been there for at least twenty-five years. It is wonderful to know that this disease has to all practical purposes been wiped out in Jordan, but it is more heartening to be able to report firsthand the loving care given the victims of leprosy. These patients have been given a home and made to feel at home. You won't find them sitting in corners and turning their heads away from visitors. They welcome guests, converse with them and are more than pleased to have visitors inspect their living quarters.

There are two married couples, each couple with a private house. These married folks invited my husband and me into their living quarters. They did not know ahead of time that we were coming. Their houses were immaculate. They were not self-conscious or shy, and invited me to take a picture of them. Patients who are able to are given chickens to raise and are

allowed to realize whatever money comes from the sale of eggs.
Patients in whom the disease is arrested are given freedom to
go out into the community as they wish. Handicrafts are taught
in the hospital. Some little money may come to the patients
from their work. If the patients are able to help with chores
at the hospital, they are paid for their time, and they have a
certain amount of independence. They are treated like a family
and *they are happy*. I doubt that you could find anywhere more
enlightened care of the unfortunate than in this small "home"
in Jordan.

The only thing that distressed me about the hospital was
that the women in charge had been asked to welcome into
their fold the two small boys with an incurable skin disease.
As we understood it, this disease was not contagious, but heredi-
tary. It is probably understandable that the easy answer to
dealing with such unfortunate children is to put them away
where they will not perpetuate the skin condition by bearing
children of their own, but it is awfully hard to see young
children so completely shut off from normal contacts with others
of their own age.

As leprosy seems to have been brought under control, so
malaria is losing its grip thanks to a rather careful check on
still waters that breed mosquitoes. Village wells are covered with
a coating of kerosene that discourages the growth of larvae.
Cholera and the plague have been gone from Jordan for many
years. There is still tuberculosis but there is also a sanatorium
to help the victims. It is south of Bethlehem. The heavy, deep
cough of many Arabs may suggest that some tuberculosis goes
undetected. The cough could also be a cigarette cough since
Arabs smoke continuously and their local brands are strong.
Undulant fever is found in Jordan. Most milk is not pasteurized.
The doctors told me that many of the natives have learned to
live with recurring attacks of dysentery and worms.

If I were wealthy, I would certainly give a bundle of money
to Jordan for public health information on the care of eyes.
Eye disease is perhaps more apparent to the tourist than any

other single health problem. You will see more blindness in one day in this country than you have seen in a lifetime in the United States. You see blind eyes among the old, the middle aged, the young, and the babes. It is more than depressing; it is appalling. One American doctor who had offered a year of his service to a Jordanian hospital said that he had seen more types of blindness and more cases of each kind than he could have experienced in his entire career in the United States. Trachoma is one cause of this. Just ordinary infection is another. The custom of Jordanian mothers of putting oil on the babies' eyes has not turned out to benefit the baby. The oil attracts flies. The eyes become infected, but until they fester, the baby is not taken to a doctor. By the time the doctor has a chance to help the baby, the eyes have become permanently damaged. The doctors said that most of these eye infections could be cleared up easily in the early stages. Malnutrition is another cause of blindness in young children. This type of blindness can be cured by proper diet. Jordanian mothers nurse their babies too long, and their milk is not sufficient since the mother's diet is inadequate.

On the other hand, there are times when mothers' remedies apparently work. A Jordanian visiting nurse was with a family at the time when one of the young children fell and came running into the house with a bad gash across his forehead. The nurse tried to explain to the mother that the child had a serious open wound that needed to be thoroughly disinfected. The mother scoffed, pushed the nurse aside, led the child to the stove, took a handful of warm coffee grounds, and smeared them around the wound. The bleeding stopped almost immediately. A few days later the nurse stopped back at the house to see how the child was getting along. The forehead seemed to be healing very well without any sign of infection.

Since the finest fruits and vegetables are available in Jordan, what is the reason that the natives suffer so often from nutritional deficiencies? The answer might be that the Jordanians cannot afford to buy the more nutritious foods or that they destroy the vitamin content in cooking. It is true that typical Middle Eastern dishes rely heavily on marrow and eggplant, neither a great supplier of vitamins. Rice is still the greatest part of the diet. In poor families, the slaughter of a lamb is a luxury reserved for special feasts. One of the fine doctors employed by a religious welfare group talked with me briefly about the health problems in Jordan. He finds rickets and night blindness among his patients, and saw lack of vitamins A and D as the problem. Here is a strange paradox. Foods with vitamin A are abundant in Jordan. Carrots are a drug on the market. And as you well know, the sun shines in Jordan until you have to hide from it. Of course, the Arabs do hide from the sun. They keep their bodies almost completely covered summer and winter. They feel that clothing both keeps them warm in winter and insulates them from the heat in summer. At any rate, the ordinary Jordanian suffers from a lack of two vitamins that seem to be in oversupply.

The Clinics

Many Jordanians can now live with the advantages of adequate medical help. There are health clinics, both on wheels and permanently stationed in the cities, that offer medical care free to those who cannot pay and inexpensively to those who can pay. In the cities these clinics are jammed with mothers and babies. To protect the young, the clinics offer free milk to mothers (similar to Similac) and advice on child care. The growth of babies is kept on charts giving measurements and weight. It is hoped this will mean stronger children in Jordan in years to come.

My husband and I visited the Jerusalem clinic by appointment one day only to find that the waiting rooms were so well filled with mothers nursing their babies that we could barely make our way through the place. We apologized to the nurse for coming on such a busy day and explained that we could return at another time. The nurse laughed away our apologies with the explanation that the clinic usually looked that way. The babies had all been previously checked, and the mothers were now enjoying their "social hour." They liked to sit around and talk, then nurse the babies until the children fell asleep, whereupon the mothers went home.

Precautions for the Tourist

In spite of the fact that well-qualified doctors and nurses are fighting a valiant battle to improve the health of persons in the Holy Land, the bald fact is that this land of Jordan is one country in an area of the world that abounds in diseases against which protective health measures have not been taken. The myriad public health laws that protect the American in his native land are lacking in Jordan.

It may be that the lack of concern for the laws of sanitation can be laid in part at the doorstep of the Muslim religion. The Muslim concept that "what is the will of God will inevitably happen" and "what is not the will of God will not happen" accounts for what Americans would term inexcusable carelessness among most members of the Muslim community. It is certainly true also that at the present time those persons engaged in growing, handling, or distributing food products have little knowledge of the preventive measures that would reduce the spread of disease.

For example, one of the most patronized salesmen in the Holy Land is the vendor of beverages or juices. In Jerusalem alone, there must be a dozen or so of these salesmen and they are among the most engaging characters on the Holy Land scene. They dress themselves ingeniously in the most bizarre costumes. They have strapped to their backs huge canisters, gleaming gold or silver, bedecked with bells or tassels. As these beverage vendors stroll through the streets, the tourist is well aware of their presence because they clink together small porcelain cups— an announcement to "come and get it." "It" may be tea, lemonade, or water. If the tourist chooses to "get it" he will notice that the vendor swishes a little water around in a well-used cup before he refills the cup with a fresh drink for his new customer.

The hawkers of vegetables, fruits, breads, and candies are similarly unconcerned about whether or not they pass along a few germs to their customers. These hawkers know their merchandise well. They play with it all day, arranging it, rearranging it, patting it, piling it up in different order. What falls on the ground is picked up and put back on the cart. A few spills on the ground may not be serious for vegetables that will ultimately undergo thorough cooking or peeling, but spills for bread, cakes, candies, or fruit fall in another category entirely—deadly serious.

Jerusalem streets have some pretty gruesome stuff deposited on them in an average day. The tourist can see contamination in full bloom. If it is true that we must all eat our peck of dirt before we die, it is easier to do it in the Holy Land.

If you are traveling in the Holy Land, it would be well for you to take a good look underfoot and to reflect that all of this washes into cisterns during the rainy season. Even in a clean hotel, it is not wise to reach for a glass of cold water. It is much wiser to slip a chlorine tablet into that glass and wait thirty minutes before drinking it. If you have been assured that the water has come from a spring, there is no assurance that you can safely drink it.

Jordan has more than its share of typhoid, hepatitis, and dysentery. The tourist may think that he can rest easy about typhoid because he has had shots. Yet I have known Americans who for some strange reason contracted typhoid in spite of having had the typhoid-paratyphoid shots given tourists. Jordanian doctors scoff at our American typhoid shots as being ineffective against the typhoid of the Middle East. On the other hand, some American doctors with whom I talked felt that there was not a "different strain" of typhoid in the Middle East but that the protective shot usually given in America is not effective for more than a six months' period and that for some individuals the immunity lasts for a lesser period.

Infectious hepatitis is so prevalent in Jordan that it would be considered an epidemic in America, and yet the natives treat this damaging disease as little more than a cold.

You will read that amoebic dysentery is not to be found in Jordan. Perhaps a more careful statement would be that amoebic dysentery is not indigenous to Jordan. People do have amoebic dysentery in Jordan and it is possible to be exposed to it.

The tourist will certainly be exposed to skin diseases. As he visits the shrines, his eyes will see that many of the little children dancing around him in the streets, stroking his hands and begging for *baksheesh,* live with sores on their faces and in their hair. As mentioned previously, trachoma is common in Jordan and the tourist should be cautioned against rubbing his eyes. Sunglasses are a good preventive against inadvertently rubbing the eyes and are necessary as well to protect eyes from the excessive glare of the sun on the stark landscape.

To give himself all the protection he needs in Jordan the tourist should *a.* not drink any water unless he knows it has been properly boiled or treated with chemicals, *b.* wash his hands a la Lady Macbeth (some meticulous tourists also scrub their shoes each evening), and *c.* eat not one particle of foods that have not been thoroughly cooked, or in the case of fruit, skinned. Cabbage slaw and lettuce may look very tempting, but if you could see the conditions under which these vegetables are grown, you would know that no salad of them could be clean unless it had been reduced to a soggy mass by cleansing chemicals.

Among the American women I knew who were living in Jordan temporarily it was an everyday practice to dump all groceries into a chlorine solution for at least half an hour before storing them in the refrigerator. Even foods like potatoes, bananas, and oranges were given this treatment lest young children handle them and then put their fingers into their mouths.

Unless the tourist is willing to be a good watchguard of his own health, he will most likely find himself confined to his hotel room while the rest of his tour party bid him "So long" and head off for a day of fun and adventure.

VI Samaria

Samaria, a district north of Jerusalem and west of the Jordan River, has been favored by the forces of nature to receive a healthy portion of Jordan's meager supply of water. In winter and spring, it is lush with green growth, and one of the loveliest sights in the Holy Land suddenly appears before you as the road from the south enters Samaria. The hills that have converged on the roadway for so many miles open up and far beneath you spreads a broad expanse of a valley farmland—a patchwork of well-ordered crops, the plain of Lubban.

A modern legend has been born in these highlands overlooking the plain. Our driver told us that during World War I, the Arabs were annoyed by the presence of many German troops in the area. A wily Arab, having gained for himself the confidence of the German commander, persuaded him that a silent night march would place his troops in an excellent tactical position by morning. The march was duly ordered. The Germans, following the Arab guide, set out in the black of night through the maze of hills. When the hills abruptly gave way to the valley, the Arab front runner stood aside and watched as the whole German force marched its way over the precipice to sudden death. This is a most interesting story. But it is *just* that, a story. When I cocked my eyebrow at my narrator in skepticism, he adamantly reiterated that the story was unquestionably true: his father had told him— indeed, his father had *seen* the carnage. Remembering how Arabs love to spin yarns about their ability to best their enemies with cunning, my husband and I let the matter drop. Our confidence in the intelligence of the German soldier was not hanging in the balance. In fact, a further glance at the descent into the valley

from our vantage point confirmed our original impression that
the descent was a slope—a steep one to be sure—but hardly in
any sense a precipice.

Jacob's Well

Somewhat better documented is the tradition surrounding the
first ancient site at which tourists stop. This is Jacob's well near
the modern town of Nablus. We are told in Genesis 33:18, 19
that Jacob with his two wives and children set up housekeeping
for a time near the city of Shechem. (The ruins of the ancient
city are a few minutes' walking distance from the well.) According to the Bible, Jacob bought a plot of land here for one
hundred pieces of money and pitched his tent. Surprisingly
enough, the *well* is not mentioned in the Old Testament.
Apparently the Gospel writers had more information about
Jacob's well than we can read in the Old Testament, because
the Gospel According to John makes two references to it. First,
John says that Jesus in traveling through Samaria came to the
field "that Jacob gave to his son, Joseph. Now Jacob's well was
there." Then, in the course of Jesus' conversation with the
woman of Samaria, the woman asks Jesus, "Art thou greater than
our father Jacob, which gave us the well and drank thereof himself, and his children, and his cattle?" (John 4:5-6, 12).

Jacob's well in the Holy Land is considered by many pilgrims
as far more than a mere curiosity—an ancient well that still serves
cool water from a depth of seventy-five feet. To many it is a
most sacred spot and to some persons there is even a feeling
that drinking water at the well is a great privilege, perhaps a
spiritual blessing.

Shechem and Jacob's well are closely associated with the
patriarchal covenant with the Lord. At the beginning of the
narrative of the patriarchs, God called Abraham to move to a new
land. Abraham complied. He was led to the land of Canaan, but
specifically to Shechem, at that time a Canaanite town. There, the
Lord appeared again to Abraham and promised to give the land

to his descendants. Abraham built in this area an altar to the Lord. Then, he moved his tribe farther south.

Many years later when he was ready to marry, Jacob was urged not to marry a local woman, but to seek out one of his own kind. So it was that he left Canaan to travel to the land of Haran, home of his forefather Abraham. During this journey the Lord appeared to Jacob in a dream and made to the young descendant the promise formerly made to Abraham: "the land whereon thou liest, to thee will I give it, and to thy seed" (Gen. 28:13). Jacob continued on to Haran. There he acquired not one wife, but two wives, two maids, eleven sons (Gen. 32:22) and flocks. With this household, he left Haran and returned to Canaan. During the return journey, Jacob encountered a man near a stream called the Jabbok. He wrestled with this man all night. Then toward morning, Jacob discovered that he had been wrestling with the Lord. For Jacob's struggles, the Lord rewarded him by blessing him with a new name, "Israel," to show that this man, Jacob, was now in a new relationship with his Lord. Jacob moved on to Shechem where he also erected an altar to the God of Israel.

The sons of Jacob were well acquainted with Shechem; we read in the Bible that they tended their father's flocks near the city. It was not far from Shechem that the brothers conspired to sell Joseph into slavery. And, many, many years later, Joseph returned to Shechem. The strong traditions surrounding this area of land were known to the Israelites, who dutifully brought back from the land of Eypt the mummy of Joseph and buried it at Shechem "in the parcel of ground which Jacob bought from the sons of Hamor, the father of Shechem for an hundred pieces of silver: and it became the inheritance of the children of Joseph" (Josh. 24:32).

Jesus and the Samaritan Woman

Because of the close association of the city of Shechem with the covenant between the Lord and the patriarchs, it is quite natural that Jesus, well acquainted as he was with the Scriptures, knew the significance of Jacob's well. Jesus paused there for a drink during the early days of his brief ministry. A Samaritan woman came to the well to draw water. Jesus asked her for a drink. The woman was surprised that Jesus, to her eyes obviously a Jew, should ask a favor of a Samaritan woman, but Jesus ignored the woman's concern over this breach in social customs. Instead, he turned her question, "How is it that thou, being a Jew, askest drink of me which am a woman of Samaria?" (John 4:9), into a spiritual lesson: if the woman knew who Jesus was, it would be she who would ask him for a drink—a drink of living water which would fill her like an eternal spring and quench her thirst for all time. As the Gospel story continues, Jesus confounded the woman with knowledge of her past life and revealed himself to her as the Messiah.

Since this well was still revered as a site associated with Jacob in the time of Jesus, it is not surprising that early Christian pilgrims founded a church on the site. Eusebius mentioned that a church had been built on this spot. The Bordeaux pilgrims (A.D. 333) and St. Jerome (400) also mention visiting the shrine. Later, when the Crusaders came to the Holy Land, no substantial or adequate structure remained for they built a three-nave church with the well directly below the altar. It is assumed that this church was destroyed by the forces of Saladin.

In modern times, this site has become the property of the Greek Orthodox Church. A rebuilding of a church was interrupted by World War I. The unfinished church still stands. Down the steps beneath the church, there is a pleasantly decorated sanctuary surrounding the well. The well is shallower than it was but still deep. Most visitors seem unable to resist the temptation to drop a pebble into the well and wait to hear the delayed splash. Many persons drink from it; a metal cup is attached by chain to the well for the purpose. Some pilgrims seek a less-used part of the rim of the cup to sip the water. Since, however, every pilgrim appears to boast that he cleverly turned the cup around and drank from the opposite side, it might be the part of wisdom to drink from the normal spot on the cup and find there the least used surface.

About five hundred yards north of Jacob's well is the site marked by Muslim tradition as a possible resting place for the bones of Joseph.

The City of Shechem

Close by are the ruins of the city of Shechem. Since Shechem figures so prominently in the patriarchal narratives, you might be interested to know that archaeological excavations have shown that Shechem was a very large city during the period of the patriarchs—in fact, it was at its height in size and power. It is interesting to speculate how this city came to be located where it is—low, on a plain. It sits before a strategic pass connecting the Mediterranean coastline with the plains of the Jordan Valley. Directly to the north is Mount Ebal; directly to the south, Mount Gerizim. If this pass were to be used by invaders, it would seem that Shechem would be quite vulnerable to attack from the slopes of either mountain. Why was the city not built on the higher ground so readily available? Why was it not cuddled against the foot of one of these mountains? Was the city here because of a good water supply? In its ruins there is evidence that there was an efficient water system. Was the city located exactly here because of a religious shrine—a sacred spot that had to be jealously guarded? There is evidence of shrines, sacred stones, and temples at various periods in the city's history. At any rate, Shechem needed to be strongly fortified and apparently it was. Excavations led by Dr. G. Ernest Wright of Harvard University, over many seasons at Shechem, have laid bare an interesting maze of walls of various ages, a mammoth three-part city gate controlling a roadway into the town, a series of houses, and a giant of a wall, called by the early German excavator "Cyclopean," because it is made with such large stones. The Shechemites are believed to have started to fortify their city in the

latter half of the eighteenth century B.C. The Cyclopean wall
seems to date to 1650 B.C.

As previously mentioned, both Abraham and Jacob erected
altars to their God at Shechem. Perhaps in memory of its
connection with the patriarchs, Joshua also honored Shechem by
choosing it as the scene for a most significant ceremony in
biblical history. After his early military successes, he gathered the
tribes of Israel together there and led them in a covenant
ceremony that brought the tribal league into existence. This
tribal league was the beginning of the nation of Israel (Josh.
8:30-35, 24; cf. Deut. 11:26 ff).

Joshua erected "a great stone" under the sacred tree in the
sanctuary as a memorial testimony to the covenant of the tribes.
Some scholars suggest that an annual festival commemorating
the renewal of the covenant persisted at Shechem as long as
northern Israel survived as a nation.

Solomon's son, Rehoboam, recognized the importance of
Shechem to the northern tribes when he went to that "covenant
shrine" to seek support in his attempt to be crowned king of
the unified Israel. The northern tribes rejected Rehoboam and
took Jeroboam as their king to effect the division of the monarchy.
Jeroboam made Shechem his capital city (I Kings 12:25).

About 870 B.C., Omri, king of Israel, was seeking the ideal
site for his capital. He found what he wanted not too far from
Shechem. It was a beautiful plot of land in the hill country,
surrounded on three sides by slopes and valleys. This was an
excellent defensive position for a city. Here Omri built Samaria.
As Samaria grew in importance, Shechem declined.

The Sweets of Nablus

Nearby Nablus is a modern town, reportedly the home of the
finest sweets produced in the country, although its major source
of income is the soap industry. Nablus is the largest town in
Samaria but not to my eyes, one of the attractive towns in the
Holy Land. Its houses look like white mausoleums stacked in

layers upon the hillsides. Its streets are crowded with people intent on their errands to office buildings, banks, or markets. The mood of the town is brusque. Yet Nablus has to offer to the tourist one small jewel of a confectionery shop where the customer is allowed to look over the shoulders of some fine artists while they work.

The artists are men who have learned how to put together sweet syrups, pistachios, almonds, walnuts, rosewater and orange-water flavoring, and tissue-thin pastry dough and to make of these ingredients a variety of delicious sweets. Their laboratory or kitchen is of the "Gay Nineties" vintage when vats of flour sat on sawdust-covered floors, great bins held the sweetmeats, and the baking was done in an earthenware wall oven. These artists bake as your great-grandmother used to. They do not measure to level quantities. They dip into a vat, take out a scoopful. Add liquid. Perhaps add another half scoopful. Shake the seasoning into the fillings or sweetmeats out of a huge bottle. They know by feel, by texture, by smell, by taste, how to turn out perfect delicacies each time. Believe me, it takes no talent at all to throw all the ingredients together and end up with one sticky, sloppy mess. The dough is particularly taxing to handle. It is so thin you can see through it, and it must be handled quickly while it is moist. If it becomes dry, it will be brittle and crack when you try to fold it or tuck it in to hold a filling.

The bakers use only flour, water, and salt to make the dough. The dough is divided and prepared into flat circles, about the same size that the housewife would use for a two-crust pie. The baker rolls this dough with amazing swiftness and firmness. He changes rollers several times, each time changing to one longer and thinner, until he stretches the dough to a circle about *four feet* in diameter. For *baklawa*, the baker uses many layers of this dough, usually fifteen layers below the filling and fifteen layers above it. To save time, he will flatten fifteen circles of dough and roll them all to maximum size at the same time. Flour sprinkled between the layers of dough prevents the layers from sticking together. When the dough is thin enough, the baker will trim it to fit the size of his pans, add nutmeats flavored with rosewater, place more dough on top, and bake it. After the pastry is baked, it is glazed with a thick rosewater syrup. The dough is like puff pastry. It will be crisp, but not the least bit tough in spite of all the rolling and sometimes, slapping and pounding.

For pastry that does not need such thin dough, the baker works on a marble counter. Here he works a circle of dough by slapping it on the counter, pulling it to stretch it, picking it up by one edge, twirling it over his head as if he were handling a lariat, slapping it down again on the counter, and stretching it. This amazing demonstration is accomplished with true grace and rhythm, so practiced is the baker artist. When the pastries are ready to be baked, the baker slides them to the proper spot in his earthen wall oven with a long-handled tool.

Nablus is noted particularly for its fine *baklawa*. In addition, the shop offers at least a dozen other Arabic sweets. For a small price, the customer may select an assortment of five pastries. Tourists who wish to sample the sweets may appreciate a warning that the portions are most generous. Each one of these sweets will supply them with many times their maximum daily requirement for sugar. Each one is also guaranteed 100 proof in pure undiluted calories. Our Arabic friends were able to polish off the whole plateful with relish. For the uninitiated, like myself, two is about the limit the digestive system will tolerate at a sitting. The usual liquid accompaniment for the sweets is water. The sweets are rarely offered as dessert. They are snack foods during the day.

Refugee Camps

Just on the outskirts of Nablus, directly across the street from Jacob's well, is a refugee "camp." This is one of several such settlements in the Holy Land, each housing a number of former Palestinians who for a variety of reasons lost their homes in 1948 when Israel and Jordan became separate countries. You will be asked not to take pictures of the "camp." The Jordanian tourist literature states that the tourist may photograph any area in the land other than military installations. This literature should also warn the tourists that the natives are overly sensitive about photographs which they feel will show the country in a bad light. If the tourist tries to photograph the refugees he will be greeted by open hostility, although it would seem that the more the world is aware of the misery of the refugees, the more eager all peoples would be to correct the condition.

The average refugee father in the Holy Land today is the head of a household that has lost its home, lost its land. In many cases he now has lost his dignity as a man because he has no employment and can no longer be the breadwinner for his family. He is accepting the support of the United Nations which maintains all the refugee camps in Jordan on a budget of approximately $35 a person *per year*.

The typical refugee home in the camp is a one-room plastered mud brick (adobe) house with a courtyard. It has a roof of sheet metal held on by rocks. This home will be one of many, almost touching one another, that line both sides of the narrow streets in the camps. The refugee father and his children will be wearing used clothing sent over from the United States.

You notice that we call these villages "camps." This label is deliberately used by the natives to call attention to what many refugees hope is a temporary status. Many still dream of, and plan for, returning to their homes in present-day Israel.

Enforced Idleness

Perhaps the most depressing aspect of the refugee camp is the idleness among the men. A woman can usually busy herself with her home, her food preparation, her children. For the men, there is little to do other than sit and talk. Why don't they use a little initiative and find themselves work? It has been alleged that these refugees have deliberately been kept in idleness to dramatize the need for Israel to compensate its former citizens for their land. The refugees do want compensation and have appealed many times to the United Nations for help in effecting such a settlement with Israel. The plain fact is, however, that the refugees are idle because Jordan does not have sufficient opportunity to integrate all these people into its present labor force. Originally, the refugees that came to Jordan numbered almost 600,000. Thanks to a good birth rate, they are still increasing despite a good 20 per cent who were absorbed into the local economy. Since the present figure for the total population of Jordan is given variously at between a million and a half and two million, this means that the refugees are about 40 per cent of the inhabitants of Jordan.

If you travel through the land of Jordan and see its cities, you become aware that most businesses are family operations. Two, three, or four persons may be involved in the operation of a shop. There is no need for additional help. If the need did arise, the person selected to fit into the shop would doubtless be still another member of the same family.

A few factories are now operating in the country, but those employing over ten men can be numbered on your fingers. It may be that the growth of industry in the land will open up opportunities for many more men, including the refugees. Industry is still in its infancy in Jordan. At the time of the separation, Transjordan was almost entirely an agricultural country, and agriculture still accounts for 75 per cent of the labor force.

Refugees Outside the Camps

Not all refugees live in camps. There are many former Palestinians who, because of superior education or specific skills, have obtained fine positions for themselves. These refugees have put down roots for themselves in Jordan. Many have gained considerable stature in their new homeland and they are to be found in positions of influence in the national government and in the cities. While many of these former Palestinians speak in public about the possibility of regaining their former country (they call it "occupied Palestine"), in private some of these citizens express acceptance of the situation that exists. They feel, "Let's go ahead and make the best of our country as it is and forget about what is past and done."

For those persons of lesser abilities, lesser education, or less opportunity, who remain unemployed, the problem is complex. If a refugee is offered employment and he accepts, he must surrender his ration card to the United Nations. If the term of employment turns out to be short-lived, the refugee finds himself truly out on a limb. He is no longer eligible for United Nations support, and is worse off than before. Unless he has some assurance that he can consider himself permanently employed, he would rather accept the United Nations ration which assures him his family will not starve.

There is one project under way near Zerqa to resettle refugees on land that is presently unused. With irrigation, this land will produce. Homes are being built here (at a slow rate, to be sure), and it is hoped that the refugee farmer will be able from his yield to buy both house and plot of land.

The Home of Jezebel and Ahab

North of Nablus, the tourist can see a site that was a great city in Old Testament times and again in the New Testament times, but known in each by a different name. The Old Testament town took the name of the district, Samaria. You may remember Samaria best as the home of Jezebel, devotee of Baal, who was so successful in introducing idolatrous worship to Israel. She dealt with the Jewish prophets ruthlessly, killing some and forcing others to flee to the caves; in particular, she frustrated Elijah. He carried on a running feud with her for the souls of his countrymen. Jezebel threatened to annihilate him.

How did Jezebel come to such a position of influence? She married Ahab, the son of the King Omri who had ruled Israel for six years from his home at Tirzah. Seeking a beautiful site for his capital, he purchased the site of the future Samaria for two talents of silver. Since a talent was a measure of weight, approximately seventy-five pounds, two talents must have been a fairly respectable sum. Omri began building Samaria about 880 B.C., but lived only six years after he had moved his capital. Ahab finished building the city. To please his wife Jezebel, a Phoenician princess, Ahab built a temple to Baal in Samaria. Worse, Ahab was attracted to the religious beliefs of his wife. This was anathema to Elijah—that the king of Israel, the chosen people, should so desert the God of his forefathers. Elijah predicted just punishment on the house of Ahab. Ahab is killed in battle and "dogs licked up his blood" (I Kings 22:37-38). His son and successor Ahaziah falls through a lattice and is bedridden for the balance of his life (II Kings 1). As for Jezebel—eunuchs throw her down from her window, horses in the court below trample on her, and scavenging dogs leave "her carcase . . . as dung upon the face of the field" (II Kings 9:30-38).

Even though a second large city was built on this site much later in history, archaeologists have found enough of Omri's Samaria to know that it was a great and wonderful place. The palace was built on the highest point of the land and must have been at least two stories high, if Ahaziah fell that distance. It must have been splendid inside. The Bible calls it Ahab's "ivory house" (I Kings 22:39). Excavators have concluded that it had wood paneling and furniture inlaid in ivory and probably decorative boxes and toilet articles so fashioned. The masonry of the palace is said to equal the finest found in the Holy Land.

What happened to the city of Samaria? The Bible says it grew in pride and corruption until the Assyrians captured it in 721 B.C., the time of the end of the kingdom of Israel. In the annals of Sargon, the Assyrian commander duly records that he conquered Samaria and took with his booty twenty-seven thousand persons.

Later the territory was occupied by Babylonians, Persians, and

Greeks. Still visible today from the Greek occupation is a huge, magnificently constructed watchtower. This tower is considered the best Greek structure in the Holy Land. It is believed to have been one of a series of such towers erected for defense.

Jesus' City of Samaria

Next on the scene, after the Greeks, were the Romans. Who built himself another great city during his years in the Holy Land? None other than the master builder, Herod the Great. Herod named the city Sebaste, the Greek translation of the name of the emperor in 30 B.C., Augustus. Sebaste would have been the "city of Samaria" as Jesus saw it. There was plenty to see in Sebaste. Since the city was in honor of Augustus, Herod erected a temple to him. This temple, the pride of the city, had a courtyard, a fourteen-foot stairway leading to the sanctuary, and in the sanctuary, an altar and statue of Augustus. Elsewhere in Sebaste, Herod carried out the Roman city formula—forum, colonnaded streets, theater, stadium, and so forth.

The ruins that the tourist sees at Sebaste today are almost entirely Roman, but there is one section of Israelite wall still standing.

During the fourth century A.D. when Constantine was shepherd of the empire, Sebaste claimed that it possessed the tomb of John the Baptist. The Christians built a church over the tomb and also a shrine over the spot where, they claimed, Herodias had hidden John's head. (As an added item of interest, the Umayyad mosque in Damascus claims to possess the head and has a shrine within the mosque over *its* burial site.)

Antiquities for Sale

Right at the ruin of Sebaste is the present-day threshing floor for the town of Sebaste. During the harvest season, tourists have the opportunity to observe at close range the ancient threshing process. When my husband and I visited this area, we were fortunate enough to find the threshing floor being used by a friendly group of villagers who were pleased with our interest in them and allowed us to take pictures.

Also at Sebaste, antiquities dealers have set their small stands. They have a smattering of small pots, scarabs, ancient glass, etc. Many tourists like to take home souvenirs of the archaeology of the Holy Land and, if they feel so inclined, they might try to bargain here. If the tourist wants to be certain that he is buying *authentic* antiquities, he should either take an expert with him to judge the merchandise or buy from a recommended shop after he has been introduced to the shopkeeper. Real antiquities are an important source of income to dealers. Most Jordanians know the worth of antiquities and *all* dealers know their worth. They know exactly where the antiquities have come from. If the tourist is offered an antiquity for a very small price, he should beware. If the antiquity were genuine, some city dealer would already have bought it and paid more. Certain persons are known to have made copies of antiquities, buried them in the ground for a time until they looked aged and mellowed, and then tried to pass them off as real. For a genuine lamp, pot, juglet, or piece of Roman glass, the price will be high, but far less than the price would be, say, in New York City.

Occasionally a native will stumble upon a tomb and try to sell the antiquities himself. From such a man, it is possible to get a bargain. However, the tourist might not get his bargain out of the country. Jordan has strict antiquities' laws. All finds of antiquities are to be reported to the government. If the antiquity is unique or rare, the government will want it for a museum; if common, it will be released for public sale.

My husband and I did know persons who purchased authentic pottery at very reasonable prices. As they were archaeologists, however, they were able to clear the pottery through the Department of Antiquities before packing it in their luggage. It is important, too, for the tourist to know that antiquities not purchased through proper channels and proved by bills of sale might be taken away at the border.

Sebaste

The walk back from the ruins to the present town of Sebaste is a short walk through narrow streets lined with the old style stone houses. The people who now live in Sebaste are used to tourists who roam the town. The natives will be sitting in the doorways of their home conversing with their children and neighbors. They will be most cordial if the tourists keep their cameras in their cases. It is very tempting to try to capture on film these colorful families and their simple homes. Most tourists who try to "sneak" a picture or two will probably find that the natives are very alert. When the camera shutter clicks, it will photograph a street that is suddenly completely cleared of people—it is astonishing how quickly people duck into the nearest doorway.

At the center of Sebaste are local restaurants where visitors may refresh themselves with soft drinks. The finest view of the town is from a roof garden restaurant now unfortunately closed to the public. Whenever the group from the American School in Jerusalem was in this region, we enjoyed the hospitality at the roof garden and spent more time there than we had intended because it was so fascinating to observe the day's activities in Sebaste. For example: the tinkle of bells that heralded the approach of a camel caravan, the caravan drawing water from the well and later winding its way up into the hills. For another: the never-ending procession of women making repeated trips down from the hills to the well and carrying back to their homes enough water for the next tubful of laundry. For a third: the town's children playing in the water of an overflow trough and never too proud to make room in the trough for an occasional thirsty goat or lamb.

Why has the roof garden been closed to the public? Simply because many tourists, in an attitude of Western superiority, have passed cutting remarks about the natives. The tour guides, the proprietors of shops, even the Jordanian chap sitting next to you, are apt to understand English very well. They resent remarks that are unflattering.

The Riddle of the Samaritans

Who are the Samaritans? Long articles and books have been written by scholars who have delved as best they could into ancient history to answer this question. According to the Samaritans themselves, they are remnants of the ten tribes of Israel, the children of Jacob. At the time of the destruction of northern Israel, 721 B.C., many Israelites were carried into exile by the Assyrians. The Samaritans claim that some Israelites were left behind and that they are the descendants of those who remained. When the later exiles, now called Jews, returned to their former home after an absence of seventy years in Babylon, they denounced as foreigners the inhabitants of Samaria. According to the returnees, Samaritans had mingled with the alien colonists settled in Samaria by the Assyrians and their blood had become tainted by intermarriage and acceptance of pagan superstitions. This quarrel led to bitter hatred between two branches of Israelites. The Samaritans built a rival temple on Mount Gerizim and proclaimed themselves the true keepers of the word of God.

Exactly when this schism took place is not known. Reliable authorities say the Samaritans as a separate group can be traced back only to the time of Alexander the Great, 332 B.C. This is not to say, however, that they did not exist as a separate group prior to that time.

There is a good reason to suspect that the schism could have been earlier than Alexander. The Samaritans accept as valid only the first five books of the Old Testament, the Torah or Pentateuch. It is suggested (even by Jewish sources) that Ezra canonized the Torah c. 397 B.C. Prior to Ezra none of the Israelites would probably have specified that the first five books of the Old Testament constituted Holy Writ, but anytime *after* Ezra, it would have been possible.

The Samaritans have kept their bloodline pure through intramarriage over the centuries. Today their number has dwindled so that intermarriage with brides who convert is allowed. In all, there are about three hundred Samaritans today. Half live in Jordan near Nablus; half, in Israel. All make the annual pilgrimage to Mount Gerizim—those from Israel with the special permission of the two states—for the Samaritan Passover.

Samaritan Passover

If you were in the district of Samaria at the right time of year, you would be able to attend the Samaritan Passover. The Passover is observed as at the time of the schism: in accordance with the procedure laid down in the Torah. Preparations begin on the tenth day of Abib, the lunar month that begins in our month of April and that opens the religious year. The Samaritans ascend Mount Gerizim and set up tents on a plain slightly below the summit. The exciting ceremonial and sacrificial meal takes place on the fourteenth.

The high priest and young men of the Samaritans graciously welcome tourists to the ceremony with a cup of hot coffee or tea and are most willing to give you detailed explanations about themselves, their beliefs and practices. Since they consider themselves the "purists" of Judaism, it is most interesting to learn about their rituals and chants that they allege have not changed in twenty-five hundred years.

The sacrifice of the lamb follows the old prescribed rules. The Samaritans purchase eight sheep, seven of which will be sacrificed, one for each clan. These sheep must be without blemish, males of the first year, and they are given special care with emphasis on thorough cleansing of the lambs. On the day of the ceremony, the Samaritan youths put on special attire— white gowns, trousers, girdles, and sandals tied with a string to their feet. Their first task is to draw and store enough water for the sacrifice. The water is to be heated and used to facilitate plucking or fleecing the animal. Fires are made in holes in the ground, three feet deep, for later roasting the animals. Just before sundown, the whole community gathers at the spot of sacrifice while the priests chant an ancient refrain. At the conclusion of the prayers, the high priest slits the throats of the lambs. He must do this quickly and skillfully so that the animals will not utter a sound. The lambs are then fleeced and hung on poles, then opened and internally cleansed with great care lest a bone be broken, which would be against the decree from God. Finally, the lambs are impaled on sharp poles, salted, put into the fire, and roasted in the ground for about three hours, and eaten by the faithful around midnight.

To see meat packaged and laid out on refrigerated shelves in the supermarket is not in any way an emotional experience, but it is quite a different matter to watch seven frantic sheep, overpowered by men, submit to having their throats slit. It is a compensating emotional factor to acknowledge that many of the Samaritans need the nourishment of this much fresh meat. For some reason, they do not appear to be a strong people physically. The young men are slightly built, emaciated, and lacking in muscle tone. The special costumes may have accentuated the lean appearance, but to an American used to athletic-looking young men, these boys seemed to have very thin, underdeveloped chests and protruding stomachs. In fact, you wonder if some marriage to outsiders may not be mandatory to improve the physical heredity of the Samaritans and perpetuate the group.

That the people are in modest circumstances is obvious from their anxiety to sell the tourist their postcards and literature about their tribes (unfortunately misprinted on the pamphlet to read, "By The Tripe of the Samaritan Priests in Nablus"). They welcome your taking pictures, and expect a gratuity. This commercial aspect of the Passover Feast gives the whole ceremony overtones of an annual church bazaar.

For tourists I recommend as a followup to the Passover Feast, a picnic of their own. If they are willing to go another mile up the narrow mountain road at night to the top of Mount Gerizim they will have a delightful meal in the light of a full Passover moon.

Where Joseph Was Sold

There is one more antiquity in the district of Samaria that the tourist might like to see. If there are enough daylight hours left to travel a few miles north of Sebaste, he might spend those hours at the excavations in Dothan. Dothan has biblical fame as the city where Joseph was sold into slavery by his brothers. There is nothing of Joseph to be found in the city, but much of ancient history. Dothan is a very large site. The top and slopes of the mound occupy as many as twenty-five acres. In various sections on the mound, the tourist can compare styles of construction from Early Bronze Age up to modern Arabic. First settled about 3000 B.C. Dothan was a city on the caravan route during the time of the patriarchs, and a large city throughout the Roman period.

The most amazing "find" at Dothan was a burial chamber that must have been a virtual Forest Lawn for countless ages of Dothan inhabitants. Excavators have uncovered many levels of burials here and know that there are more beneath. Close to three thousand pottery artifacts already have come from this site.

The excavations at Dothan have been carried out under the direction of Mr. Joseph Free and Wheaton College, Illinois. Each season, Mr. Free has brought groups of students to the Holy Land so that they might have an opportunity to learn more about archaeology. My husband and I on one of our visits came to Dothan on a Sunday morning when only a few students were at the site. These students showed us around the mound, explaining the significance of the ruins and the amazing collection of artifacts. Then they invited us to join them in a

Sunday service. Dothan is a beautiful site. High on a hill, it overlooks some of the lovely productive plains of northern Jordan. We settled ourselves in chairs on the veranda of the living quarters of the archaeologists. We were handed Bibles, and here in this wonderful Old Testament setting, we opened our Bibles and listened while five young archaeologists led us in worship.

The Miserable Border Towns

Some citizens of the Holy Land are worse off than the refugees. These are the persons living in border towns between Jordan and Israel. There are several such towns not too far from Nablus and Sebaste. Although they are sprinkled all along the border, few tourists in Jordan are permitted to visit any of them—they are too close to a zone where shooting accidents may occur. Tourists need not fear that they might wander into such an area. Police patrols on the roads will halt all traffic at a goodly distance from any area where there might be danger. Unless a visitor can prove that he has official business to proceed beyond the checkpoint, he will be turned back. For reasons of pride, the Jordanians do not want tourists to see how the people in the border towns must live. When a halt was called to the active fighting, the truce line in many cases separated a village from its farmland, sometimes from its water supply. The villagers, mostly farmers, were left with no means of self-support. Since they do live in their own homes, they technically cannot be called refugees and thus are not eligible for United Nations relief. Church-related welfare groups have tried to help in the border towns, and the Red Crescent (the equivalent of our Red Cross) gives whatever aid it can. I visited six of these border towns, and I'll try to give you a composite picture of their worst and best features.

At their worst, the towns are inhabited by people who are miserably dirty, miserably ragged, and underfed. They are openly hostile, even toward persons trying to furnish aid. Their homes reflect their despairing attitude. All are of the old-style masonry, many are crumbling, none is new. Around the homes there is litter and debris. Pride in keeping up the home has gone. The towns look shabby and tired. The *muktar* (mayor) paid by the government is responsible for all arrangements to aid his community, and he does his best to keep his people fed and clothed. In the very poor towns, the people exist on bread, olives, olive oil, yoghurt, perhaps a few eggs. A few times a year, the *muktar* may be able to have sheep slaughtered so that the inhabitants can have some meat.

The children of the border towns are dressed in whatever clothing the family is given. Almost all of the children are barefoot. The men and women wear shoes, but shoes not theirs originally do not fit their feet, so they wear them with the backs broken down and slip into them as you would into a sandal. (Occasionally more fortunate Jordanians wear their shoes in this way, but by choice.) Many of the little girls wear dresses, but instead of a sweater or jacket, they top their dress with a well-worn and patched man's suit coat. I saw one little girl fall down. She had on several dresses but not a stitch of underwear. Among the men, most wear surplus army coats, usually patched and ragged. The women wear the traditional Jordanian dress, but the dress has seen long, long service.

Without money, the people of the border towns cannot move. They have property but no one would buy it to enable them to resettle elsewhere. Most other Jordanian towns are using their full quota of manpower for the jobs available, and do not want any squatters.

At one poor town, the men gathered in an empty stone building to hold a short meeting. My husband and I were present with a group observing the operation of a mobile medical clinic that stops in the town weekly. The men were obviously upset; they evidently felt they should be eligible for more material help than they were getting. The children in this town, not aware of exactly what was going on, became upset because their fathers were upset. The youngsters outside the meeting knew that, in some manner, this loud talk and agitation was directed against us. Since they had nothing else to do, they gathered around our carry-all and began spitting at it and the few who had remained in it.

No practical answer has yet been found to solve the misery of border towns. The people sometimes sneak back into the fields (now in Israel) to snatch fruit, vegetables, or cereals for their families. The Arabs of the border towns do not accept the fact that these farmlands are no longer their own. It galls them to see their enemies reaping a harvest from trees that were planted by themselves. But if they are spotted across the truce line by the Israelis, they may be shot.

I saw one child climb onto the roof of his house. There, growing between the stones, were bits of grass and weeds. The child picked and ate them.

In some of the border towns, religious groups furnish the schools with food to ensure that the children have a hot nourishing meal at noon. Some of the local girls who have assumed the task of helping and teaching the young do a beautiful job of keeping clean and trim a barely adequate schoolroom. They follow directions for the use of the foods and give the children the warmth and kindness of personal interest. It is inspiring to see how much one dedicated person can do with an absolute minimum of material supplies.

After we had seen so many faces that were gaunt and filled with resentment, it was a relief to visit another border town that seemed to have an entirely different attitude. Here the people knew that we were in some way connected with the free medical help they were receiving, and consequently, they were warm and friendly toward us. They also seemed content and relaxed, even though they were in poor circumstances. It could be that this more mellow attitude had been fostered by the *muktar* of the town, a most charming man who spoke not a word of English but conversed with us genially and freely through an interpreter.

Visit with the Muktar

The *muktar* invited us into his home, where as an official he is responsible for entertaining guests. There was one large room in his home for this purpose. It was well appointed, all things considered, with a couple of dozen chairs, all of the wooden dining-room type fashionable in America about thirty years ago. As in most Arab homes, if there are chairs they are set smack against the wall—a practice that comes from the tradition of the tent where the sheik seated himself at the head and arranged his guests in order of their importance along either side of the tent. Consequently, in a modern home, the host will take a center seat on the short wall of the room, and his guests will be seated in a rectangle around the room. This arrangement is not too conducive to sprightly conversation. Rather than yell across the room, the guest usually occupies himself with his neighbors on either side. In the center of the room, the Arabs usually place a table with flowers on it.

Our *muktar* had a radio in his reception room. Around the walls were pictures of his children, for he was very proud of his handsome family, seventeen in all. After our chat, he led us out through his garden and offered us flowers when we admired them. The guest in an Arab home must be careful not to voice admiration of objects within the home. Some Arabs still follow the tradition that what the guest admires must be offered to him. Our host shared with us his coffee, tea, cigarettes, and chocolates.

I might add that this *muktar* is not old. He is a youthful middle-aged man. When I noticed that he slipped into the medical clinic at the close of the day, I mentioned to one of the medical team that I was surprised that a proud Muslim of his station would admit that he could need medical help. The answer came with a wink and a smile, "He just picks up a little Geritol. He needs it. He has three wives." I did not see any of these wives. They prepared refreshments for us, but they stayed discreetly behind slightly opened doors, peeking at us.

Don't Go Overboard with Praise!

Because the people in the border towns are so hampered by their lack of material needs, the visitor tends to go overboard in expressions of sympathy, appreciation, and encouragement. At one border town, the inhabitants asked us if we knew about their spring. We were assured that this marvelous spring had produced water for generations and that towns for miles around could share in its life-giving flow even in times of drought. We took the short walk from town to the foot of a hill to see this underground spring. The water came forth in a sure, steady flow, and several women were filling their old-style water containers, goatskins. After they had filled their goatskins, they hoisted this slippery load on their shoulders, and as it dripped cold water down their backs, they scrambled back up the hill barefoot as they were by the shortest but steepest route over rock, sand, and pebbles. We knelt at the spring, took some water in our hands, noting its clearness. We nodded our approval and repeated again and again those few Arabic adjectives that we knew, "very fine," "beautiful," etc. One of the natives, watching our effusiveness, spoke to our guide. The guide turned to us and interpreted, "He wants to know why you exclaim so. Do you not have springs in your country?" That simple and direct question left us with no easy answer.

Sometimes we were able to communicate with unexpectedly pleasant results. In one small town, we were being shown the method of malaria control. The schoolboys questioned us about where we were from. Our answer that we were from the United States brought from them very enthusiastic response, "Yes, yes . . . United States . . . good friends" . . . (they pointed to a group of men working on a road) "money . . . United States." It was very thrilling for us to know that in this very small community the natives knew that money to improve their town and their country came directly from the United States. As representatives of a generous country we were raised to an undeserved pedestal by our group of young admirers, but it was humbling to acknowledge to ourselves that our contribution to this project was probably no more than a fraction of a penny. We examined the road work and praised the workmen, who were working entirely by hand, no machinery.

We often found that these young boys, encouraged by the false notion that all Americans have much money to give away, felt that if they became friends with an American, it was surely possible that the American might take them back to the United States to live. Preposterous as this notion is, it is still sad to see the light go out of a young man's eyes when you must make it clear to him that this prospect is not a possibility. Many of these young boys think that an American may be able to help him to find work in Jordan. Archaeologists do try to give work to as many native men as possible. When the boys are asked just what experience they might have had, they admit that they have had no experience, but each one feels certain that he would be very good at "bossing the other men."

Incidentally, the youth from the small towns were usually amazed that I, a *woman*, knew how to read and write.

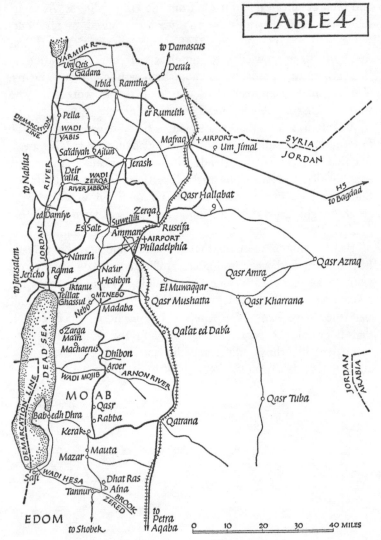

TABLE 4   Jordan East and North of Jerusalem

VII The Road to Jericho

Jerusalem to Jericho is not a long ride, but it is packed with interest for Bible students. The road out of Jerusalem winds around the Mount of Olives to Bethany. And even in those few minutes before you reach Bethany, if you look closely at the roadside on the left, you see some open tombs. Dating from the time of the Maccabees, they were discovered by accident in 1950 when a cave-in occurred on the road. The continuing historical discoveries, accidental or planned, make living in the Holy Land a very exciting adventure. Suddenly one day you hear a rumor that someone has stumbled onto an antiquity. The curious rush to the site. What is it? How old is it? How do you interpret it? Do you think it will be significant? Every day holds the promise of a new revelation from the past and as you know, some very exciting finds have been made in Jordan. Archaeology is still a new science, just a little over a hundred years old. Of the known biblical sites in Jordan, only 2 *per cent* have been fully excavated. Think of the marvels yet to be uncovered!

The Tomb of Lazarus

In Bethany, the tourist has no problem finding the church dedicated to Jesus' miracle of raising Lazarus from the dead. At almost all hours of the day, a score of tourist taxis are lined up here, their first stop on the way to the Jordan Valley. The church is modern, built in 1952–53, but it has incorporated into it the remains of former churches built on this site. The dome of the sanctuary is filled with beautiful mosaics retelling the story of the miracle. Outside the church there are some excavated rooms believed to be the home of Mary and Martha, and beyond, up a narrow path, is the tomb. This tomb is well below ground, some two dozen steps straight down, and you need a candle to find your way around. You may step into the tomb itself, if you wish, but the more usual procedure is for the visitor to stand in the anteroom while the guide steps into the tomb with his candle, outlining the shape of the tomb and relating the famous story (John 11:38 f). One day when my husband and I visited the tomb, a photographer followed us down into the tomb. This I assume is also not unusual because he wished to take our picture in front of the tomb of Lazarus. As tourists, we learned to overlook these small commercial ventures because we realized it is necessary for many Jordanians to use all their resources to earn a living. Impossible to overlook was a much more unusual gimmick of the photographer—his attempt to make our visit to the tomb more dramatic by calling out periodically, while the guide told the story of the miracle, "*Lazarus, come forth!*" I regret that Lazarus did not.

The town of Bethany is always in a hubbub of activity. It is one town in Jordan where you can be sure of running down the inhabitants or its children, if you are so minded. Everyone is on the road. Many shops open right onto the street, and this is a major highway. The storekeepers are usually seated on stools along with a group of friends right on the roadside, and there is a steady stream of persons afoot, sometimes leading a burro, carrying supplies to or from Jerusalem. Vendors stroll along the street, some with pushcarts, others with a metal tray filled with wares atop their heads and a tray stand swinging in the crook of an arm.

Entertainment on the Road

In the Holy Land, it is not necessary to search out the spectacular sights to keep yourself entertained. The simple daily life of the people of the country can be enchanting. Just at the outskirts of Bethany, I witnessed a refreshing transaction. A young boy had been picking greens along the roadside, and when he had gathered a handful, he sat down and began to nibble a few. He spied a nut vendor and hailed him. They exchanged a few words. The vendor set down his stand, put his tray of nuts on it, reached in his pocket for a piece of paper, folded it into a cone, filled it with nuts, handed it to the boy, took in exchange the handful of greens, stood them up like a small palm tree in the middle of his tray of nuts, put the tray back on his head, picked up his stand, and shuffled off down the road. The young boy, happy with his nuts, started to run up the road. Spying me watching him from the car, he sallied over, pressed his face against the window and screwed up his eyes and forehead to get a good look at me. He ran his hands all over the car, feeling the metal, chrome, windows, tires; then he thumped the car with his fist to see how solid it was, and satisfied, sauntered off down the road.

This harmless curiosity is not found only in children. We rarely stopped to ask directions that we were not immediately surrounded by people who pressed their noses to the windows, so anxious were they to inspect the car and the tourists. My impulse was always to raise the camera and take a shot of them, but I never had enough nerve. We learned to keep our doors locked because often the people decided they would ride along with us. They are not too busy and a ride in a car is a treat. We often did take along a man who offered to show us the way, and on only one occasion did a man take us to where *he* was going rather than our own destination.

Almost anyone walking along the road will hail you for a ride. Most commonly, off-duty Jordanian soldiers will be looking for a lift into the cities. When a soldier hails him, the motorist feels he must stop because the soldier might be an official road check. For various reasons, the motorist is often officially stopped on the road and asked where he has come from and where he is going. For instance, we were trying to find our way to the monastery of Mar Saba, an old and remote institution perched in the hills above the Dead Sea. As we left the main road to start off into the wilderness, we encountered a police post and were halted by a young Jordanian officer. "Where do you go?"

"To Mar Saba." "I go to Mar Saba," and with that he stepped into the car. We drove on over a miserable road that had deteriorated to pure bedrock and it became apparent that the young officer had probably gone with us for our safety's sake. Because the road was so horrible, we did not arrive at the monastery until dark.

The monastery is an unusual sight—a stark cloister in the middle of nowhere. Women, of course, are not allowed to enter. After we had seen the outside of the building, I was ready to turn back to Jerusalem. The soldier was most dismayed. He had counted on a visit and a cup of coffee with the monks. Naturally, he and my husband would have the social hour. I would sit in the car. I was not having any such arrangement—sitting in the wilderness in the dark—so we started back.

When we returned to the police post, nothing would do but that we join the young officer and his family for dinner. This we could not do since we were expected back in Jerusalem. Explain as we would, we could not console the young man for our insult to his offered hospitality. A refusal of hospitality is not lightly accepted by any Arab. It is an offense and we tried to be careful not to put ourselves in a position where refusals were necessary. Many is the cup of coffee or tea we have drunk, well aware that tomorrow we might regret it. However, on those occasions when we could take the time to sit down and try to communicate in snatches of English or Arabic with our Jordanian friends, we found that time more than well spent. These people, whether peasant or aristocrat, are the most warm-hearted, the most kind hosts you could ever meet.

Only One Wife?

At times, communication between persons of Eastern and Western cultures reminded us that we think differently. We had stopped at the so-called "inn of the Good Samaritan" to look around the remains of a caravansary. The guidebooks had mentioned that on the floor there were mosaics, but they turned out to be not worth the investigation. Bits of floor would have been a more accurate description of what remained to be seen. Stationed at this spot is a Jordanian policeman. He checks traffic when directed to do so, but when he is not busy, the days at the post are long. We found him in a most genial mood. He invited us to sit and have a cup of tea with him and two friends. These gentlemen spoke no English and since I understand so few Arabic words, I was content to let my husband carry on the conversation while I contemplated the walls of the building, the floor, and occasionally the policeman's horse which was nibbling grass just outside the building. As I glanced back at the conversants to see how the talk was progressing, I found all eyes in the room had turned on me. I began to listen. The three Arabs were eying me rather speculatively and my husband was obviously quite amused. I caught enough of the conversation to realize that my husband was explaining that he had only this one wife and that I would be the only one until I died. The policeman had two wives thus far and the other two gentlemen did not commit themselves—except that all three were commiserating with my husband on this limitation placed on men of the West. When this distasteful (to me) conversation ended, we left the police post with warm handshakes all around—except from me. Mine was limp and cool.

The Good Samaritan Inn

The Good Samaritan inn (Luke 10:34) on the road to Jericho is actually not the inn of biblical tradition, but a ruin of a caravansary converted into a Turkish police post. Now a Jordanian police post, this landmark is on high ground, halfway between Jericho and Jerusalem.

History tells us that there was from earliest times a fortress here to offer protection to wayfarers. They may have sought a haven from the threat of robbers, but they may also have sought refreshment and physical respite from the change in air pressure and climate between the two famous cities. Jerusalem

is approximately twenty-six hundred feet above sea level; the
Dead Sea, thirteen hundred feet below. The city of Jericho is on
slightly higher ground than the Dead Sea. As you travel these
few miles, your ears inform you that you have encountered a
change. You notice as you go down, winding through the hills,
that the temperature is getting warmer than it was in Jerusalem.
(Going in the opposite direction from Jericho to Jerusalem,
we frequently felt thoroughly chilled.)

The landscape presents a panorama in several shades of brown.
This ancient land has not carried its years gracefully. It looks old,
used up, cantankerous. The hills are barren and choked by outcroppings of rock that have been swept bare by centuries of
untamed winds. Where the hills are solid rock, the striations are
curved and sagging as if they had settled into eternal discomfort,
yielding to the jolting demands of earth tremors. It seems to be
an undue hardship that the Holy Land was fated to carry on its
back a disproportionate amount of the world's supply of rock.
In other lands, the rocks differ; some secrete gold ore or diamonds
or silver. But not Jordan. Jordan rock is rock to the core—limestone, chalky marl, and basalt. It is not an exaggeration to say that
if a good world market were found for just plain stone, Jordan's
economy would go into the black overnight.

At times down through a crevice in the hills you see the deep,
deep blue of the Dead Sea. On down you go, steadily down
until you emerge on the flat expanse of the Jordan Valley. Far
to the north you see a precipice that has been selected as the
Mount of Temptation where Jesus fasted for forty days before
beginning his ministry (Mark 1:12, 13). A monastery is placed
there today. Far to the south you see the hills which sheltered
Qumran and contained the caves where the Dead Sea Scrolls
were secreted.

Racing Camels and Horses

A side road to the Dead Sea and Qumran passes Jordan's race
track, a tourist attraction, where during the cooler winter months

horse races are alternated with camel races to the delight of tourists and natives. If camels are not comic enough just plain as they are, you should see them run. We had been assured that "Oh, yes, camels can run like the wind—just like a horse." Camels don't run like the wind. In a contest, they would never give a race horse a gray hair. They were never put together for speed. Camels may have a certain charm as they amble along in their undulating gait, their lethargic shuffle, but they are ridiculous when they try to have a real go at it—clomping along at fourteen to twenty miles an hour. They may determinedly thrust their necks forward and point their noses straight ahead, but when they pick up those heavy, heavy hooves that hang from their skinny, skinny legs, and flap them up and down, up and down around the track—they just don't have it. They look like a gawky adolescent trying to brave it through an ordeal. The jockeys wear the native costume, the robe and *kaffia*, and differ in their choice of where best to sit on a camel. Some use large saddles and sit directly over the hump. Some use a sloping saddle and sit slightly forward on the hump. Some use practically no saddle and sit far back, just above the tail; how they stay on their mounts is a mystery, halfway down the rump of the camel as they are.

The wealthier Bedouins who attend these races are marvelous to see. They are beautifully dressed in black robes, gold braid trim, and white *kaffias*. These gentlemen consider themselves the aristocrats of the land, and have great dignity. It is easy to imagine that they live as did the sheiks of old—in tents lavishly furnished for comfort, plush Oriental rugs and soft cushions spread on the floor, coffee brewed for them in brightly polished copper pots, hookahs filled with water and tobacco, awaiting their pleasure. The younger upper-class Bedouin, immaculately attired, is a gentleman who in every sense fits the idealized picture of the romantic desert prince.

These gentlemen at the track have doubtless come to watch their own horses race. There is a box office for placing bets and it is well used. Since the crowd is not large at the races, it is simple to tell by the shouts of joy or anguish just who has won or lost and to what extent. The intervals between races are filled with music supplied by a band. The British influence is shown by an abundance of bagpipes. The band is dressed in the blue serge uniform and the red checkerboard *kaffias* of the Bedouin army of King Hussein. Government dignitaries sometimes attend the races, and King Hussein has said he would try to attend to further encourage tourist attendance.

A short distance from the track is the Dead Sea hotel and casino where there is nightlife for the tourist. Gambling is advertised. The favorite daytime activity is to lie on the sand and sun yourself or to test the remarkable buoyancy of the salt laden water.

In many countries of the world today, people find it thrilling to sit in partially reconstructed amphitheaters of a past civilization and enjoy concerts and drama. I doubt that the drama of such a moment can be more compelling than the drama of sitting in this race track in the Jordan Valley. Here you sit in the grandstand with a small group of excited people who are enjoying an informal afternoon. You look out in any of several directions at the view. What do you see? Just such sights as these: *a.* salt flats and castle-like salt formations that in prehistoric times lined the floor of a great sea that covered the entire Jordan Valley; *b.* its vestigial remain, the Dead Sea, beautifully blue, the setting for tragedy when God visited his wrath on the cities of Sodom and Gomorrah; *c.* the red hills of Moab, whence Moses viewed the Promised Land he would never enter; *d.* the hills of Ammon, the scene of Israelite warfare against the strong Ammonite kingdom, a plague to the Israelites before the armies of Saul and David quelled it; *e.* the hills of Judea, the setting for both the birth and the death of Jesus, in the Judean cities of Bethlehem and Jerusalem; *f.* the hills above Qumran, the site of the greatest biblical discovery of our time—scriptures two thousand years old, older by a thousand years than the earliest Hebrew manuscripts known—the Dead Sea Scrolls. This is *some view!*

You may be a person who likes to stand outside at night and view the stars—it gives you a sense of the proportion of man to the universe. In the Holy Land, the visitor is constantly aware of proportion. At almost any spot he stands amid the scenes of our earliest recorded history. "A thousand ages in Thy sight / Are like an evening gone" becomes a deeply felt truth, not merely the poetic expression of even such a hymn writer as Isaac Watts translating the ninetieth Psalm.

The Dead Sea Scrolls

On the northwest corner of the Dead Sea there is a small pocket of land containing ruins that formerly were not considered significant. Scholars had looked at the surface ruins and had concluded that they belonged to an old Roman fort of no particular interest to biblical students. This small pocket of land was in a desolate area far from a good supply of water. On the edge of the Dead Sea, far below sea level, it was hot and sultry for most of the year. Probably no one had ever lived in the place. The area was quite well protected. To the south a cape jutted out into the sea with a spring nearby. To the west, high cliffs sheltered it. On the north, the area was open. Certainly for centuries no one had been in this area other than Bedouin shepherds and their flocks.

On a most memorable day in 1947, one of these young shepherds made in the cliffs above Qumran a discovery that was to electrify biblical students all over the world and whet the appetites of thousands and thousands of laymen who have hungered for more evidences of religious history. Without question it has brought fresh interest to the Holy Land as a country to be included in a travel itinerary. The discovery was the Dead Sea Scrolls. Over the years, *eleven* caves have been found in the vicinity of Qumran that contained biblical scrolls. And what was written on these scrolls? Most importantly, biblical Scripture— portions of the entire Old Testament that we have today with the exception of the Book of Esther.

Why should such a find of Scripture be so exciting? There has always been speculation that there was room for error in the transmission of our Bible. Copyists can make errors. Translators may change the meaning of passages by misinterpretation of key words. The Dead Sea Scrolls date a thousand years earlier than the oldest previously known Hebrew manuscript. Scholars were anxious to examine them to see what textual difference could be found. Thus far, *no* differences have been found that in any way alter significantly our understanding of the Old Testament. Also from the caves came two halves of a copper scroll describing hidden treasures which some scholars feel might be the treasury of the Temple and some most interesting documents that pertained to the life of a religious sect of two thousand years ago.

The Qumran Monastery

Following this unprecedented discovery, archaeologists took a long hard look at the Roman ruins at Qumran. Certainly this literature did not belong to the Romans. Perhaps it would be wise to see what lay beneath the fort. When the area had been cleared, the remains of a large fortified monastery were found. Most impressive among these ruins were the huge cisterns fed both by rainwater and by aqueducts which channeled rain water from the hills to the monastery. From the conclusions that were drawn about the uses of other structures in the monastery, it would seem that the monks had here a self-sufficient operation. Members of the sect made their own pottery. They had a forge. They had a grain mill, a bakery and laundry. From their literature, we know that they engaged in farming. There were rooms in the monastery large enough for assemblies and one that was evidently the "library." Furnished with inkwells, a table and benches, it was probably here that the manuscripts were faithfully copied.

The Essenes

Who were these people and why were they here? Most persons accept the deduction that the monastery belonged to the Essenes, a group of Jews who differed in their beliefs from the Sadducees and the Pharisees. The Essenes flourished in Palestine during the century preceding Christ's birth. Earlier during the second century B.C. some of them had retired to this remote spot and built the monastery. Coins found in the excavation indicate that people lived here more or less continuously for about one hundred years before they deserted the monastery about thirty years before the death of Christ. The date of the abandonment coincides with the known date of an earthquake. In 4 B.C. the monastery was apparently rebuilt and reoccupied. The rebuilding may or may not have been effected because of the death of Herod the Great the same year. In A.D. 69 the monastery was completely destroyed by the Romans when their legions came to the Holy Land in strength to put down Jewish rebellions against the empire. It is believed that just prior to this destruction, the Essenes stored their "library," well protected by linen wrappings in capped pottery jars, in caves in the nearby cliffs.

Why did they never retrieve their library? One guess is that the community was massacred. If some refugees made it to safety, they apparently did not want to risk returning to the caves. Some refugees may have been converted to Christianity and thus did not find it imperative to cling to the old scriptures.

It is possible that this marvelous treasure of literature had already been "dipped into" by accident before its twentieth-century discovery. There had been a report in A.D. 800 that some old Jewish manuscripts had been found in the area near the Dead Sea.

Community Life and Beliefs

From the writings of the early historians, Josephus, Philo, and Pliny, scholars knew much about the Essenes but it was important to find definite information about them in "their own handwriting." Since the discovery, volumes have been written on each phase of their interesting community life. Briefly, the community considered itself the "true covenant of God." It would appear that they studied the Book of Habbakuk assiduously and considered it had great significance in explaining events in their own day. To preserve the purity of the community and to grow in perfection, the Essenes evidently felt the need to be separated from worldly influences. Members of the sect appear to have practiced the rules of purity prescribed in the Torah, conditions laid down to ensure at all times that the Israelite army was pure and ready for the holy war the Essenes anticipated. A complete plan for the final war between the "Children of Light" and the "Children of Darkness" was written into a scroll. This scroll lays out a rigid schedule for the total of forty years to be spent in disposing of each of the enemies; it describes the equipment and weapons to be allotted each fighting unit; it details religious services and prayer to be used at each juncture of the war. The scroll even calls for sabbatical years, five of them, when no man will be allowed to engage in warfare.

Membership in the sect was granted only after a long probationary period. The growth of a member to perfection was considered a slow and gradual process, and possibly the probationary period was necessary to ascertain whether or not a prospective member could live up to the discipline required by the community. A rigid hierarchy was maintained among the brethren. Each man was honor bound to obey his elders and the bidding of the majority. A man was seated at the dinner table according to his rank in the group. His position in the army was determined by this same rank. His right to speak in a group was considered a privilege and was limited by his rank. His participation in religious ceremonies could not be expected until he was found by his elders to have attained a certain level of perfection. Days at the community were spent in prayer, purifying bathing in cold water, labor, and Scripture reading.

The Essene community lived in some ways as did the early Christians described in the Book of Acts. They practiced community ownership of property. Members of the sect who engaged in farming, herding, bee-tending, or handicraft turned in any profit received to the treasurer of the sect who bought goods for the whole community and distributed it as the need arose. The elderly were given comfort and care. Marriage was not forbidden, but it was not encouraged.

In one art the Essenes were not perfectionists. Archaeologists found the masonry at Qumran very poor. The various rooms were so patched and altered that it was difficult to find clearly the original plan of the monastery.

You might be interested to know that from an accounting of the fragments of biblical books found near the Essene community, the most numerous (and perhaps the most popular) were the books of Deuteronomy, the Psalms, Isaiah, and Genesis.

Some scholars have been quick to associate John the Baptist and Jesus with the Essene philosophy. John, of course, lived as they did, without material possessions. He identified himself as a "voice . . . in the wilderness" calling men to God; the Essenes applied the same phrase to themselves. John seemed to place great importance on "washing for repentance"; cleansing by washing is also prominent in the practice of the Essenes. Jesus' tie to the Essenes would be, first, that Jesus sought out John, perhaps an Essene, at the beginning of his ministry. He also decried the unequal distribution of wealth and had great sympathy for the poor. He commissioned his disciples to baptize (a cleansing washing), and while he often tongue-lashed the Sadducees and the Pharisees, he did not seem to castigate the Essenes.

To Get to Qumran—

Because of its location, there is no ideal time to visit Qumran. In the summer, the heat is most oppressive near the Dead Sea. In the winter the heavy rains wash down from all the hills of Jordan to collect in this lowest spot in the country. The narrow plain immediately north and west of the Dead Sea becomes a

quagmire. Our first attempt to visit Qumran in the winter was
a disaster. We had called the tourist police to inquire about
the terrain and had been assured that the track leading to the
ruins off the main road was open. As we (a group of about
fifteen) approached the flats that lay between us and Qumran, it
was obvious that no ordinary car was going to be able to travel the
few remaining miles to the site. The track glistened with a fresh,
smooth coating of silt.

We had at our disposal one Land Rover and its intrepid Arab
driver. This fearless man had transported archaeologists into the
most forbidding areas of the Holy Land. He had forded streams,
crossed gulches, and maneuvered through boulders. He proposed
that he run a shuttle service for us, taking first the men and returning for the women and children. Inspired by his confidence,
we quickly loaded our male members plus their lunches and
camera equipment into the Land Rover. Then we stood off, bid
them good-by, and nodded approval to the promise that the
driver would be back for us in a short time. The Land Rover
eased off the main road into the track, plowed ahead for about
fifteen feet and sank. The deceptive layer of silt was in fact a
deposit of at least three feet of muck. We had strong rope with
us, but all of our combined pulling-power on the rope could
not budge that vehicle. We finally had to send an SOS to army
headquarters in Jerusalem to rescue us with a truck and winch.

The payoff was that as we languished by the roadside, a dejected group of sightseers, another Land Rover breezed up alongside us. Driving it was a jaunty Englishman. His glance surveyed
our difficulty. He stopped and in the most clipped British ac-
cent called out, "Anyone for Qumran? Hop in!" We all shook
our heads, negative. Off he sailed down the main road while
we watched him with malicious curiosity, awaiting the painful
moment when he, too, discovered that there would be no visitors
to Qumran that day. Our little game was spoiled when Jordanian
soldiers at a post down the road stopped him before he could
dip his Land Rover into the wheel-choking slime.

Herod's Splendor

If a man were affluent enough to have one home in Jerusalem and a second in Jericho, he could shuttle the forty-five minute drive between the two and enjoy fine climate almost the whole year 'round. Because of the thirty-five-hundred-foot difference in altitude temperatures vary widely in these two cities on any given day. Jericho will always be the warmer.

One of the first men to discover the resort quality of the Jordan Valley was the onetime ruler of Palestine who left not one stone unturned if that stone could be used to enable him to live in the manner to which he was accustomed. This man was Herod the Great. In the Jordan Valley, at the foot of the hills where a gorge empties its rain water into the flat land, Herod built himself another palace. This must have been a splendid home. Since Roman aqueducts along the gorge brought sufficient water to the area, he was able to fashion the most spectacular garden for his home. It was a sunken garden, terraced in part. Fifty niches in the walls surrounding the garden held statues which were reflected in a watercourse flowing quietly through the garden. In addition to this lovely and probably private garden, Herod built a spacious palace. Its excavators found that one of the buildings in the complex had a grand staircase one hundred and fifty feet long. For the rest of Jericho Herod furnished pools, parks, a hippodrome, and an amphitheater. Herod died here in 4 B.C. Weather has taken a heavy toll of this excavation and little remains on the site today that can be identified by a layman.

The Old Roman Road

Just west of Herod's Jericho (called New Testament Jericho to distinguish it from the more famous Old Testament Jericho and the modern town a few miles to the north) is the old Roman road to Jerusalem. In a bad state of repair, it is a nightmare

to travel in an ordinary car, but passable by Land Rover. There
are several reasons, however, for attempting this route. It follows
along the most beautiful gorge in the Holy Land. The cliffs rise
several hundred feet above the bed of a stream, the Wadi Qelt.
Along the gorge ruins of the old Roman aqueduct are visible.
Several miles from Jericho is the monastery of St. George, an
amazing structure that appears to maintain its grip on the cliffside
by suction. The monks who enter this isolated cloister spend their
lifetime within its walls and are buried there.

Finally the Roman road is the one Jesus would have traveled
as he made his final trip to Jerusalem to be crucified. It was
in the New Testament Jericho that Jesus met Zacchaeus, the
publican, and rested in his home (Luke 19:1–10).

The Jordan River

Two other sites are importantly connected with the ministry of
Jesus near Jericho. One is a bend on the Jordan River chosen
as a probable scene of the Baptism and the other is the Mount
of Temptation where Jesus pondered his mission immediately
after the baptism.

The tourist is often dismayed when he sees the river site for
the first time. During the dry season the Jordan is little more
than a creek heavily overgrown with rushes. There is a picnic
ground beside the stream and a few wooden stands where merchants sell soft drinks, fruit, etc. During the winter, however, it
is a far more presentable river, wider, with a swift current, and
in flood, it can sweep over the picnic grounds, tables, vendors'
stalls and all.

The Jordan, so often described as the lifeline of the Holy Land
(and it *is*), cannot be compared with such mighty forces of
water as the Mississippi or the Tigris. It is wide only as it leaves
the Sea of Galilee where the width is ninety to one hundred
feet. It quickly narrows to the stream that weaves a sinuous path
along the sixty-five-mile length of the Jordan Valley to the Dead
Sea. In its entirety the river is a little over two hundred miles

long, and its depth varies from three to ten feet. It can be comfortably forded in many places.

The Jordan is *the* river in the Holy Land and it is *the* river to which Jesus traveled to meet John and to give tacit approval to the ministry of John by requesting John's baptism (Mark 1:9; Matt. 3:13). The fourth chapter of Matthew relates that immediately following the baptism, Jesus walked to the hill country (a good long walk, by the way) to spend time in meditation and prayer. As mentioned previously, there is a site selected in the hills to commemorate this event. From this perch in the cliffs, Jesus could have overlooked not only the Jordan Valley and the river, the hills of Moab and Ammon, but he would have seen the fabulous city of Herod. He could have looked out over the hill country and pin-pointed other kingdoms that were flourishing settlements in his day. On a clear day, he might have seen Mount Hermon's snow-capped peaks in distant Lebanon. This would indeed have been a most secluded and fitting setting for the temptations that may have beset Jesus.

Earlier in this same area of the Jordan Valley, Joshua had led the children of Israel across the Jordan River on dry ground. Joshua 4:20–24 tells that Joshua placed twelve stones in Gilgal on the bank of the river to tell all succeeding generations of men that the Lord had made it possible for His people to enter the Promised Land. Gilgal became the rallying point for the military campaigns of the Israelites and also a great sanctuary. We might wish that Joshua had been able to cement his twelve stones into a permanent monument so that they would remain for us today. There are several ancient mounds in the immediate area of Jericho that might be Gilgal, but until excavations unearth more positive evidence, the location of Gilgal is unknown.

The Missing Walls of Jericho

If the location of Gilgal is in doubt, most scholars feel that there is no doubt about the location of another city whose name is almost synonymous with that of Joshua—Old Testament Jericho.

The mound of this old city lies on the north edge of the modern town of Jericho. Joshua's siege of the town may be one of the best-known stories in the Bible thanks to its immortalization in song—"Joshua fit the battle of Jericho . . . and the walls came tum-bl-ing down."

Early in the twentieth century scholars became eager to verify the Bible by archaeological exploration. Tell es Sultan (the old mound) was one of the first sites excavated in Palestine. It stood to reason. Jericho was a huge city. It had been enclosed by a strong fortifying wall. If this wall had fallen flat, there must be evidence of it still to be found. It has since been regretted that these early archaeologists set about their exacting task with such zeal. Lacking knowledge of today's more cautious digging methods, lacking the new science of exact dating of pottery, the earliest archaeologists tore apart a section of Jericho with the result that it is now lost to scientific scrutiny. Later an archaeologist of the thirties was convinced that he had found the walls of Jericho of Joshua's time. Archaeologists in the fifties claim that these walls, damaged by earthquake and fire, belong at least a century prior to the time it is believed that Joshua entered Palestine. Traces of the city walls that allegedly yielded to Joshua's trumpets are non-existent. In fact, there is almost nothing left of the city of Jericho of Joshua's time except a smattering of pottery.

What does this mean to the archaeologist? It suggests several possibilities. *a.* Joshua so thoroughly destroyed the city that nothing remains of it; *b.* he exaggerated the extent of his military victory (many towns fell peaceably to Joshua and perhaps a small Jericho fell to him without a fight; only later did these ruins of an older and larger settlement at Jericho become the traditional site of Joshua's victory); *c.* this is not the town called "Jericho" by Joshua. Until further discoveries in the Holy Land throw more light on the story of Joshua's invasion, the question must be left in doubt.

Digs at other cities mentioned in the Book of Joshua as the

sites of great military victories have shown similar damage and this destruction is all dated to the same time, the thirteenth century B.C., which does tally with the date scholars ascribe to Joshua's invasion. Among these cities are Bethel, Lachish, and Hazor (Joshua 8:9, 10:31, and 11:10).

"The Oldest Walled City"

If evidence of Joshua is missing from the mound at Jericho, much is still there to interest the tourist. Advertised for years as the "oldest city in the world," Jericho will perhaps now have to alter that claim to read "the oldest walled city in the world." Recent discoveries in Turkey reveal that some cities flourished on the Anatolian plain as early as 7000 B.C. Jericho claims this same date for its earliest settled occupation. A well-built Neolithic tower thirty-five feet thick and a defense ditch cut out of rock testify that these early settlers were prepared to defend their town. Their houses were relatively well built with plastered walls and floors. The section of the mound calculated to date from the Neolithic period (the Late Stone Age when man first discovered how to make pottery) is forty-five feet high and encases twenty successive layers of these earliest mud brick houses. Also dating from Neolithic times are some startling skulls, covered and shaped by plaster to resemble a living human head. Whether these skulls were so preserved for religious purposes, reverence for the dead, or as examples of artistic sculpture is not known. The skulls are displayed in the Jordan Museum at Amman.

A study of the many levels of occupation has suggested to archaeologists that the last time Jericho was a truly large city was three hundred years before Moses. The Exodus is usually dated 1290 B.C.

Perhaps the most important conclusion drawn from the excavations at Jericho is that scholars have had to revise their previous opinions as to the earliest date that man settled in communities and houses. It was several thousand years earlier than anyone had guessed. The settlement at Jericho has also changed the previous picture of what type of country the Holy Land was when Abraham entered it. It was more sophisticated than scholars had thought.

A Modern "Ancient" Town

The mound of ancient Jericho, as mentioned, is a "collection" of mud brick towns one on top of the other. It is interesting that at the foot of the mound, the tourist can see firsthand what a mud brick town might have looked like when it was inhabited. This mud brick town is a refugee camp. It is a very large one and the persons who live there are managing to endure with only the bare necessities of life. Twentieth-century conveniences that we take for granted are not available. To all intents and purposes, these people do not live differently from the ancients who settled at Jericho.

When we first saw this crowded mud brick camp of one-story dwellings, we asked what the families did to try to keep their homes cool during the summer. The answer was "nothing." By the middle of May, it is already hot at Jericho. There will be scarcely a cloud in the sky until October. Temperatures will be consistently above 90°, above 100°, often above 110° F. No wonder the people here and all over the Holy Land rejoice when, in the fall, they see the first rain clouds form in the skies. If the Arabs have one strength to admire above their other qualities, it is certainly their ability to accept, to endure, to wait out miseries.

Difficulties with Education

The United Nations has tried to give the refugees good clinics to protect their health and schools to equip the children to earn their living when they are grown. A solid education for the younger generation may in time spell out the answer to the refugee problem. The boys seem to take their education quite seriously. As we drove along the roads in the Holy Land, and particularly those near Jericho, the streets were often crowded with groups of boys reading their lesson books. These boys can present a traffic hazard because they are really studying and sometimes they are unaware that a car is approaching. We have puzzled over this method of studying, but perhaps the answer is a simple one. Conditions in a one- or two-room house are not conducive to study. The rooms are probably crowded, and too much noise in the home precludes concentration. It is certain that lighting conditions are not the best for reading, let alone Arabic print. Outside, there are no benches to sit on to study. So-o-o, the boys walk. They know that their only chance for a better life is to learn, and if they learn enough, they may be able to go on to a university.

Until recently, going to a university meant leaving Jordan. Now Jordan has started a university at Amman because it desperately needs to keep its educated young men. But even if a boy should find it necessary to leave Jordan to get the education or the job he wants, his leaving may not mean that his future earnings will be totally lost to Jordan. Family ties are so strong that a portion of the boy's earnings will filter back to the rest of his family. The majority of refugee boys are not aiming toward a university education, but for a skill in a trade that they can put to immediate use.

The Spring of Elisha

From the mound of Jericho, the tourist has a clear view of the traditional spring of Elisha (II Kings 2:19–22). The men of the city complained to Elisha that while the city was pleasant, the water was bad and the land unfruitful. Elisha threw salt into the spring and made its water sweet. Certainly the traffic to and from the well today suggests that its waters are very pleasing. Hundreds of women gather at the well in the morning and evening hours—this scene is one of the more arresting sights of present-day Holy Land. The gowns are so colorful, their white headdresses so becoming in contrast to their dark eyes, skin, and hair, and their carriage as they balance tins of water on their heads so poised—every tourist wishes to have a picture of this scene. While the women are sometimes amused, perhaps flattered, by our requests for their pictures, the menfolk are adamantly and vehemently opposed to sharing their wives and daughters in this manner with strangers.

The Oasis that Is Jericho

Present-day Jericho is still a pleasant city. It is a city where bougainvillaea grows and blooms all year round and trims the houses with splashes of purple and red. Jericho has shade trees, palm trees, and flowering shrubs. It is truly an oasis. The area surrounding the city is rich in citrus groves and banana palms. We are told that in prehistoric times this whole valley was lush with growth and was a comfortable home for the elephant, the lion, and the hippopotamus. This is extremely difficult to imagine. While the Jordan Valley is lush with growth in comparison with the rest of the land, there is scarcely a thicket that would conceal an animal of any size today, let alone furnish the privacy needed for rearing the young animals. It is claimed that there are wild pigs in Jordan. We did not see any.

The Vision of Musa Al Alami

Much of the food production that you now see in the Jordan Valley is the result of the hard work and the imagination of one man, Musa Al Alami. Shortly after the partition of the Holy Land into Jordan and Israel, Mr. Al Alami began an experimental farm in the region of Jericho. He envisioned an aid program whereby Arabs could help other Arabs by teaching modern farming skills to refugee boys. His vision has paid off handsomely. Proper handling of both the land and the crops has resulted in a fine yield of produce in the Jordan Valley. Visitors are welcome to stop to see his model farm and Boys' Town.

Here at the farm and throughout the valley tourists can see the amazing fertility of the Holy Land. The testimony is seen as well in all of the city markets. It is a challenge to recall finer horticultural specimens raised by any other country. Cabbages and cauliflower less than a foot in diameter are rare. Carrots are husky affairs, equal to four or five of our slender tapers. Red radishes match the carrot in shape and size. Markets are generously furnished with eggplant and the smaller green marrows, staples in the native diet. The citrus fruits look beautiful on the outside, but the exterior cannot prepare you for what is inside—they are utterly delicious. It can be said without equivocation that no one can know how superb an orange can taste until he has sampled the tree-ripened fruit from Jericho. There is no "color added" in Jordan to fool the customer that the fruit is ripe. This fruit *is* ripe and it is sweet and it sits easily on the stomach. If Jordan could grow enough to supply us, and ship them to us quickly enough, the oranges would capture the market. The lemons, too, in Jordan put ours to shame. They are large, bursting with juice and that juice is properly tart, not sour. Watermelons are delightful, also sweet from that constant dose of Jordanian sun and they serve as a welcome thirst quencher when water is not available. Plums are so sweet and juicy that you cannot bite into them without a napkin under your chin. Jordan grows excellent apples, grapes, apricots, and figs.

In fact, there are only two foods grown in Jordan that are not superior to those found in our supermarkets. One is the banana. While the flavor is good, the banana is very small, not much larger than your finger and it looks as if it had not been ready to leave its mother. The other inferior produce is corn, a new crop in Jordan. Perhaps there is not enough moisture here

for good corn because it is tough and dry. While it is certainly
not up to American tastes, the natives relish it and buy it as
finger food from vendors who strip it to order, pop it into boiling
water and serve it on the streets.

The Scarcity of Meat

If most of the produce in the Jordan Valley is superb, I must
reluctantly admit that the meat falls short of meeting a high
standard by "a right smart plenty." Beef is scarce, pork is non-existent because of its prohibition by Mohammed, lamb is available,
but very strong. In fact, since it has been so often recommended
that Jordan get rid of its goats, I suspect that I unwittingly helped
the cause on many dining occasions.

To westerners the meat markets are a horror. They deal
almost entirely in lamb and goat and carcasses of these animals
are hung in the open air, if indeed any *souk* can be described
as having open air. Of course, they will ultimately be thoroughly
cooked. The whole carcass is not too pleasant a sight but it pales
to insignificance alongside the other portions of the animals
offered for sale. Nothing is wasted, including heads and un-
mentionables. We in America also use these things but usually
we disguise them in sausage so that we are not treated to a display of animal inner anatomy. A whole row of bloody goat
heads will curb the appetite. And at that, I don't believe they
look so bad just cut off the animal as they look as I once saw
them in Damascus: skinned and boiled, a skull with tidbits of
meat stuck in the sockets. We have become accustomed to
meats wrapped in cellophane, sterile, cloaked in anonymity with
no suggestion that this is a part of an animal that has recently
been slaughtered. The Jordanians have sensed our reaction to
their meat markets and they are most resentful of the tourist who
tries to snap pictures of a row of lamb carcasses. They need not
worry overlong about the tourist's pictures. The *souks* are so
dark and so crowded that it is almost impossible to engineer a

decent picture. Heads bob into the middle of your lens and shoulders brush yours as you try to steady your camera. It is not altogether accidental.

A Caliph's Palace

Just outside the city of Jericho, there is a palace. This is a *real* palace but it was not built by King Herod. Nor was it built by the Israelites, nor the Greeks, nor Constantine. It is far more modern. It belonged to an Arab, one of the sultans of the Umayyad period (661–750) who were affluent and who knew how to live sumptuously. Caliph Hisham Ibn Abdul Malik lived here at Jericho in the eighth century. The palace sits in the midst of the sultan's game preserve, a walled estate where he could retreat to enjoy the pleasing climate. That the sultan had fine living quarters and a columned courtyard might have been expected. That the sultan had luxurious baths and an elaborate system of pipes to bring hot water to these baths may be a surprise. As did the Romans, the sultan made a leisurely ritual of bathing. He had an entrance room to the bath, as well as cold rooms, hot rooms, and retiring rooms.

The most beautiful room in the bath complex is the smallest. It boasts what many call the most beautiful mosaic in the world. This hideaway, where it would be supposed the Caliph retired from his bath, is lighted through a filigree arch of intricately carved stucco which forms one wall. Around the edges of the room, there may have been soft cushions. The mosaic on the floor, is still as fresh in color as the day it was laid. The tree that nearly fills the mosaic is exquisite. Blue leaves outline the shape of the tree. The remaining foliage is an attractive arrangement in various shades of greens and cream. Rosy pomegranates dot the tree. Beneath it, in brown and beige, two gazelles feed peacefully on the tree while a third succumbs to the strong jaw and claws of a lion. The entire mosaic is rimmed with mosaic tassels to suggest that this was a carpet on the floor.

Bits of colored glass once fitted into the carved stucco window still lie in the sand around the palace. For this lovely palace was destroyed by an earthquake while the sultan was still enlarging it. When you see how possible it was for some people to live very well in the Holy Land, you wish it were still possible for more people to live well there today. All of the Middle East is earthquake country. The Holy Land has always had its share of this calamity of nature and will undoubtedly have a few more. If there is to be another earthquake, how fortunate it would be if the tremor were to divert some of the vast oil supplies of other Middle Eastern countries into Jordan. What a blessing that might be!

In the eastern desert of Jordan, there are other impressive Umayyad castles. They were used as hunting lodges when game was far more plentiful in the Holy Land. Lions, gazelles, and hawks were fair game for the caliphs. Horses for racing and hunting were also bred. (The Bedouins still go hawk hunting in the desert. Hawks are used to hunt rabbit and deer, and as the wild predators command a high price on the market, some Bedouins earn their living by trapping and training them. The common method of trapping is to use doves or rabbits as bait, enclosing them in mesh. The trained hawk seeking a tasty meal also becomes enmeshed.)

Driving into the Desert

If you wish to drive out into the desert to inspect the castles of the Umayyad sheiks, or to see firsthand the interesting life of the Bedouins, you must hire a good guide. Desert roads are sand tracks with hundreds of branches leading from them to small settlements. After the first few turns in the track, an amateur pathfinder could find himself in real trouble. All sandy hills look alike, especially when you look at them from the opposite way you originally viewed them. The persons who live in this area speak only Arabic. They would not understand what visitors were doing on the desert, let alone give them directions for returning to civilization.

We stopped at one of the desert police posts to ask directions to one of the castles. These desert outposts are interesting to see. They usually sit up high and are substantial cream-colored structures. Usually, horses are tied nearby. These outposts look for all the world as if you had stumbled into a past age as depicted in the movies when the French Foreign Legion maintained such posts to keep peace among the tribes.

The young man on duty did speak a little English, and he was marvelous to see. He wore a long brown robe which was flapping in the wind. At his waist was a wide red belt filled with bullets and on his head was the Bedouin *kaffia*. We asked to take his picture; he refused, but suggested that he might allow one if we came back late in the afternoon when he was off duty. Even with the explicit directions he gave us, we could not find our way though the castle was only a few miles away. We "chickened out," gave up hope of seeing the castle, and hastened to return to the macadam road that we knew led to a definite destination.

The Alexandrium

You may drive north through the Jordan Valley by either of two roads. Each has its own beauties. The one that leads directly north from Jericho follows a path close to the hill country on the west side of the Jordan River. For some distance the road is dotted with small villages; then in the more open country, Bedouins pitch their tents close to the hills, in the spring in rather large groups. There is not much of historical interest on this route save one infamous monument. This is the Alexandrium, highest hill in the area, where Alexander Jannaeus (103–76 B.C.) maintained a fortress. The Arabs call the hill *Qarn Sartabeh*, "fortress of the slayer," after the Maccabean who apparently killed his share of enemies. Long after Alexander Jannaeus, Herod used this fortress. As mentioned earlier, signals could be sent from the Alexandrium to the Herodium near Bethlehem. Herod was as entitled to the Arabic name of the fortress as Alexander

Jannaeus. Herod maintained a family burial plot here and buried in it at least three relatives for whose deaths he was directly responsible—the brother of Mariamne one of his wives, and two of his sons by the same wife.

The ascent of the Alexandrium is for those who need to prove that they are hale and hearty. A good pace will take you to the top in an hour. There are ruins of the old fort on top, but the better recommendation for the climb is the view from the summit: a panorama of the Jordan Valley, cut by the zigzag path of the Jordan River; the Dead Sea; and in all directions the hills of Jordan.

The view of these hills can be described in two words— absolutely barren. Not a tree is in sight anywhere. There are a few small bramble bushes if you want to count them as shrubs. They don't amount to much even when they are full grown to their foot-high, foot-wide status. The brambles serve two good purposes. They provide nibbling food for goats and they provide momentary warmth for shepherds. On cool days and nights, shepherds gather a few of the bushes, set a match to them and in the "pouf" of flame that follows, warm their hands.

The group of archaeologists with whom my husband was associated dug some caves in this hill area. When they were on location, they tried to bargain with the cook to arise early at least one morning to fix a hearty breakfast of pancakes. To help the cook get a good night's sleep, the archaeologists offered to prepare their own supper the previous evening. What would they fix? Just something simple—they would probably roast wieners on a stick. The cook stopped the whole plan immediately when he posed this unanswerable question, "Just where do you think you will find a stick?"

Arabs Behind the Wheel

The other road of the Jordan Valley is on the east side turning north off the Jerusalem-Amman highway after you have crossed the Jordan River. I traveled this road many times, and not often without having my hair stand on end a couple of times. The road is narrow and not in the best condition, but that is not the problem. The traffic is not heavy, so that is not the problem. The problem is the Arab drivers. Every Arab is quite certain that when he takes to the road, no one else has a right to be on it. This attitude finds overt expression in two ways: the driver lays a heavy hand on the horn to give warning, loud and clear, that he is coming through; and second, he maintains the center of the road until you can literally see the whites of his eyes. Hopefully, one car will give way. That car will always be the car of the tourist. An Arab driver is not averse to nudging you to the side of the road.

This insistence of the Arab driver that he must maintain the center of the road may be a type of face-saving or it may be a form of the game sometimes called "chicken." Whatever it is, I have no taste for it. I often witnessed a similar game on the streets of Jerusalem where some brash young taxi drivers amused themselves by brushing the clothing of pedestrians with the fenders of their automobiles.

Just why any Arab would chance damaging his car in such ridiculous games is a puzzle. All cars in Jordan are imported, and unless customs have been circumvented by some means, the car owner has paid 100 per cent duty to the government. This duty makes a car a major investment for any Jordanian. I might also add that the cost of car insurance in the Middle East is extremely high. The attitude of some of the drivers may account for high premium rates.

The Evil Eye

If I sometimes cringed while driving up the road east of the Jordan, there were other consoling factors that made the trip a delight. The road cuts through many towns, both prosperous and poor. Most interesting is the variety of dwellings that can be seen so close at hand. The stone homes I had seen many times before, but it was unusual to see bands of gypsies in their vari-colored tents. They are easy to identify because they do not use the black goatskin tents of the Bedouins.

One village is formed of whitewashed adobe beehive-shaped homes, reminiscent of a type of village common in Syria, also settlements where the houses resemble Indian pueblos—made of mud with protruding roof beams. The occupants of these homes many times decorate their windows by outlining them with a wide swath of yellow, blue, or white paint. This decoration is more than a beauty mark. Superstitious occupants count on the marking to ward off the evil eye. The painted window frames are found on homes other than the pueblo type. I tried to find out if there was any significance in the color selected, but could get no answer other than that it was a matter of personal taste. The people hate to admit that they are supersti-tious and yet the evil eye legend is rife. When I questioned a city dweller on why it was that I saw no cows in Jordan when I knew there were some, he, without thinking, answered, "If a man has a good cow he keeps it always inside." The second question, "Why would a person keep a cow always inside?" was not so immediately answered. The gentleman slowly and de-liberately gave this answer, "Because a man can take better care of a cow inside." A more honest answer would have been that if a cow is a good milk producer, a man will let no one see her lest he put an evil eye on her and ruin her milk.

Irrigation

Along the road north is one of the most refreshing sights in the Holy Land. A farmer will open the gate in an irrigation ditch to water his crops. The water comes from the Jabbok, a tributary of the Jordan. Far to the north, on the Syrian border, another tributary, the Yarmuk, has been harnessed to provide irrigation for the Jordan Valley. This is the first, and a highly successful, attempt to bring more water to the valley. The results are apparent—a green, green valley filled with growing crops. Rounded hills in the middle of the plain, often the sites of ancient cities, are covered with growing wheat.

Emotional Men

In the mornings, the streets of the villages swarm with people. The men will be gathered in small groups carrying on the most heated conversations. They yell and shout at one another, cuffing each other. The observer tends to shrink away from these groups because it does seem that real violence might break out at any moment. It won't. The men may not be discussing anything more serious than where to go for a morning cup of coffee. If you watched them for any length of time, you would see that Arab men give full vent to each small emotion. You should see one of them when he spies a friend coming along the street! He will call out his friend's name in the most anguished joy. He will run up to meet him. The two will fall into each other's arms, kiss each other, perhaps walk off down the street holding hands. No need to raise your eyebrow. It is customary in this country that the men greet men with kisses and men greet women with a handshake.

The Status of Women

As the men are overly voluble, so the women are overly taciturn. We are apt to pity the Middle Eastern woman who is so dominated by the males of her family. Jordan is only now talking about giving women the right to vote. They have long believed the woman belongs in the home. The majority of the people consider it a disgrace for a woman to work outside the home. Much this same situation prevailed in our country not too long ago. Great grandmother was privileged to perspire over a hot stove, to exercise her arms on the washboard, to scrub and sweep—but to work in an office, never!

It would certainly be presumptuous to assume that the inferior

position of the average Middle Eastern woman in society makes
her unhappy. It is perhaps fairer to say that the above-average
Middle Eastern woman is the one who suffers more. The educated woman in Jordan often finds herself stymied. The majority
of her countrymen and women do not necessarily respect her.
They look on her as a strange breed. They don't understand
her. They may be suspicious of her. She has overstepped her
bounds, and she must travel in the select company of the few
other women who are like herself. Among them she can be open.
She can express her feeling, her opinions, discuss politics, world
affairs. In a gathering of men and women, she must again assume
her mask of inferiority, wait on the males and set her mouth
in a vapid smile.

There are very few activities for the educated women in Jordan. Most of them can afford to have household help, so they
have many hours to fill. There is a Jerusalem women's club that
meets once a month to hear a speaker, and there are some adult
activities in connection with the YWCA. Lacking are the myriad
school and church organizations that so fill the Western woman's day. The educated woman in Jordan does not yet have social status. At the moment she feels frustrated and a little useless, but she will find her way just as did the women of the
West.

At present, it is the women of the towns and villages who
feel comfortable and at home in the culture the area has so
long known. As I've said, the villages swarm with people in the
mornings, but shortly after noon, there will not be a person out,
they will have retired to their dwellings to observe the siesta
during the heat of the day, and the villages will be closed up
tight as a drum. Late in the afternoon the streets are aswarm
again.

Succoth and Zaretan

Of historic value to the tourist, along the road are two Old
Testament cities that have been excavated. Many other cities

on this plain will be explored one day. The first is Deir 'alla, believed to be Succoth. The name "Succoth" (meaning booths) was given to the site in honor of Jacob who made booths or sheds here for his cattle as he was traveling back to Shechem from Haran. As you stand on the top of the old mound, you can see the brook Jabbok. If you followed this stream to the east, you would come to the spot where it is believed Jacob wrestled all night with the Lord. Further Old Testament fame associated with Succoth comes from Judges 8:5-9, 14 ff, where Gideon punishes the rulers of Succoth because their city would not supply food for his armies, and from I Kings 7:46, where the chroniclers report that bronze vessels for Solomon's temple were cast at or near Succoth.

The second city excavated in this area of the valley is Sa'idiyah, believed by some to be the biblical Zaretan. It is not far from Deir 'alla. The tourist visiting the excavation who now recalls the distance he has come from Jericho—about twenty-five miles—will appreciate the grandeur of the act of the Lord that enabled Joshua to cross the Jordan dry shod, for when Joshua led his people across the Jordan to the Promised Land, the river backed up to form a lake all the way to Zaretan (Josh. 3:16, 17). Zaretan was a well-known city, known to have been inhabited from the time man first used copper, circa 3500 B.C., and through the time of the Israelites.

Recent excavations under the direction of Dr. James P. Pritchard of the University of Pennsylvania have turned up some remarkable finds. The most striking is a double stone stairway once covered with wood beams from the top to the foot of the mound. This stairway was completely underground and thus hidden from an enemy: it is believed it was used to reach the water supply, the stream at the foot of the mound, when the city was under siege. Other surprising finds were some bodies preserved in bitumen, unusual in Palestine, and a woman's skeleton generously furnished with a long carnelian necklace, also unusual in the relatively poor Palestinian populace of the Bronze Age.

The Archaeologists' Search for Biblical Sites

As you drive through Jordan, you will probably see some "diggers" at work; more than half a dozen archaeological excavations are undertaken in the Holy Land yearly. As a rule, the diggers will be laying bare a portion of a mound that is obviously not a natural formation, but rather a wart on the landscape—a rounded hill that has become covered with dirt. The mound is an ancient dwelling place, abandoned because of war, or fire, or earthquake, or of insufficient water or disease.

Why have archaeologists decided to dig here? What are they looking for? They are seeking more information about the ways in which our forefathers lived. A particular site is chosen for excavation as the result of calmly calculated, scholarly guesswork. If it is an old biblical town, the archaeologist has undoubtedly obtained clues from the Bible that point to this location as the probable site of the town. Perhaps other ancient literature mentions the town, and the clues to its probable location fit this site. Perhaps the natives have a name for this mound that seems to fit what is known of the biblical town.

Does this mean that scholars do not know the exact locations of the famous cities of the Bible? Yes, it means exactly that. This small portion of land, so overrun through the ages by Assyrians, Babylonians, Persians, Greeks, Romans, Byzantines, Arabs, Crusaders, and Turks has suffered so much destruction, so much dispersion of its inhabitants that it is difficult to trace by historical records any continuity in the known geographical locations of towns, even the more famous. The users and usurpers of the Holy Land were concerned with using the land to suit their own purposes. If it suited them to war on a neighboring site, to flatten it, and to use its stones to build a city a few miles away, this is what they did, and they did not leave behind a marker announcing to posterity, "This was the town of Jericho which will be important to your study in the twentieth century of our invasion of Palestine." So now the archaeologists are asking the land to regurgitate what it has swallowed up during the ages—the residences, the shops, the temples, palaces, the fortifications, and perhaps the literature of the people who lived so many years ago.

When the archaeologist finds a mound, how does he know where to start to dig? Does he just take a shovel and start in? No indeed! This would be the most certain way to destroy completely any archaeological evidence. Before anyone begins to dig, a lot of study and thought is focused on the site. Does anything remain above ground that would give a clue to fortification walls? Is there any evidence of how this city was originally laid out? Where might the water supply have been located? Are there any known tombs in the area? What is the evidence supplied by bits of pottery on the mound? Small soundings will be undertaken—small areas dug to see if the guesswork is correct. Are there really houses in this area? Is this stone outcropping the top of an old city wall? Then, after all surface evidences and literary records have been studied again, the archaeologist will lay out a grid pattern over the areas to be excavated. A foreman and crew will be assigned to one or more squares. Then and only then will the dig begin, a tortuously slow process wherein the surface is carefully peeled away inch by inch. Evidence of occupation will appear. This evidence may be a floor, pottery, a wall, bones, or dirt that has changed color or texture. The digger will take great care to explore any level of occupation horizontally before proceeding farther vertically. Any artifact of human occupation will be sorted from the dirt and labeled, noting the exact location where found and the date it was found. In areas where there might once have been grains or coins, the dirt will be sifted through a fine sieve before being carried away to a dump. Any small item overlooked in a dig may be lost forever. No shovelful of dirt taken from its original position can be reconstituted as it was. For this reason, archaeology is tedious work, to be undertaken only by those persons with patience and deep knowledge. It also takes knowledge to judge where to dump the dirt that has been taken from the excavation. More than one archaeologist has winced when his suspicions were confirmed that an important part of an excavation was leading the diggers directly to the area under the dump pile. What do they do in such a crisis? They have to take the time to shovel away the whole pile.

The good pick man or shovel man must have a "feel" for the texture of dirt so that he can distinguish immediately between "fill" dirt that has sifted in through the ages and the hard packed dirt of a floor. Too energetic wielding of a pick ax can cut a gash through dirt that represents hundreds of years of human occupation. Not only is it necessary to dig cautiously and to record meticulously every small find—it is essential to sketch the area dug at the end of each day's work and to photograph it, if the findings warrant a permanent record on film. The sketches, photographs, and other records, will be given to the archaeological architect who, happily, will be able to cull from such data a substantial idea of the over-all plan of the city at any given age.

How Old Are the Finds?

How does an archaeologist know the age of the materials he finds? In Palestine, dating relies heavily on the evidence of pottery. The ordinary cooking ware of men from the earliest times, be it found only in small pieces, varies greatly in texture, color, shape, timbre. To the pottery expert, a collection of pottery all taken from one level of the mound, will give almost indisputable evidence of the date of that human occupation. Rims, handles, decorations give excellent clues to the time the pottery was probably made.

To give an idea of what the various dating terms mean, let's suppose that a mound in Palestine has been occupied continuously from the Stone Age. (Let us quickly add that scholars do not agree on the exact span of time to be assigned each of the periods listed below should be confined. For our purposes, however, the chronology will give the reader a general, over-all picture.) The surface of any area in the Holy Land is most likely to produce Islamic culture since the Arabs have lived on the land continuously since they overran the Middle East in the seventh century. One later culture is of interest to the archaeologist: that of the Crusaders who overran the country in the eleventh and twelfth centuries, but their influence was short-lived. The Turks came later, too, but they converted to the Muslim culture. So, from top to bottom, in the earth of the Holy Land, excavators might expect to find:

Islamic: 636 A.D. to the present time.

Byzantine: 323–636 A.D. This period dates from the time when Constantine the Great christianized his empire until the Muslim invasion.

Roman: 63 B.C.–322 A.D. This is the period during which there were such strong leaders as Julius Caesar, Herod the Great, Hadrian, and Nero.

Hellenistic: 331–62 B.C. This period starts with the conquest of Egypt by Alexander the Great.

Iron: 1100–331 B.C. This period is usually divided into three Ages: Early, Middle, and Late Iron. It covers much of the history of the Old Testament from the kingdoms of Saul, David, and Solomon to the reigns of Nebuchadnezzar and Belshazzar of Babylon and kings Cyrus and Darius of Persia.

Bronze: 3200–1100 B.C. This period also is divided into Early, Middle, and Late. Abraham appeared during the Middle Bronze Age, and the Exodus of Moses and the conquest of Canaan by Joshua mark the end of the Late Bronze Age.

Chalcolithic: 4000–3200 B.C. This period is distinguished by man's first writing and by the use of copper.

Neolithic: 6000–4000 B.C. From this Age archaeologists date the first evidences of early village living and, late in the Age, the first use of pottery.

Mesolithic: 8000–6000 B.C. This would be the Stone Age when so
                 far as is yet known, man used nothing other than
                 stone for implements. Man planted some foods, but
                 he was primarily a hunter and fisherman. This period
                 is also called Pre-pottery Neolithic.

Since we usually think of Stone Age man as primitive and un-
intelligent, it was astonishing when a huge defense tower discovered at Jericho was dated to 7000 B.C. On the Anatolian
plain of Turkey, a quite civilized urban society, dating to
7000 B.C. or earlier showed remarkable talent for sculpture and
frescoes.

The dating of the various ages set down here are measuring
tools for the Holy Land. Other areas in the world progressed
through Stone, Copper, and Iron Ages at varying dates in history. For instance, in the United States the Indians north of
the Rio Grande could be described as living in the Stone Age
when this continent was discovered in 1492.

The Significance of Archaeology

What of real significance has archaeology accomplished? Is archaeology just a fascinating pastime? Some of its champions
have in jest labeled it "grown-up sandpile." Has archaeology
justified the time and money expended in pursuit of buried
history by producing information that is a distinct contribution,
for instance, to our knowledge of the Bible? Without qualification, the answer is yes. The person who thinks he can teach
biblical history without being well-grounded in the additional
information supplied by archaeologists—information that has a
direct bearing on our ability to understand the biblical stories—
is cheating himself intellectually and giving to his pupils only
half a loaf. Our Bible, you see, is a biased book. To use a
present-day analogy: it was not wirtten by newscasters whose
duty it is to give a succinct account of a day's events; it was
written by news commentators who after they have appraised a
day's events, interpret the meaning of a selected few of those
events.

The Bible and Its Authors

The Bible writers ignored news devoid of spiritual significance. News that could have spiritual meaning was fully exploited. The Bible makes no claim to be a complete history of ancient times or even of Israel. Rather it is a record of a selected history which our religious forefathers felt showed clearly the thread of God's continued concern with one group of people. This group of people was convinced that God had revealed Himself to them in a very special way. They treasured this revelation and assumed the responsibility of a people chosen to uphold a covenant with the Lord. They saw the Lord as an exacting parent who intervened in history to punish His children when they went astray, to protect and help them when they were in danger of being destroyed. The Bible is an account of historical events as seen through the eyes of *these* people.

In a book of this type, we find historical gaps. We sometimes find apparent duplications of stories, as if the final "editors" did not wish to choose between two varying accounts of the same event and thus included them both. We find passing references to customs and traditions that, lacking further clarification, remain at best utterly confusing. The layman who has attempted to read the Bible and has set it aside because he was unable to comprehend truly all that he read need not feel deficient in intelligence. Early in this century many biblical scholars grappling with biblical perplexities were coming up dry. Dedicated to the search for truth, they felt that to maintain their intellectual integrity, they had to be cautious about the historicity of the early books of the Bible and to point to David as perhaps the first truly historical figure presented in the Bible. This was not cynical skepticism on their part. On the basis of what was then known, the patriarchal narratives and the Exodus were beyond understanding as stories of a real people. The customs of these ancients, their business codes, their worship practices were so different from any other known or accepted practices that the scholars were at a loss to make sense of them. The whole story of Abraham's origins and travels, for example, seemed confused. It was more like a sentimental legend fondly told by a people many generations later.

Many persons have never questioned a word written in the Bible. They have accepted the book on faith. If there were contradictions or confusions it would not matter to them because they had already accepted the premise of the Bible that God was concerned with His creation. Other persons do not have this facility to accept on faith alone. They need to know that the Bible is factual. For these latter persons, archaeology has supplied the dimension they sought.

"The Other Peoples"

Other peoples living in and around the Holy Land also left records. Archaeologists have learned much about their cultures and from them has come new light on the less clear portions of the Bible. Many of the old cobwebs have already been cleared away and many more will be in the future. During the past forty years archaeologists have recovered so much information about ancient history that the scholars cannot keep up with the diggers in the task of deciphering and interpreting it all.

In the Holy Lands, the archaeologists have made possible the recovery of several ancient Near Eastern languages. A wealth of written material, now decipherable, has revealed the legal codes of the ancients, their business transactions, their rituals, their religious beliefs, their Wisdom literature, their historical and legendary narratives. This information is of more than moderate interest to us because it is now recognized that in many instances, the customs, the business traditions, the legal codes, and sometimes the worship practices were identical or similar to those accepted by our patriarchs. These other peoples have spelled out for us many answers that we sought about the kinds of persons who were the forerunners of the tribes of Israel.

These extra-biblical sources have also proved very valuable in contributing to the understanding of the Hebrew language. As counterparts have been found to Hebrew words in the similar languages of neighboring lands, previously non-translatable Hebrew words now take on new meaning. For further reading about the many details that enabled scholars to unravel the mysteries of the patriarchal narratives, the reader will enjoy Dr. W. F. Albright's *The Biblical Period from Abraham to Ezra*, Dr. G. Ernest Wright's *Biblical Archaeology*, and Dr. John Bright's *History of Israel*.

As of the present time, scholars have learned that there was an invasion of or immigration to Palestine at about the time they now suspect Abraham went there. Almost every scholar agrees that Abraham and the other patriarchs were true sons of their times (say 2000–1700 B.C.) since the oral and written traditions were accurately preserved. It is worth mentioning that the customs and traditions of the patriarchs would have been as archaic and puzzling to persons living at the time of the United Monarchy (?1004–?926 B.C.) as they have been to us. Yet, rather than tamper with the tradition and alter it to be more comprehensible to them in terms of their changed culture, they kept it as it was. This integrity of the early scribes as revealed by archaeology has made it possible for scholars finally to confirm that the patriarchal narratives make excellent historical sense when viewed in the light of what is now known of the period.

Later Biblical History

Turning to later biblical history, we note that the route of the Exodus has escaped scholars thus far. There are theories about the probable movements of this band of religious refugees. Unfortunately, a people on the move do not necessarily leave permanent traces of their wanderings or their resting stations. There is no doubt that the Israelites came to Canaan. Archaeologists have on many excavations viewed the evidence of Joshua's destructions of cities. They also have found no destruc-

tion in cities like Shechem and Gibeon where the Bible records
that Joshua took the cities without a battle. One telltale evidence of a city occupied by the incoming Israelites is poor
masonry. The Israelites may have been fine fighters, but often
where archaeologists have found a level of inferior building of
walls and houses above better buildings of the Late Bronze Age,
that level dates to the Israelite invasion.

In the Holy Land, archaeologists have unearthed and have
claimed to identify many old biblical towns. Among these are
Jericho, Shechem, Taanach, Samaria, Dhibon, Gibeon, Megiddo,
Hazor, Bethel, as well as the many others mentioned throughout
this book.

For the period of the prophets, extra-biblical sources have
had much to tell us. We can better understand the powerful
sermons and prophecies of the prophets when we have a more
complete idea of the environment in which they spoke. Dr.
G. Ernest Wright explores this subject in his book *The Old
Testament Against Its Environment.*

The Scrolls and the New Testament

When we approach the time of Jesus, we already know a great
deal about the society in which He was living. Missing was the
evidence of a strong anticipation of a Messiah. The New Testament suggests this, but the New Testament was written *after*
the fact. The Dead Sea Scrolls provided the answer to that
question. The literature found at Qumran showed quite definitely that the Essenes were looking for a coming Messiah—
even to the point that they engaged in a messianic meal.

The Dead Sea Scrolls, coming directly from the culture at
the time of Jesus, have made some of Jesus' statements understandable. Jesus once said, "Ye have heard that it hath been
said, Thou shalt love thy neighbour, and hate thine enemy"
(Matt. 5:43). To our knowledge, no one had ever said such
a thing, but indeed it was said in the Qumran literature where
the brethren had been admonished to love the brethren but

to hate those outside the fellowship. Again, Jesus said, "Which of you shall have an ass or an ox fallen into a pit, and will not straightway pull him out on the sabbath day?" (Luke 14:5). Our answer today would be with the Pharisees, "Of course we would pull an animal out on the sabbath." But it was expressly forbidden to perform even this task of mercy on the sabbath in the Qumran literature, lest the sabbath be profaned.

Many books have been written about the relationship between the Gospels and the Dead Sea Scrolls. Suffice it for our purposes to say that the discovery of the Scrolls has added immensely to a richer, warmer, and fuller understanding of the New Testament.

Can the Bible Be Proved?

The question that most laymen voice to the archaeologist is, "Can archaeology prove the Bible?" Inasmuch as archaeology has confirmed so much biblical history, the answer to that question would be yes. Archaeology will continue to confirm biblical history as more discoveries and recoveries are made. If the layman really means by his question, "Can archaeology prove that God appeared to Abraham and Moses?" "Can archaeology prove that God exists?" "Can archaeology prove the resurrection of Jesus?", the answer is obviously no. To know exactly what motivated Abraham and Moses, would it not be necessary to talk personally to them? Or would it be sufficient to look at the biblical record and to decide from the actions of Abraham and Moses that their motivation was out of the ordinary? Similarly, we cannot reasonably expect to encounter Jesus and question him as to the accuracy of the Gospel writers' interpretation of his life. We can look at the record and note that a dispersed and dejected group of disciples at the time of Jesus' death suddenly took on new life—actually caught on fire with their enthusiasm to go out and preach and teach as they had never done while Jesus was living among them. They were willing to be martyrs rather than to deny what they were preaching about Jesus. What could archaeology dig up that could tell us more about that faith they preached?

The biblical record, from Abraham through Paul, deals with *real* people, *real* places, and *real* events. Left to the reader of the Bible is the *interpretation* of those events.

Will More Information Be Found?

Is it possible that we will ever find more of the Bible, particularly more Gospels—more of the teachings of Jesus? Until a few decades ago it was thought that there was no possibility that any new literature concerning the life of Jesus would be forthcoming from the Holy Land. The discovery of the Dead Sea Scrolls has now opened this question again. More manuscripts two thousand years old may be found. Since the Essenes protected their literature and secreted it in caves when enemies threatened, it is possible that early Christians may have done the same thing. It has been known since the fall of Jerusalem in A.D. 69 that many Christians fled to a city of the Decapolis in northern Jordan named Pella. Because this city continued to be inhabited for centuries in the Byzantine period, archaeologists, knowing well that tons and tons of Byzantine debris cover the town level of the early Christian era, have been reluctant to excavate. Since removal of the top layers by a bulldozer is not considered scientific, the excavation will require much labor, time, and money. Would any early Christian literature be found here? Possibly. As for caves—many in Jordan have not been fully investigated, let alone excavated. But undoubtedly there still are manuscripts of importance to us undiscovered in Jordan and other nearby countries.

VIII The Capital and Its Surroundings

Amman—Its History

Amman is the capital of Jordan. It was once a capital city of the Ammonite kingdom, about 1200 B.C., when it was called Rabbath Ammon. Biblical students may remember the town best because of its association with a dishonorable act of King David. The Ammonites had angered David because of their disrespectful reception of goodwill ambassadors that David had sent to the capital. David ordered his army to attack the town. It was during the siege that David became enamored of Bathsheba and used his prerogative as king to get rid of her husband, Uriah. David ordered Uriah to be placed in the midst of the fiercest fighting at Rabbath Ammon and Uriah was killed.

In the third century B.C. Amman came under the control of the Egyptians. Ptolemy II rebuilt the town and named it Philadelphia. Of its early history, there are almost no visible ruins. Herod took the town about 30 B.C. He swept aside the buildings then standing and fashioned in its place a typical Roman city.

The Modern City

Amman is far more interesting as a modern city than as a site of some ruins from the past. It has built so rapidly in the past fifteen years that it gives the impression of being fresh, clean, and lively. Amman is very proud of its brand new university, the first in Jordan. It is a stunning, all-white stone structure located in one of the newer sections of town. The city also boasts the finest hotel in Jordan, the Urdon. It is beautiful, a luxury hotel with a swimming pool. Amman has night clubs and must be considered the "swingingest" spot in the country.

From Jerusalem, there are two routes that lead to Amman. The direct route is the main highway, the regular Jerusalem-Amman road. Far more interesting is the longer and much slower route which turns north off the Jerusalem-Amman road to head up the Jordan Valley, then turns east to pass through es Salt and on to Amman. The road to es Salt follows a stream through a valley that is planted with crops. The latter road winds through hills that are scenic at all times of the year and in early spring indescribably beautiful.

The Magnificent Flowers

I am certain that anyone who has an interest in the Holy Land has heard that the flowers in the spring are lovely. I would go further than that and say that the Holy Land produces a yearly miracle of bloom that is breathtaking. While this miracle is enacted in many areas of the Holy Land, one of the most beautiful backgrounds for the display is the es Salt road where the hills are solid banks of wild flowers.

From May to October, these hills are brown as can be. Then, in late fall, the skies, which have not produced a drop of moisture for six months, may suddenly open and rain torrents on the land. In some areas this rainfall may measure sixteen to twenty inches. The land responds. It is amazingly fertile. The hills turn green and in every spot that holds enough dirt to support a seed or bulb, a wild flower springs to life, blooms its heart out. Thousands of tiny, tiny flowers carpet the land in a patchwork of purple and yellow. This display changes weekly as new varieties of flowers find it their turn to come to life. The blooms reach a crescendo of color in April when the reds, blues, purples, and whites of blossoms fill the hills and valleys with overwhelming beauty—a magnificent exhibit of nature's ability to upstage the best of us in garden planting.

As is true in the States, the first flower to poke through the ground in the Holy Land is the crocus. Jordan has many varieties of the crocus and they are very small. They spread their little petals almost flat on the ground and they may not measure more than an inch in diameter but they mass themselves in such quantities that they coat the ground. Later, the iris will arrive, then the tulips, buttercups, anemones, lupin, grape hyacinth, cyclamen, poppies, and many more. The hollyhock is native to Jordan and it grows like a roadside weed. It has been said disparagingly that many of the blossoms in Jordan are just weeds. True! The weeds grow because there is no spraying program to restrain them, but you should see how spectacularly dozens of varieties of thistles can brighten the landscape.

The most precious beauty among the flowers is the cyclamen. This delicate flower with its gracefully recessed, fuschia-tinged, pink petals is just about the size of an African violet blossom. The delicacy of the flower is accentuated because it is so often found in crannies of rock, or massed along fences and walls. Second in beauty is the anemone, again a delicate flower in pastel colors, white, and a brilliant red. The anemone is believed to be the "lily of the field" of the Bible and it can be repeated today that Solomon in all his glory could not match the beauty of a field of anemones.

Many persons who travel to the Holy Land like to arrange travel plans to arrive there when the weather is dry and moderately warm in May. If they were willing to risk a few showers and arrive the first of April they would be treated to a gorgeous and overly generous spring flower show. The Holy Land is strikingly beautiful at that time and more than a match for any man's idealized vision of the "Promised Land." When the show is over, it is completely over. The first day of hot sun, or the first strong sirocco wind, shrivels the flowers. The land reverts to brown. Yet it is fair to say that the land retains a certain magnificence in its more usual brown ugliness.

Whether or not the tourist can arrange to see the Holy Land when it shows its most beautiful face, he still should consider coaxing his taxi driver to drive him to Amman via the es Salt road because it is most picturesque.

The City Roads

Amman, for the tourist who is driving his own car, is a city of utter frustration. The downtown section is situated in a valley. There is one main street through the center of town. From this very busy street, you can look up to the residential areas of Amman, scattered over seven high hills. Each of these hills is served by a road that leads up to it from the downtown section, circles the hill and winds back downtown. There is no road communication between the hills themselves, and the roads in the downtown section are not well marked. I assume the natives know them well. The uninitiated, however, find themselves picking out roads leading out of the downtown section by the eeny-meeny-miney-mo method. My husband and I started several times toward what seemed to be roads leading up to the old citadel of Amman and each time we found ourselves on a different hill where we had no recourse other than to circle the hill and go back into the downtown section. The downtown section is a bottleneck, a continuous stream of automobiles and people plus a few policemen who try to keep the two apart. These policemen have the most actively strenuous job in the country. They are whirling dervishes.

Amman Antiquities

While the tourist is participating in these repetitious forced excursions through downtown Amman, he may as well look around. He may pass by one of the best preserved antiquities in the country, a huge Roman theater. The theater was built in the second or third century A.D. It had an original seating capacity of six thousand, and is directly across the street from one of Amman's leading hotels. There are other Roman ruins in Amman and if you stick with the challenge of getting to them, it is possible to find yourself eventually at the old citadel of Amman. Some stretches of the walls around the citadel date

perhaps from the eighth century B.C., the others are ascribed to
Herod's city. There is a square building calculated to date to the
Arab occupation of the sixth–eighth centuries A.D. Its use is unknown. There are ruins of a temple to Hercules that also belonged
to Herod's city.

The Museum

Beside the temple is the Jordan Museum, small, well lighted
and arranged, displaying the cream of the more recent archaeological finds in Jordan. These choice pieces are but a smattering of
the artifacts now in the museum's possession. It is hoped that
eventually a much larger museum will be built here and many
more of the historical finds of the Holy Land put on display. At
present, they rest undisturbed in storage rooms. The present
displays include the copper scrolls and benches of the script
writers from Qumran, the most curious plastered heads and a
tomb from Jericho, many clay figurines that are typical "art," of
Ammonite to Nabatean periods, some good statuary, exquisite
Roman glass, and some lovely jewelry (obviously imports as
Palestine is poor in raw materials for fine jewelry).

The Wealthier Part of Town

Wandering about the hills of Amman, you might by chance come
upon one of the beautiful residential areas, containing the homes
of the wealthier natives, the ambassadors to Jordan, and foreign
personnel working or on assignment in Jordan. The embassies
are here as well. This section of town, an eye-filling sight, may
be a preview of what all Jordan could look like, given an improved economy. The homes are all built in the Jordanian
manner, of white or soft pink stone and are most tastefully
ornamented with metal work on the doors and windows. They
are landscaped with the native flowering shrubs and vines that
seem even more colorful against the stone background.

The King's Palace

You would not *by chance* find yourself at the king's palace in
Amman. The palace complex occupies one of the hills and it is
a large estate with homes for all of the king's immediate family,
a guest house, and the palace itself which includes the king's
office, reception rooms, and a theater. Visitors are allowed to go
to the palace, but they are well screened previously by guards at
the foot of the hill. From there, they are given an escort who
will not leave their side until they are again returned to the guard
house.

While the palace and its grounds are most pleasantly landscaped with flowers, trees, and pools, the palace is not so grand
or luxurious as the word "palace" would suggest. The portion
inside that visitors are usually permitted to see is well appointed
but utilitarian. The only suggestion of luxury would be the plush
Oriental rugs. In the reception room, visitors are offered a cup of
coffee. Uniformed members of King Hussein's guard serve the
typical Bedouin coffee, the bitter beverage without sugar.

In case you, as a tourist, go to the Amman palace, I must
warn you that when you have finished the coffee, you must hand
the cup back to the gentleman who served you with a slight
wiggle-waggle of the hand. This is the customary signal that you
have had enough. Ignorant of this custom, I handed my cup to
the soldier by stretching out my hand and arm in a straight line,
whereupon the cup was immediately refilled.

Outside the palace doors, Jordanian soldiers stand at guard.
When the king is in residence, guards wear a very colorful uniform, the black and red robes and cossack hats of the Circassians.

Shopping and Customs

Shopping in downtown Amman presents a problem. You have
heard it said on television that shoppers wish that someone
would line up all the stores of like kind in one place so that

the customer would not have so much walking to do. Middle Eastern cities have followed the theory of the Yellow Pages for years. All the tinsmiths are side by side. All the goldsmiths are gathered together in one arcade. All the shops selling materials for clothing are in the same block where both sides of the street are generously draped with fabrics. In shopwindows of another block there was nothing displayed other than watches and clocks. If a person can find the section of town that he wants, shopping is easy. This lumping of like merchandise together is supposed to make it easier for the customer to compare and bargain. My husband and I compared plenty and we bargained plenty, but in the Holy Land the American stands out. Our shoes, our clothing, and our manner give us away immediately. You can see dollar signs gleaming in the merchant's eyes when an American walks into his shop, and the price is higher than it is to persons of any other nationality.

If you want to know how much more you are charged as an American than as a Jordanian, let me give you some examples. The Westerners who live in Jordan all employ native household help. The help does all the grocery shopping. The employer can easily pay his help out of his monthly savings on groceries alone.

We priced an attractive Oriental lamp in one of the shops. The quoted price to us was $60. We asked a German friend to price the same lamp. The first quoted price to him was $45. This means that the lamp is probably properly priced at around $30. We had heard it said in jest that what is sold for ten cents to the Jordanian, costs the Germans twenty-five cents, and the Americans a dollar. Perhaps that jest is not far from the truth.

We found that it was wise procedure to deal consistently with one shopkeeper. When he became acquainted with us, his prices assumed more normal proportions. If he were out of the shop momentarily, it was not advisable to try to deal with his employees. They would put the prices back up. If we told them that we had paid less on a previous occasion, the assistants would exclaim that we had indeed been favored—the shopkeeper had made for us a "very special price." This is nonsense. One druggist's assistant tried to charge me $3 for a $1 lipstick refill; $5 for a $2 can of hair spray. The Westerner calls this downright cheating. The Easterner calls it cunning and is proud when he can better his adversary.

I was amused to read a very up-to-date description of shopping in Eastern countries in the 1912 Baedeker *Guide to Palestine and Syria,* "As Orientals attach no value whatever to their time, the transaction of business is always a long and tedious process. Unless the purchaser is prepared to pay whatever is asked, he will have to exercise the greatest possible patience. As a rule, a much higher price is demanded than will ultimately be accepted, and bargaining is therefore the universal custom. This is emphatically the case in making purchases in the Bazaars. As the trades and handicrafts of the same kind are generally congregated together in the same quarter of the street . . . it is an easy matter for the traveller to move on to the next dealer when he thinks he is being treated unfairly. If the purchaser knows the proper price of the goods beforehand, he offers it to the seller who will probably remark 'it is little' but will nevertheless sell the goods. A favorite expression of the Oriental shopkeepers is 'take it for nothing' which is, of course, no more meant to be taken literally than the well known 'my house is thy house.'"

True. Every word. The straightforward "fixed price" mentality of the Westerner runs into a formidable obstacle in the Oriental bazaars. The exasperating process of bargaining at length is still practiced in Jordan. It is a pleasure to the Easterner, and the tourist who will not "play the game" actually insults the shopkeeper. If the tourist simply pays the first price asked, the shopkeeper regards the customer as a fool.

Most shopkeepers run a leisurely business. Their shops are not so packed with customers that they must run an assembly line to the cash register. They enjoy trying to outwit you. This is a part of their culture, but as a customer, you are a guest in the shop, and you may spend the greater part of the day there if you wish. Not long after you enter the shop, the shopkeeper will send out for coffee for you. Until the coffee comes and you have drunk it, you are a captive audience. The owner will show you all his merchandise, tell you about his country. If you can relax and enjoy it, you will have a great time shopping. Once you have accepted the coffee (which has actually been forced on you) you may feel obligated to make a purchase of some kind. Do not make the mistake of worrying whether your bargaining might cheat the merchant of profit he needs. Your bargaining is merely a method of establishing what is the correct asking price for any piece of merchandise. If you do not pay the "going rate" you will not walk out of the shop with the goods.

One of the frustrations of tourists is to return to the hotel with an armload of purchases and find from checking with other tourists that the price paid was too high. If it is possible, forget it. We Westerners are in no way a match for the Eastern merchants. You *will* be overcharged. Perhaps it is best to accept the fact beforehand, put it out of your mind, and refuse to let it spoil your fun.

You do not need to make a large purchase to waste your money. The price of a pack of cigarettes, a bottle of wine, a bar of soap, a candy bar will be higher for you than for an Arab. On necessities, find out in advance the proper price. Hand it to the shopkeeper and he will take it. If you ask the price, it is bound to be higher and you will be letting yourself in for an argument. If the merchandise has a price tag, the numbers will be in Arabic—not too helpful to Americans. You will never see items marked "on sale." In fact, Eastern merchants use an opposite tactic from Americans. If business is bad, the merchant will not reduce prices to move his merchandise, but rather put the price up and try to make a whole day's profit on one customer.

What are the typical items for which the tourist may haggle with the shopkeeper? Jordanian shops are filled with shellwork, wood inlay, and carved wood articles. Bibles with olivewood covers are very common. The carefully carved Nativity scenes in olivewood are expensive ($100 to $200). Many women like the embroidery work. You may buy just the embroidered pieces or native dresses. While the Holy Land offers a plethora of jewelry in combinations of brass, copper, silver, and semi-precious stones, it is the gold that is the best buy. Jerusalem shops, particularly, are well stocked with gold jewelry. It is expensive, but a bargain compared to the standard price in America.

In modern Jerusalem, the shops will rather proudly exclaim that they are "modern"—they have fixed prices. Translation: the prices have been set for the tourist trade. If the tourist laments that he yearns to own this lovely article but cannot pay quite so much, coffee will be sent for and the bargaining will begin.

The Customs Office

My husband and I had occasion to go to one of the customs buildings in Amman to straighten out a matter of possible duty on our automobile. Since we were tourists, it was necessary to learn about government regulations that require that a car be taken out of the country every three months or be subject to 100 per cent duty. The customs office is a very busy place, or at least it was the day we arrived. The courtyard was filled with Arabs, sitting and chatting, waiting for some affair to be settled. As we approached the doorway, our interpreter started into the building first. As he crossed the threshold, a soldier barred his entry momentarily during which time the man was thoroughly frisked from shoulder to toe. I was next in line. My eyebrows must have shot up almost to my hairline. I stood stock still, musing on how a lady handles herself in such a situation. The soldier stepped aside and motioned me through the door. Whew!

Inside, the whole first floor lobby was packed with Arabs sitting cross-legged on the floor passing their waiting time in spirited conversation. We picked our way among them and went upstairs to one of the offices. The customs official we met had stacks and stacks and stacks of papers on his desk. He greeted us courteously and offered us a chair. It was fascinating to watch the work going on in this office. Stack at a time, the official went through the papers, affixing a signature to some, or whamming down a stamp on others. (The Arabs never just press a stamp to a document. I believe they are fond of more muscular activity. They *wham* it down.) At any rate, when a stack had been inspected, the official rang for a boy who would pick it up and carry it to another office. While he was carrying it out, other boys brought more stacks in. How this custom official ever understood all that he was doing is a mystery. This almost frenzied sorting of papers, interrupted by telephone sessions, went on at a lively pace for fully an hour.

On this occasion, as well as many others, we noticed that the Arabs do not place full confidence in the ability of the telephone to carry the voice. To help the phone along, the Arabs make sure the voice has enough volume to carry by itself. If a long distance call is in progress, all conversation in the room is impossible.

We did transact our business satisfactorily. Our interpreter was wise enough to follow our papers around (probably hidden in one of those stacks) from room to room until they eventually came back to us.

I suppose it is true in almost every country, if you want to see interesting byplay, watch the merchants deal with the customs officials. Person after person enters the office, presents his case in his most engaging and charming manner while the customs official sits woodenly behind the desk, quietly but firmly shaking his head, no. You needn't understand the language.

We saw one other interesting bit of byplay with the customs, but that occurred at a border crossing. Three men in a car stopped for customs inspection. The official hauled out of the trunk of their car several suitcases packed with brand new clothing. Each of the men was wearing brand new clothing that included uncreased and unwrinkled suede jackets. The customs official backed off from the trio and looked at them, obviously perplexed about what to do about this bunch of customs cheaters. It seemed to be obvious that here were three merchants who were trying to bring into the country a supply of clothing to sell, but they attempted to pass it by customs as their own wardrobes.

The official finally decided how to teach them a lesson. He emptied the three bags out into the dirt. Then he stepped around on the clothes to get them good and soiled, tossed them back into the trunk, and waved the men across the border.

Reconstruction of Jerash

If the tourist has not become thoroughly saturated with viewing the imprints of Roman culture throughout Europe and the Middle East, he will have a rare treat in Jordan when he visits the ruins of Jerash, north of Amman. When the Romans controlled the rich caravan route from the inland deserts to the Mediterranean, they constructed ten marvelous cities along the route and these cities are referred to as the Decapolis.

One was located at Jerash. The place first conquered for the Romans by Pompey in 63 B.C. and for almost three hundred years it stood as a majestic Roman city. (Jerash is considered one of the finest examples of Roman building and city planning to be seen anywhere.) The town was devastated by an earthquake in 746, but one of the entrances into the city is still preserved. It was a triple arch or city gate erected in the honor of a visit by the Emperor Hadrian in 129. Just outside the gate there was a huge hippodrome. Inside the city were the usual forum, baths, theaters, and public buildings. In Jerash many of the tumbled ruins were not carted away to make building stones for more modern buildings. Most of them lay as they had fallen. This made possible a reconstruction of the city that is now assuming gigantic proportions.

One of the theaters has been beautifully reconstructed to seat six thousand spectators again. There is a tremendous temple to Zeus, the fallen columns of which appear to be second in size only to those found at Baalbek in Lebanon. From this temple, the visitor can look down over a unique oval forum, almost enclosed by the fifty-six Ionic columns still standing. Leading off from the forum is a colonnaded street that runs the length of the city north to south. At the cross roads, where an east-west road cuts through the town, tetrapylons are still in place. As you walk along these streets, you can discern shops with watermains beneath them, a nymphaeum with fountains, a temple to Artemis. This latter temple is also going to be a beauty when it is reconstructed. A very large stairway led up to it from the street.

Jerash also has many old Christian churches. It was here that our study group discovered a baptistry, certainly one of the earliest in Christian history and obviously far too small for bodily immersion. A person could get his feet into it perhaps. The non-Baptists among us delighted to call this discovery to the attention of our Baptist friends, who "hmmmmd" at it but did not care to make a statement. There are also in the Holy Land many possible baptistries large enough to hold a dozen men, but to my memory, none but the small variety is found inside churches.

The Department of Antiquities has built a new rest house at Jerash for the comfort of tourists. There is also a small restaurant at the entrance to the ruins. This older restaurant has an outdoor patio covered by latticed wood. Where there are no trees for shade, the latticework thickly covered by vines offers effective shelter from the sun. It was our custom to seek out these small native restaurants for lunch for they have an atmosphere that is cheering and cozy. We did not eat the food offered by the restaurants. We always had our lunch with us—sandwiches, fruit, hard-boiled eggs, foods that would not spoil. Our only purchase from the proprietor was something to drink. We were never made to feel in Jordan that it was in any way insulting to a restaurateur to have the customer bring his own lunch. We were always warmly welcomed, gladly given table space and further service if we wished it. On one occasion when we requested permission to use a table in a restaurant that was closed because of cold weather, the proprietor brought us water, the only thing he had to offer at the moment as hospitality. The kindness and courtesy of all Jordanians in welcoming the guest, customer or not, is *fabulous*.

Gadara or Um Qeis

North of Jerash there are several more cities of the Decapolis. The ten cities founded to protect Rome's interest in the trade route were located in an area stretching from the Sea of Galilee to Amman. None of these more northerly cities is excavated. One of them is associated with the New Testament story of Jesus' healing of the demoniac. This is Gadara, now called Um Qeis. To reach Gadara the tourist must pass the sites of three other Decapolis cities, Husn, Irbid, and Beit Ras. There is nothing ancient to be seen in Husn or Irbid. In Beit Ras not much is left intact of the Roman city, but it is genuinely amusing to see, built into modern structures, stones that were cut and carved by the Romans. The same phenomenon can be seen elsewhere in the Holy Land. The tourist may spot a stone bearing a Christian symbol taken from a Byzantine church built into the side of a Beit Ras house, or a door lintel from an old church, now proudly standing over the threshold of a small Arab home.

At Um Qeis, the tourist can clearly see evidence of the Romans. There is a fine theater with stone chairs shaped to fit the seated figure; a lovely female statue still sits in the front row among the ruins, propped in place by two theater chairs as if she were waiting for the actors to come on stage. Unfortunately, she has no head. Elsewhere in Um Qeis, tourists can follow the path of the main Roman road through town. Fallen columns lie by the roadside. Remains of what appear to be church sanctuaries, and of a smaller theater are on the outskirts of town. We know from historical records that Um Qeis (Pliny's Gadara) at one time had a university, but today it is a poor town of friendly people.

Um Qeis is located on a high spur of ground overlooking the Yarmuk Valley and the Sea of Galilee beyond to the northwest. The view here on a clear day is nothing short of magnificent. It is a rather dramatic spot from the standpoint of both ancient and present-day history, for it was near here that Jesus drove the unclean spirits from the demoniac into a group of swine on the hillside, whereupon the swine ran wildly into the Sea of Galilee and drowned themselves. Today when you stand on the hill at Um Qeis, you see the Sea of Galilee nearby, but altogether in Israel. You see the Yarmuk River, site of the Arabs' water irrigation project. You know that the Arabs and Jews seem to find it necessary to shoot at each other from time to time, and it is in areas just like this, where the borders are in dispute, that flaring tempers cause such unrest in the Middle East.

Ghost Town

From Um Qeis, where Jordan receives its maximum rainfall and the surrounding countryside shows it in a stand of grass and trees, the tourist may travel east along the northern border road of Jordan and in less than an hour reach the edge of the desert where there is practically no rainfall. Is there anything to see here in the desert? Let us say there is much more to see than would be imagined.

Not too far into the desert is a very large ghost town. Its outline looms against the sky as though it was still standing, and in truth, a great part of it does still stand. The rest, however, is piled up in mounds of stone on the ground. It does not appear that the desert dwellers have carried away much building stone —perhaps if someone had the patience, strength, and time this town could be reassembled as it once was.

Um Jimal, this gray-black desolate town, built of black basalt rock, was founded by the Nabateans in the first century B.C. It was a watering spot, a respite for caravans on their long route to Damascus. There being no water from springs in the area, Um Jimal had house cisterns and a very large city cistern to collect winter rains. In the second century A.D. the Romans took over the city. Archaeologists suspect that Um Jimal became a religious center in ensuing years because there are remains of at least fifteen Byzantine churches. Um Jimal was abandoned during the eighth and ninth centuries.

Um Jimal is fascinating to visit. It is so deserted, yet so intact, that the tourist feels he has stumbled on a great city that has recently been the scene of a disaster. It is a huge town. No other ruin I saw looked anything like it. The doors that swing open and closed are made entirely of the dark basalt rock, as are the roofs. In many of the buildings and houses the roofs and upper stories were supported by a series of slender rectangular stones set at an angle into the walls of the structure. This method is called "corbeling" and you may be quite familiar with it. I saw it only here at Um Jimal.

Visitors can walk the town for hours, picking out houses and churches, studying Christian symbols cut into the stone, looking at inscriptions. They can walk the town for hours, that is, if they do not first break an ankle by slipping on the ever-present building stones strewn helter-skelter beneath their feet. My wild desire was to start piling the stones back into place on the walls so that I could search the ground for other evidences of the people who once lived here. I'm sure others have had the same desire but were deterred as I was by the thought of how many tons of stone one would have to move before bare ground was visible. The walls of buildings that still stand appear to be pretty much on the same level as when built. It is probable that some sand covering has blown in over the years, but it is apparently not too deep.

Um Jimal has long been used by poor Bedouins. The walls still standing in the town make excellent shelters and the Bedouins pitch their tents against them. In cold weather the town is so well filled with Bedouins that the sightseer must take care least he invade their privacy. In warmer weather, the Bedouins take their tents outside to catch the breezes. They are drawn to this location both for shelter and because a few of the cisterns still give them a supply of water.

A small Bedouin girl approached me with a handful of coins. In such a location the tourist can be pretty certain that the coins are authentic, and the children have little to do except search for them in among the stones. I bought a handful at a fair price. Apparently, the word got around town because as I was leaving the site a young Bedouin man ran up to me excitedly with a most "unusual coin." I could well believe that he felt he had an unusual coin, one which he did not recognize at all. It was a twentieth-century Indian coin bearing a likeness of the Emperor of India, the King of England. It was certainly in far better condition than any other coin he had found at Um Jimal —if worthless as an antiquity.

Night in the Desert

My husband and I had the good fortune to go farther into the desert on this northern road—to travel through it to Iraq and eventually on to Iran. After we left the last Jordanian outpost and had checked out of the country officially, there was still a considerable territory of Jordan to cross. (We had elected to travel the desert at night as most persons do.)

As luck would have it, we saw the desert under a full moon. It was perfectly beautiful. The moon shone so brightly it seemed more like twilight, and we could see for miles across the flat land. Occasionally, we saw a fox chasing what he hoped would be an evening meal. I saw one hyena; it was not close to us but the animal is easily recognized because of its skulking stance.

After the moon went down, the desert was pretty dark. We could see the road in our headlights, and we amused ourselves by watching the sprightly desert rats scamper across the road in front of our car. These rats have quite a bit of character and personality. They stand upright with their little paws held high and run on their two hind legs. They have a perfectly erect tail with a crook at the end of it. They seemed to be playing a game with us momentarily standing on the side of the road, then scurrying at top speed to the other side of the road. They always won! We didn't hit any.

After a few hours of this, I turned to my companions in the

front seat and mentioned that I was glad to have two other persons with me. If by any chance I saw anything other than rats and cats in this isolated desert, I wanted a witness to assure me that I was not having hallucinations. I had hardly uttered the words when down the road strolled a slim, young Bedouin entirely dressed in white. I turned to one companion. "Did you see him?" The answer, "Yes." Then, to the other companion, "Did you see him?" Again, "Yes." Where on earth this man was going was beyond our comprehension. We were a hundred miles from anywhere. We had to assume that walking travelers also take advantage of the cool evenings.

A little farther down the road, we saw camels bedded down with their packs beside the roadway. Their riders were nestled close to the animals. Beyond, we came upon a group of donkeys, sound asleep, standing across the road. We stopped, honked our horn, flashed our lights, honked our horn. Not one donkey moved a muscle. We never did waken those donkeys. They stood right on the road with their eyes closed. Rather than nudge them with the car and perhaps risk damage to the car, we backed and went off the road to get around them.

There are small check posts where the traveler must stop and report as he crosses the desert. One soldier tried hard to make us understand that we must make our next stop at what sounded to us like "Atchfor." We really puzzled over this information. There was no town ahead by that name. One of the brighter members of our party came up with the correct answer. The soldier was simply trying to tell us that the next post on the road where we had to report was "H-4."

These stops are not too easy to find, since they are usually small buildings dimly lit by a kerosene lamp. One time we found ourselves trying hard to report in to what turned out to be a sleeping family. We left in a hurry when the family dog awakened. Dogs in Jordan are not to be fooled with. They are not pets. They are wild dogs taken in and fed by families for protection. They are a protection for certain. If you try to pet one of these fellows, he just might take your arm off.

Cats, too, in Jordan are not cozy little house pals. They are hunters, and they rarely purr. Goodness knows there is plenty for them to hunt, since rodents comprise the greatest animal population in Jordan. Cats of the domestic variety run wild, and it seemed that we saw almost as many roaming cats on the desert as we saw busy, scampering rats.

We had been warned more than once by others who had made this desert trip that the Iraqi border was not well marked and was easy to miss. There were three of us in our car sufficiently awake to watch carefully for it. We almost missed it. If we had crossed the border and had gone sailing on into Iraq, we could naturally be suspected of entering the country illegally for motives other than wholesome. We were driving right along when we noticed a couple of old oil barrels on the road. As we slowed to circumvent them, a soldier came running at us with his arms waving above his head. He was the border guard. Sure enough, when we looked more closely at a dark building somewhat off the road, we could see that the building had a kerosene lamp inside and when our eyes were more accustomed to the dark, we could just make out on the side of the building painted in large letters the word IRAQ.

On our return trip across the desert we were flagged down by some other travelers who had run out of gas. We let them siphon some out of our tank. Apparently the siphon is standard equipment for travelers. When we reached Jordan, we thought we might not have enough gas to make it home. It was three o'clock in the morning. We drove to the gas station at Mafraq which we had been assured was attended day and night. Attended it was, by a sleeping guard. When we awakened him, he came out to the car in his pajamas to deliver the unwelcome news that he was a watchman. The owner with the key to the pump would not be around until six in the morning. Probably all the way to Jerusalem no gas would be available. This is a problem the tourist should be aware of. It is really a good precaution to carry a can or two of extra gas in your automobile.

On two occasions we stopped for gas in the daytime only to be waved away by an attendant who shouted to us that he would not have gas until the next day. In outlying areas, one station may serve a very large district.

The Mosaic of Madaba

A pleasant trip that just about fills a morning takes tourists from Amman south to see a floor mosaic that, when complete, was a map of the Holy Land and the promontory which tradition suggests was the site from which Moses viewed the Holy Land.

The town of Madaba is a pleasant and interesting place. As the central area has been built on the top and slopes of the old tell, modern Madaba is held aloft by ancestor cities of the same name. The city appears on the flat landscape like a little peaked triangle filled with houses. The town has some biblical history but it is not particularly distinguished.

Madaba is mentioned in the books of Numbers and in Joshua. The tower was captured and occupied by the Maccabeans (165 B.C.) and handed over to the Nabateans as a token of appreciation for their military assistance. Probably the finest period for Madaba was when it became yet another stately Roman city.

The town has not been excavated, however, and the Roman buildings are not in evidence. The fame of Madaba rests on its collection of mosaic floors, some now in private homes and one in a modern Greek church. The most important mosaic, believed to date from the sixth century A.D., the time of Justinian, is a map of Palestine. This is the earliest known map of the Holy Land still in existence and as such is accepted as the best authority in the sixth century for the location of traditional biblical sites.

The map represents an amazing artistic achievement, a pictorial view of the entire country. Fish swim in the Jordan River. Palm trees grow where they would have flourished, wild life abounds in those areas that would have supported it. The names of cities are spelled out in Greek by the tesserae. Towns are represented by reproductions of houses and shrines—reproductions so faithful that the houses and shrines can be identified. The town of Jerusalem is shown as a walled city. The Damascus Gate is pictured. Two streets through Jerusalem show that they were lined with columns. In residential sections, small houses crowd one another. The houses are executed in a manner similar to the artwork of a five-year-old—they are little, roofed faces with two eyes (windows) and a gaping mouth (front door). The Holy Sepulcher shows its triple door entrance, its rectangular shape, and its dome over the rotunda. The tesserae of the mosaic have retained their vivid colors—reds, yellows, greens, blues.

Mount Nebo

Mount Nebo is a short distance northwest of Madaba. In the Bible we are told that Moses saw the Promised Land from this vantage point, and died and was buried not far off. There are ruins of a church and an ancient monastery on the site today. Following clues from a few letters of pilgrims who visited the Holy Land from A.D. 394 to 1564, an excavation was undertaken. The buildings, just as described by the pilgrims, were uncovered. The church is now being reconstructed insofar as possible from the building stones found at the site. It is small, with a double row of columns leading to the chancel, and steps leading up to the altar. Portions of the floor are covered with mosaics still in fine condition. Many of the artifacts uncovered by the excavation are stored in a work building on the site.

It is a privilege to stand on Mount Nebo and look over the Jordan Valley as Moses did so long ago. The tourist can scrutinize the scene dispassionately from a new tourist department patio. To Moses, sighting the Jordan Valley meant that an old, old man could lay down his head and rest. The task that had demanded of him superhuman physical stamina, superhuman spiritual strength, superhuman leadership throughout his adult years was finished.

The Moabite Stone

Both Nebo and Madaba are mentioned in a source other than
the Bible. This source, found many years ago, must be considered
as one of the more exciting finds in the Holy Land. It is the
Moabite Stone, a stele that contains an enemy's account of
warfare with the Israelites.

In II Kings, the Bible tells us that the Israelites, under Ahab,
were bothered by rebellions in Moab. Armies set out to put the
rebels down but were forced to discontinue when the leader of
the rebellion, Mesha, sacrificed his son to his god, Chemosh.
Just why this act forced the Israelites to retire from the battle is
not explained. So went the Israelite account.

Now we have another version of what happened during the
Moabite rebellion by Mesha himself. A vain king, apparently,
Mesha had imprinted on his gravestone a record of his accom-
plishments during his reign. His stele, the Moabite Stone, was
discovered late in the last century at Dhibon, a city south of
Madaba. Natives found the stone, still intact, and hurried with
the news to a scholar who, they thought, might buy the stone for
a good price. The scholar traveled to Dhibon, studied the stone,
very wisely took a pressing of it, then sped away to obtain money
to buy the stone. In his absence, the finders had second thoughts
about the sale. How could they realize the most money? To them
the answer seemed simple. Rather than argue among themselves
about apportioning the money from the sale of one large stone,
they would break the stone and every man take a piece and
bargain for his own share. The scholar returned to find that this
calamity had happened. The Moabite Stone was not only in
pieces—pieces of it were lost.

All of the stele that was recovered was pieced together; the
original stone thus mended is now in the Louvre. From the
pressing, the message on the stone could be translated. It was
a choice and pertinent comment on the story of II Kings. In
essence, the Moabite version of the story went like this: I am

Mesha, son of Chemosh, king of Moab, who made this high place for Chemosh because he enabled me to triumph over my enemies. Omri, king of Israel, had long oppressed Moab and his son followed in the same practices. I triumphed over him and Israel is destroyed forever. Omri took Madaba, but Chemosh restored it to me. (Mesha then names the cities he built and for which he built reservoirs. He names the cities he captured and adds that he slew most of the people living in them. One of these cities was Nebo where Mesha claims to have slain seven thousand and to have taken the objects of Yahweh worship and laid them at the altar of Chemosh.)

The town of Nebo mentioned by Mesha is south of Mount Nebo. Nebo, like Madaba, possesses famous floor mosaics.

The city of Dhibon where Mesha's stele was found has recently been re-excavated and its masonry may be of some interest to tourists.

A Modern Arab Girl

Many ancient cities in this area of the Holy Land have been deserted for years. They rise like bumps on the sandy plateau or sit in a field of wheat. The only signs of life anywhere near are a few scattered small homes. In one of those quiet spots, Hesbon, off the main road, we did some surface sharding. My husband and I were returning to our car when we heard footsteps coming toward us from the side of the tell. When the person came into view, it turned out to be a girl who could have stepped out of a page of *Mademoiselle* magazine. She was wearing a short, full skirt, a blouse, and a pink leather jacket. She had on silk stockings and high heels, and her hair was arranged on her head in one of the bouffant styles. She greeted us in English. Who was she? What was she doing here?

She *lived* here. She was a young educated Arab woman who lived in one of these small homes with her family while she taught the local one-room school. She was now dressed to go into Amman for the day. A taxi was to pick her up any minute. Her command of English was quite good. The taxi being a bit late, we had a chance to talk with her for a short time and to be introduced to her father. He was straight off the desert, a kindly man, but a typical native fingering his worry beads. He spoke not a word of English but watched us intently while his daughter explained to him what we were doing and beamed fondly at her while she conversed with us in our language. Somehow, this typical Jordanian had raised a most atypical daughter.

Kerak Crusader Castle

Just south of Dhibon the tourist may head down into one of the more awesome gorges in the Holy Land. It is called the Wadi Mojib and boasts vital statistics of a two and one-half mile width at the top and a depth of well over one thousand feet. While the road from the top down to the river at the bottom is steep and winding, it is not overly difficult to negotiate except in the rainy season when washouts occur. Natives hop on buses and travel this road daily on their way to Amman. Along the way tourists may watch for remains of Roman roads, milestones, and bridges.

Kerak, a biblical town known to have been inhabited from about 1200 B.C., but more famous for its Crusader castle, is about thirty miles beyond the wadi.

The castle, now cleared of debris and easily examined, is typical of the impressive Crusader architecture. It is a collection of long, dark, stone-vaulted rooms, lighted mainly by slits from which arrows could be sped against possible invaders. In retrospect, when we consider how tenuous was the hold of the Crusaders on the Holy Land, this type of massive building seems terribly impressive. On the west of the castle, there is a sheer drop that the Crusaders envisioned and used as a handy spot for the execution of captured enemies.

For the tourist today, the Kerak castle offers a beautiful view from its high perch overlooking a large area including the Dead Sea. To make Kerak more accessible to tourists, a guest house is being built there with restaurant and overnight facilities.

The Bedouins

As you drive out from Amman south into the desert areas, you begin to see the tent dwellers, the Bedouins, at one time the aristocrats of the Middle East. To many Westerners, the tent dweller is a fly-by-night, unreliable human being, a gypsy, who will steal anything that is not nailed down. In the Holy Land, that image of the tent dweller is completely erroneous; it is contrary to the facts.

The Bedouins who live in black goatskin tents, sometimes singly, sometimes in groups numbering up to hundreds of tents, are continuing in a time-honored culture that is in many ways more civilized than our own Western culture. These nomads, the livestock dealers of the land, count their wealth in sheep, goats, and camels. They are not aimless wanderers. They live in an orderly fashion, dwelling within prescribed regions that have been traditionally known as "belonging" to their particular tribe. The tribes need large areas of land so that they can move within their own areas to provide for themselves fresh grazing ground, proximity to water in summer, sheltered places against winter winds, and breezes to assuage the summer sun. Each Bedouin tribe knows its own land and will defend it. Each knows its own water supply and will defend it. Water arising within the domain of one tribe is considered the property of the original owner. It will be shared, but it cannot be taken. Because water can at times be in short supply, a tribe's right to its water is absolutely inviolate. (This very old "law" of the land has some implications in the political dispute in the Arab countries today. Since the head waters of the Jordan River arise in Lebanon and Syria, the Arabs dispute the right of Israel to pump the water to Israeli fields and desert regions.) In times of water shortage, it is not unusual for a tribe to ask for charity in sharing water with a neighboring tribe that has been more blessed. This help is not refused. All Bedouins have felt the agony of enduring without water the intense summer heat.

The Bedouins are very independent and very, very proud. Certainly in adjusting to the desert climate, they have proved that they have physical endurance considerably beyond the strength of most of us. This pride causes the Bedouin to look down on the *fellahin*. The two groups do not mingle, nor do they inter- marry. We have mentioned that the Bedouins consider themselves the aristocrats of the land. King Hussein is very proud of his Bedouin background. In his book he mentions that one of the fondest memories of his youth came from those occasions when his grandfather took him along to visit in the desert tents.

Responsibilities of the Sheiks

Because it is not easy to stay alive on the desert, the Bedouins have developed a code of living that has been passed down by tradition for many, many generations. This code has never had to be written out. Every Bedouin is raised on it, and he adheres to it. You may notice that in many respects the Bedouin traditions have laid the background for the entire Middle Eastern culture.

A man's first loyalty is to his tribe. He is expected to consider first not his own welfare, but that of his tribe. He accepts the authority of the sheik, the wisest man of the tribe. The sheik may have inherited his position of leadership, or he may have been chosen because he had the quality of superior leader- ship. If he was chosen, he is apt to have an aura of "luck" associated with his life that gives confidence to his people. He must have courage, for in a very large tribe there may be several "tribunals of justice." One sheik may give judgments in matters involving land; another, camels, etc. There is always one head sheik whose word will be the final authority and accepted as such if disputes do not seem to be satisfactorily settled earlier.

In small tribes, or in tribes that include only one family, the patriarch, the grandfather, will hold authority over all his progeny.

The sheik provides for all his tribe, seeing that they have material goods, money, food, and especially meat for feasts. He is responsible for any offenses committed by any member of the tribe. If one of his clan steals, the sheik will seek out the guilty party and see that the victim of the offense is compensated or given satisfaction. Formerly, it was the practice to seek out the guilty one by casting lots. (This tribal custom is also found in Old Testament law. Joshua was following this tradition when he sought out and punished Achan in Josh. 7.) Any offense committed by a member of a tribe is considered a disgrace to the *entire* tribe and not a black mark against just one individual.

In the past, it was a practice to cut off the hand of a thief. Since we personally saw no handless people in the Holy Land, it may be that this severe punishment is no longer used or that thievery has become all but non-existent because of the known punishment.

It is certainly true that punishment is responsible for the fact that there are no illegitimate children in Jordan. This offense is punished by death to both parties involved, and has practically eliminated familiarity between the sexes except in marriage. In order to eliminate temptation, girls are isolated from friendship with the opposite sex until they are given in marriage. You will never see a young girl being courted by a youth as she spends her day tending flocks.

Hospitality

The Arabs are known the world over for gracious hospitality. This custom comes from the Bedouins. Hospitality is so important to desert dwellers that if a sheik does not conform to the tradition, his neighbors will look down on him as unworthy. There are rules that have been passed down through the generations about the proper way to treat a guest. If a visitor comes to your tent, you, as the sheik, are obligated to entertain him for three days. It is not allowed to ask the visitor his name, nor is it allowed to ask him to leave before three days have passed. It is possible that this guest has come to the tent to seek protection from an enemy. If this is the case, during the three-day stay the host is obligated to guarantee his safety, even at the cost of the host's life. (For an interesting comparison read Genesis 18 and 19.) If, perchance, the guest is an enemy of the sheik, the same rule of hospitality must apply. When the three days are up, the guest must leave, and he is on his own.

What *would* happen, do you suppose, if a sheik surmised during a three-day visit that he was befriending an enemy who merited death at the hands of the host? Would the host be obliged to give him a sporting, ten-minute headstart at the termination of his visit? Would the guest, under the circumstances, sneak out of the tent during the night? Would the host allow him to steal away, or would he post a guard outside the sleeping quarters of the guest? Unfortunately, however interesting the possibilities, I have no answers to this situation.

The host is expected to feed his guest well. If he finds his larder embarrassingly empty, he is allowed to steal a sheep from his neighbor. This resort can be taken only in an emergency. A man cannot steal a sheep because he is expecting company, but if he has a hungry guest inside the tent, the host *must* feed him. If it has been necessary to take a sheep, he sends word to the owner that this act has been committed. The taker is bound to compensate the owner of the sheep within four days or pay fourfold. The taker is not allowed to steal a ram, and if the women of the neighboring tent or tribe have a pet sheep, it too cannot be taken. So, watching carefully to see that he does not break any rules, the host may bring home a sheep, and the guest will be treated to a feast. He will be made most welcome and will not be shown even by the slightest hint that his visit has caused any inconvenience. The guest will accept all marvelous hospitality and will, in turn, be ready to reciprocate to any stranger who presents himself at his tent.

Traditions

Each Bedouin tribe has its individual traditions. Since each considers its own customs superior to those of other tribes, the Bedouin father will look first within his own tribe to find a husband for his daughters. His brother's sons will be the most likely candidates. This intratribal marriage serves two good purposes: the bride's dowry is kept within the tribe, and the loyalty of the daughter to her father can remain the same except in unusual circumstances when a father and his brother have a serious misunderstanding. Bedouin girls, by the way, are seldom veiled. They wear black headdresses however, and if they have been taught to be very modest, they will turn their back to avoid showing their faces to a male. Sometimes they will pull their headdresses over their faces. Some of the women use the strings of coins from the dowry as a sort of veil. The girls are quite protected by male members of their tribe; in fact, the tribe looks after *all* its members both to give aid and protection to them and to take responsibility for any breach of good conduct by those members toward others.

A Bedouin hates to borrow. If a man has money, he will eat; otherwise, he will try to exist on whatever meager supplies he has. He will be patient as long as he can physically afford to be patient because he knows that he will never starve. His fellow friends of the desert will look after him in an emergency. It is against the code of the desert ever to borrow another man's horse, sword, or rifle, his wife, or his seal with which official documents are signed.

The Bedouins do not invest in clothing. Most of them have one outfit at a time, and if they are poor, they wear it until it falls off (or, as one might suspect, until it walks away).

Raiding and Revenge

According to desert code, a Bedouin is allowed to kill under three circumstances: he is expected to seek revenge if any member of his family has been murdered; he is expected to avenge the honor of his women and to rid his household of any unchaste women; he is expected to defend his fatherland.

In the past there were some nasty feuds between tribes resulting from the practice of seeking blood revenge. If a man has committed a criminal offense against a member of another tribe, the offended tribe will consider all the offender's male relatives equally guilty of this crime. This would include father, brothers, uncles, and sons. The offended tribe might well take the son of the criminal and kill him to satisfy their need for revenge. If this is not considered fair by the original offender, he and his male relatives might shoot the brother of the man who killed their son. This, in turn, would lead to further killings. The ultimate settlement of such an affair would probably be a meeting between the sheiks of the two tribes who would reach a mutual agreement involving a gift of livestock. Revenge is a deadly serious business in the Bedouin community, and the Arab who would not exact his revenge would be scorned by his peers. He would have lost face, and to lose face is anathema to any Arab.

Also in the past, Bedouin tribes indulged in raiding neighborhood tribes. Call this a grown man's game if you wish, but it was an accepted practice. The object of the raid was to capture a neighbor's livestock. (Women were not considered fair game in a raid. They were not to be touched.) Summer was the raiding season since, because of the necessity to be near a water source, an enemy tribe always knew approximately where to find its prey. After a raid, the victim had to rally forces within his own tribe and make plans for a retaliation. In Jordan today, raiding is passé and warfare is no longer engaged in by the tribes as the practice has been outlawed.

Since raiding was the job of the men and since men had, in addition, to be warriors in case of an invasion of the inland, they were considered the protectors of the family, the traders of livestock, and not required to do any other work. (Some men were willing to milk the camels since these cantankerous animals are considered dangerous.) The division of labor between male and female continues today. The Bedouin woman works very hard. She makes the tent of closely woven goats' hair (it sheds water), she pitches the tent, she probably weaves the material for clothing, she tends the herds, she cooks the meals, she gathers firewood, she gathers water, she tends the children. It is a part of the culture of the land that the Middle Eastern woman works very, very hard. She waits on her man.

Marriage

A wedding is a very happy occasion for the whole tribe, who feast and celebrate until the marriage is consummated. After proof of consummation has been exhibited to the wedding guests, all the guests return home happy. How is such an exhibition accomplished? Following what was apparently also an old biblical custom, the groom displays to his relatives the sheet of the marriage bed. To enable the bride to give proof of her virginity, it is customary for the mother-in-law to give evidence of her good faith in the new daughter by presenting her with a chicken head before the bride retires to the bridal chamber. This rather earthy custom, which Westerners would consider an invasion of privacy, is casually accepted by the tribes. The virginity of the bride is a matter of concern to the whole tribe.

In some Bedouin tribes it has been the custom to denude the bride of body hair before marriage. If it is available, a mixture of zinc and arsenic is used for this purpose.

Medical Practices

That phrase "if it is available" is important to remember when we consider the customs of daily living among the Bedouins. On the desert the tent dwellers had to do the best they could with what was available, and this was true of their daily diet as well as of their medical practices. In physical makeup, the Bedouins tend to be of a slight, wiry build. Certainly if one has survived to marriage age, he must have had stamina to withstand even the childhood diseases without modern medicines. In dealing with sickness, without any knowledge of medical discoveries, they experimented and used what seemed to produce satisfactory results. They learned to treat headaches by the application of leeches. Wounds were cauterized with fire. Pain was "relieved" by hot brands. Manure was the accepted poultice. Camel urine was the cure for headlice. Women who gave birth on the desert had to become philosophical about burying many of their babies, for it was not known that infection might follow such a practice as cutting the umbilical cord with a dusty stone. Some mothers, desperately trying to aid themselves with a difficult delivery, might tie a rag to the baby and attach the other end to their own foot. After the birth, the baby was rubbed with salt. In some tribes the mother, after delivery, was packed with salt and later with alum. Infant mortality was high, but the death of anyone on the desert was accepted as the will of God.

Modern Help for the Bedouins

Today, some of the Bedouins who live close to the west bank of the Jordan River are given modern medical help. Mobile clincis serve them, and certainly the message that more pleasant and effective medical methods are available must be filtering back to the more isolated Bedouins. Women bearing children must particularly enjoy having trained doctors and nurses care for them.

Many Bedouins are learning that youngsters need selected diets. Generally, they eat two meals a day, their standard diet being milk, yoghurt, dates, wheat, and meat on occasion. Clinics now offer powdered milk, protein supplements, and vitamins for youngsters. Mothers have been thrilled with the results of im- munization shots or injections of antibiotics. They are so con- vinced of the effectiveness of shots that they are disappointed if they leave the mobile clinics without one.

Mothers are discouraged from nursing their babies for an

overlong period. Boys used to be nursed until three years of age; girls until two. Since the mother's diet was insufficient, her milk could not provide the baby with adequate nourishment.

The Bedouins, who have lived in the isolation of the desert, are now broadening their horizons through the transistor radio. It is not uncommon now to see robed and *kaffied* men riding donkeys over the land and clutching in their hands brand new transistors. While the Bedouins do not have formal education, it is certain that the radio is doing for them a great educational service.

The Summing Up

If the Bedouin is to be Westernized, his culture will have to be completely destroyed. How would it be possible for the lover of the desert to confine himself to an office and an eight-hour-a-day job? How would it be possible for the Bedouin to disperse his tribe into offices all over the land and still retain a tribal loyalty? How would it be possible for the women to take a place in the Western-type business world without drawing them completely out of their chaperoned and sheltered status where sexes do not mix until after marriage? The Bedouins do not have any concept of a "proper" time for any activities. They do as they please as the mood strikes them.

One of the former officers under the British mandate, Aref el Aref, who told us many of the practices of the Bedouins in informal discussions in Jerusalem, said it was not unusual to be awakened at any hour of the night by a Bedouin with a problem on his mind. One such man called at three in the morning to pour out his heart over a grievance that proved to be of *six years'* standing.

The Bedouin treasures his freedom and leisure. He has a passion for the open air and wide spaces where he can roam at will and when he pleases. His hearth is the open fire on the desert where he can sit assembled with his Arab brothers, spinning tales. Arabs are wealthy in folklore and they are fond of using the light of past superstitions to interpret their own times. While the Bedouins are nominally Muslim, their strongest beliefs stem from their confidence in the oral tradition that has come down from the desert. They believe firmly in the evil eye that is able to curse a person or an animal, voluntarily or involuntarily. They believe that some people have abilities to see into the future and that some persons have the ability to heal. The Bedouins do not follow all the practices of the Muslim religion, but usually subscribe only to the first tenet that "there is no God but Allah and Mohammed is his prophet."

The prayer of the Bedouin is that his God, his Creator will grant him his life's needs:

a. A large tent giving shade all day where friends will come

b. A beautiful wife to cook for guests

c. Honor and no shame

d. A good mare to ride

e. A flock of sheep sufficient to serve all guests

f. Camels for milk

g. A large family

h. A pilgrimage to Mecca

i. Long life

j. Paradise

IX   Beyond the Jordan

The Way to Petra

Petra is a ghost town in Jordan. It is unique in the world. If it were necessary for the tourist to extend his time in the Holy Land for a day or so to make a trip to Petra possible, he would not regret having given this time to see one of the great wonders of this world. The usual travel arrangement is to hire a taxi to pick up your party at your Jerusalem hotel about four or five o'clock in the morning and to drive south to this old Nabatean ruin. The trip takes about four hours and you arrive just as the morning sun is sending a soft light over the ruins. (This is the best time to take pictures. Often later in the day the very intense sun will not only throw harsh shadows, it will obliterate the delicate and lovely shadings in the red rock that your eye can see so clearly.)

The drive takes you along an excellent desert road, and while many persons find the desert scenes flat and uninteresting, you can add much interest to your trip by watching for the Bedouins. You pass watering holes where goat and sheep nomads bring their flocks. You see camels, caravans, and the daily life among the tent dwellers. In addition, the railway that parallels the desert road has a long history. It once ran from Damascus to Medina, and along its famous tracks Lawrence of Arabia blew up many Turkish trains.

A car can travel only so far as the entrance to Petra. There, you must leave the taxi at the police post and proceed either on foot or on horseback. You have only about a mile to go to reach the ruins, and an interesting mile it is. When the oleanders are blooming, many of these lovely shrubs brighten the roadway leading to the *siq*.

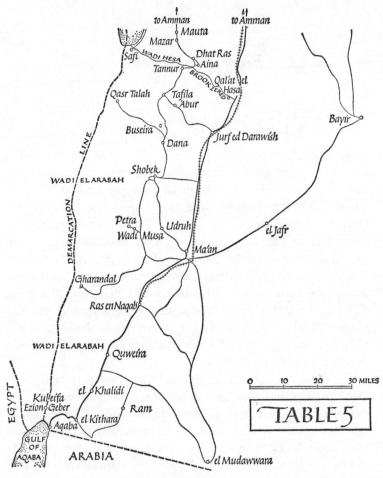

TABLE 5 Southern Jordan

Tragedy at the Siq

The *siq* is a defile in the high, rocky hills surrounding Petra. It is a natural channel cut into the cliffs by water, and the path you travel is actually the bed of a dried-up stream. The *siq* is not wide. In places it narrows to six or eight feet. The cliffs on either side rise to a height of two to three hundred feet. This defile makes a neat little funnel that traps rain water that flows down the barren slopes of the hills. A few years ago this charming and unusual gorge became the setting for a major tragedy. A group of French pilgrims walking to Petra were caught unawares by a flash flood. Heavy rains in the hill country had sent a torrent of water swirling into the *siq*. The walls were so straight and slick that the travelers could not find toeholds by which they could climb to save themselves. My memory is that about twenty persons lost their lives in this dreadful accident. After the tragedy, the tourist department sought precautions against a recurrence. A safety device was easily found. It had existed and had been ignored. The old Nabatean dam, built two thousand years ago, had once served this purpose for an ancient kingdom. As you enter the defile, you can see to your right the old dam, now repaired to divert errant or sudden torrents, and to render them harmless by channeling the waters back down a slope into another valley.

The Wonders of Petra

Your exit from the *siq* and your first glimpse of Petra is so unusual (almost awe-inspiring) that it must be experienced to be appreciated. It is a visual *sensation*. The Nabateans must have had a keen sense of drama to have planned and carved a perfectly magnificent structure to greet you when you enter and to set the tone for the splendor that the entire city would have to show you. As you walk through the *siq*, the path turns often. You never see far into the distance. This is an hour's walk, and the tourist becomes accustomed to glancing ahead only to see more of the same type of channel. At the last turn of the *siq*, however, he again peers ahead, and there— outlined by the opening in the rough rock of this narrow defile, looking close enough to touch—stand huge, stately rose-colored pillars and the beautifully carved façade of an old Nabatean tomb. This is a tremendous building, one of many such in Petra, carved entirely from natural stone. This stunning view of a tomb (called the Treasury) alone is worth the ride to Petra.

Petra is what you might call a cemetery par excellence. Many of its ruins are tombs with elaborately carved façades. The tombs have all the grandeur of a temple to the Roman gods. Petra also has temples, a banquet hall, a theater. It at one time had a nymphaeum, baths, paved roadways, columned streets, and arches. But Petra is different from any other splendid ancient city. It was carved meticulously from the most lusciously colored rose sandstone, the substance of the hills of Petra, and the temples and tombs were carved front to rear right into the "living stone."

The Nabateans

Who were the people responsible for this most unusual city? They were the Nabateans, who first appear in history as an identifiable tribe in the sixth century B.C. At that time they were rather typical Arab nomads, tent dwellers of the desert who dealt in trade but disdained agriculture. They were a sizable group who spread themselves over the southern area of the Holy Land in the territory known as Moab and Edom. Today this area might be described as including all of the land bordered by Aqaba on the south, Amman on the north, the Dead Sea on the west and the present border on the east. This includes the Wadi el Arabah and part of the Israeli Negev. The area was the very heart of the caravan route from Egypt to Damascus.

The Nabateans were well aware of this fact. Petra by its

location was a perfect base of operations for a tribe of caravan looters. Whether the Nabateans stumbled upon this vast chasm of Petra or invaded it, hidden as it was among precipitous cliffs four thousand feet high, they made of it a cozy, safe hideaway from which they could dart out, pounce upon caravans laden with riches and dash back with their treasure without danger of reprisals. In time, the Nabateans found that a better system of extracting booty was to guarantee the caravans safe conduct and collect a fee for so doing. This control over a portion of the caravan route led to their political control over the entire caravan route and extended the influence of the Nabateans up into Syria.

Petra remained their capital city. With their riches, the Nabateans started building their beautiful creation in the fourth century B.C., but it was not their only artistic achievement. Khirbat Tannur has a Nabatean temple excavated and amply described by Nelson Glueck in his volume *Deities and Dolphins*. The Wadi el Arabah has excellent Nabatean ruins and Palmyra in Syria is a second beautiful monument to Nabatean artistry. Since the Nabateans had cultural contacts with Egyptians, Greeks, and Romans, they borrowed from each ideas for building beautiful cities and they emerged master city builders. Their talent for sculpture was considerable. Their attention to intricate carving of attractive design is apparent. Their engineering was remarkable. They were marvelous storers of water. Their reservoirs and aqueducts brought enough water into Petra to support a large agricultural program. Their water systems into the Negev were sufficient to support large cities. Nabatean pottery is highly prized, for it is far and away the finest native pottery ever produced in the Holy Land. It is as thin and delicate as the finest china. The best is decorated with fine lines and delicate feathery designs.

The Nabateans grew into a kingdom, and they had several strong and influential kings about the time of Christ. Their capital at Petra served them well until the Romans came into the Middle East. In A.D. 106, Petra became just another city in the Roman Empire. About 300 Petra started its decline into the shell of a town that it is today. Petra became a Christian city in its declining years and was destroyed by the Muslims in the seventh century.

The Thousand-Yard Plain

A walk skirting the thousand-yard-wide plain inside the Petra hills will show you, in the cliffs, the stunning beauty of the tombs cut straight into the rock. The walk through the plain will show you traces of a rather grand city, Roman in essence. A walk to the top of the cliffs will bring you to the religious "holy of holies" of the Nabateans, perhaps a place of sacrifice and worship.

Near the altar of the high place, we were treated to a most fascinating sight. Sitting on the lovely red rock as if he owned the whole hill was an exquisite, vibrantly blue lizard. He was a slender fellow about ten inches long. He moved about his business, paying no attention to us. He was so elegant and handsome, so striking in this setting, that we felt we were intruders— that we were privileged to watch some sort of regal creature. It seemed to be beneath his dignity to investigate us or to retreat from us. He ignored us completely.

A second surprise at this remote Nabatean shrine was that a young Jordanian, anticipating perspiring and thirsty tourists, maintains a soft drink stand here. He has no ice up here on top of the cliffs, but he sets his bottles in the shade. This is a soft *warm* drink stand, but the beverage is at least a thirst quencher.

There is a tradition that Aaron, brother of Moses, is buried on top of one of these hills. Muslims rather jealously try to guard this shrine for there seems to be a superstition that persons other than Muslims should not visit the tomb.

Petra is well worth seeing, but unless you are a student of Nabatean history or archaeology, one day will be sufficient time for you to take in the flavor of the city. We had an almost comic experience in discomfort during our stay in Petra.

We had planned to go to Petra several times during the winter but for various reasons, we did not actually make the trip until June. Southern Jordan can be very, very hot in June. It is not necessarily so, but it *can* be. It was, when we went— to the tune of about 120 degrees. There is a hotel within the city at Petra. It is called a "camp." This label, we assume, is a mild warning that the guest must not expect first-class accommodations, although the prices are strictly first class for Jordan.

The Battle with the Sun

To repeat, it was *hot*. We had arrived in the early afternoon, during the heat of the day. We were not too uncomfortable walking through the *siq* because the cliffs provide some shade and we walked at a most leisurely pace set by the weary little burro that carried our luggage. At the exit from the *siq*, we stepped into the brilliant sunshine that filled the plain, or valley, of Petra. We still had a mile to walk to reach the "camp." Here at Petra, again on the desert road south and at Aqaba we were given a splendid "opportunity" to catch the full meaning of the old Babylonian religions that worshiped the peace and beauty of the moon and despised the sun as a ravisher. This Middle Eastern sun is not the same as the sun we love in Ohio.

At home, the sun is a distant golden sphere that warms and strengthens and gives welcome light and brightness. Here in the desert of the Holy Land, it is a wicked, white searing blast of heat from the heavens—a vicious enemy, a predator. It gives no respite. There is not a cloud in the sky to soften or shade its full force. We have been used to heat that is miserably humid, cloying, and sticky. This type of heat cannot be compared in the same breath with dry heat. The dry heat that we experienced must have been a little foretaste of what it is like to perish in the desert. The sun parches you. It truly *attacks* you, so steadily sucking the moisture from your skin that in time you would be nothing but a flesh-covered bone.

We had walked only a few hundred yards when our daughter cried out, "Oh, I have such a headache." Covering her head was some relief. No wonder the Arabs carry their shade on their backs in heavy layers of clothing that will not allow the sun to touch their skin. No wonder they wrap cloths round their heads to shade their brains. If the nape of the neck and the top of the head are not covered, a man's battle with this sun is not going to last very long. I use the word "battle" advisedly. A person is quite conscious of steeling himself to withstand the onslaught of that sun—not that it does any good. That monstrous sun has all of the power on its side. The only recourse for the wise tourist is to hide from it—to seek out even a slender thread of shade and rest.

Hotel in Petra

We were greatly relieved when we finally reached the "camp" and the hotel, about a Class "c" model, but a haven to us at this particular moment. We deposited our luggage in our rooms and reached for the water tap. No water. Our hotel was apparently having a problem. Its pump was broken. Water was in short supply. (Some hotels in the Holy Land are operated in partnership with the government. We found more than once that the investor who undertakes to manage an establishment considers himself responsible for only those perfunctory duties that pertain to simple day-by-day operation. All heavy maintenance work, all outlay of further monies become the responsibility of the "government." Thus when a tourist complains about bad service, he can expect to receive a shrug of the shoulders and the reply, "The government has not fixed it.") This, the broken pump, was the fault of the "government." Water had to be brought in by burro and it would take some time. It did. It took about an hour!

We washed off quickly in the cold tap water from a roof

cistern and it was a good thing we did not dawdle. Just as we finished, the tap finished yielding water. The system seemed to be that if the guest wanted water, he had to ask for it. The pump would not be fixed. The water was doled out in minimal quantity to the cistern in the roof by hands and buckets method. Okay! Somewhat refreshed, we set out to see a few Petra sights before dinner.

When we returned to the hotel and asked when we might have dinner, we were told we could eat immediately. The short-order cook arose from his chair on the veranda, told us he would call when he was ready, went to the kitchen and turned on his primus stove. While we waited on the veranda, we watched a young Arab musician who was entertaining the other hotel employees. When the musician first appeared, we thought he had just wandered in, but it is probably true that he is a standard fixture, local color for the tourists. He was dressed all in white. He had a most primitive instrument, a gasoline can with a string attached. This was a homemade imitation of a *rababa*—a square-shaped, long-necked, one-stringed violin. The instrument produced a whining thin tone, not pleasing—but Arab music to my ear is at best a succession of distortions. The talent of the minstrel lies not in his performance on the instrument but rather in the wealth of folk songs he knows by heart. Since we could not follow the language, we did not understand the songs. The Arabs sing of many things—work, watering, death, weddings, any phase of desert life. They say that the rhythm of many folk songs is set to the gait of the camel.

In an amazingly short time, our cook set before us a really fine dinner. The meals were the only saving grace to our three-day stay at the "camp." As soon as dinner was over, we retired to our rooms to read more about the fabulous city of Petra. We had hardly seated ourselves and opened our books when we found ourselves in total darkness. Once again, we had to seek an explanation. It was simply this: the hotel found it necessary to be very sparing of electricity because it had only a small generator. Lights were provided only during the dinner hour. If we found it necessary to grope down the hallway to the bathroom during the night, we would find a candle in our room. Okay! It was eight o'clock in the evening, hardly our usual hour for turning in, but it had been a long, hot day. We'd rest and start out early in the morning after a good night's sleep.

Unfortunately, we were the only guests in the hotel. We were also the only persons who turned in for a good night's sleep. The boys who ran the hotel went out on the porch, just below our window, turned on a kerosene lamp, and settled down to a good old thigh-slapping game of some kind. They had a wonderful time. They roared and shrieked with laughter until well after midnight. Peace at last? Nope. Nighttime at Petra is the time for dogs and cats to enjoy the social hour. We had dog fights, howling cats, and braying donkeys most of the night. Promptly at six in the morning, deliveries to the hotel started—mostly canned goods strapped on the backs of burros, as many clanging cans as they can carry.

I am certain that the Petra "camp" is not always as nonconducive to comfort as we found it, but I suspect it never reaches a really acceptable standard of service. We had friends who visited it in the winter. They nearly froze to death with too few blankets, no heat, and no hot water.

In the morning we traded experiences with a tourist we had not previously seen. His experience had pretty well matched ours except that his guide had talked him into spending his nights at Petra in the "atmospheric" way—in the caves. The "camp" has outfitted a few nearby caves with beds, washstands, etc. For this delightful experience the guest pays the same price per day as he would for a hotel room. Our friend, a native of Tennessee, in addition to staying awake during the night with the noise, had battled mosquitoes and bugs, and was ripe for revenge. This he accomplished by getting his guide up early in the morning, insisting on seeing all of Petra and pushing his guide almost to exhaustion while he, himself, refused to show the slightest sign of annoyance from thirst, fatigue, or heat. We later saw this same Tennessean in Istanbul. He was still taking in all the sights, still full of vim and vinegar.

So, to sum up, Petra is one of the outstanding sights not only in the Holy Land, but in the Middle East. You can easily see it by driving down for the day and returning after dark. And there is now, just outside the entrance to Petra, a new guest house.

The Treacherous Arabah

If you travel south from Petra to Aqaba, you rejoin the desert road, through country as devoid of scenery as on the way to Petra. Civilization is sparse here. We had never traveled the road before and did not know that a short way from Petra, the scenery changes drastically and without warning. The area immediately south of Petra is so flat and barren that you do not realize that you are driving on a plateau well above sea level until suddenly you find yourself on the edge of a vast chasm filled with massive and strange rock formations extending east, west, and south as far as the eye can see. This is your first, truly sensational view of the Arabah, the infamous desert that is the southern extension of the Jordan rift. The road now descends abruptly, way, way down two thousand feet into the chasm which you will travel all the way to Aqaba.

The Arabah is a spooky place. It looks as if it doesn't belong in time and space. It has a flat sand floor from which rise hundreds upon hundreds of elongated eruptions. The eruptions are not soft, mellowed mounds of sand. They are bunches of rock, strikingly colored yellows, oranges, reds, and browns. A haze surrounds the entire area. The Arabah has a fascinating but malevolent beauty. It sits quietly and lurks, if that is possible. It invites, almost dares you to enter and explore its beauties, yet it is a treacherous maze. It could swallow you. What a freak of nature it is! With the sunlight playing on the haze, the chasm seems to shimmer—just as if it were a living evil soul, capriciously beckoning to you, yet all the while mocking you with suppressed laughter because you dare not accept its challenge.

The Nabateans made friends with the Arabah. Ruins of their towns and shrines are scattered throughout it. A good guide can find them and return you safely to the main road. We knew friends who hired a guide to escort them to some, but they had a rough moment when the guide temporarily panicked because he thought he had taken a wrong path. But the most popular trip into the Arabah is to see a natural wonder, the Wadi Ram, a cavern cut by water through the rock, said to equal in many ways the beauty of the Grand Canyon; it is northeast of Aqaba and is most easily reached from there.

Aqaba

The port of Aqaba is not visited by many tourists. It is a six-hour ride from Amman, but just a couple of hours from Petra. Situated at the southernmost reach of Jordan on the gulf of the same name, Aqaba is an unusual spot where the tourist can stand on Jordanian soil and look out to Israel, Egypt, and Saudi Arabia. The town of Aqaba has little to offer the tourist, but west of town are a guest house and a hotel that cater to the tourist who enjoys the sea. Plans for the development of this entire area are fantastic for this underdeveloped nation. Here it is hoped to build a small "Riviera"—a model town with boulevards, gardens, palm trees, and apartments. The first step in completing this ambitious plan has been accomplished: concrete roads and boulevards are being laid out.

Aqaba has a good hotel. It is well furnished, and it provides private and modern bathroom facilities that work. The hotel offers complete bar service and excellent dining. The staff is polished and courteous. During the winter the climate at Aqaba is most inviting and it is quite probable that a tourist would enjoy the sunshine, a good rest and pleasant surroundings there.

As at Petra, we went to Aqaba out of season. We experienced

some discomfort, but on the other hand we stumbled into one of the most delightful experiences of our stay in Jordan. The discomfort at Aqaba came from the heat.

The day we arrived, the breeze was coming from the gulf and the resort was absolutely delightful after the heat of Petra. Late in the afternoon the wind shifted. Immediately behind the hotel is the Arabah, the desert we'd just traveled, the desert shown in the film "Lawrence of Arabia," the desert so beastly hot in August no man was believed able to cross it, but Lawrence did, to surprise and defeat the Turks at Aqaba. When the whimsy of air currents decides to send you a taste of that scorching breath from the Arabah, the climate at Aqaba is a trial to endure. The thermometer in the shade registered 46° Centigrade—114° Fahrenheit. As one employee whispered to me, "It can be hell here in the summertime!" He was right. The metal in the chairs on the veranda was so hot we could not sit on them. The rooms were an inferno. The hotel advertises "air conditioning," but doesn't have enough generators to operate the units except for limited periods of time.

Encounter with Royalty

In the morning, we decided to enjoy the beach. Aqaba has a fine sandy beach. For the comfort of guests, beach chairs are placed along the waterfront in shade. The shade comes from picturesque grass roofs supported by poles. The view is very pleasant. The water is clean, very blue and cool. The view from the beach, as noted earlier, includes three nations other than Jordan, but the view turned out to be even more interesting than that for us. We had noticed a motor boat skimming the water and towing some water skiers. In fact, the skiers made such a pretty sight in the water (especially one man in a bright yellow life jacket) that I reached for my camera and took a few pictures. One of the skiers, the one in the yellow jacket, slipped out of his skis when the boat neared shore and walked up on the beach to where we were sitting. As he called

out to us a hearty "Good morning," we looked up and recognized the very muscular, deeply tanned young king of Jordan,
Hussein. This completely unexpected encounter with royalty
both pleased and amazed us. We were the *only* persons sitting
on the beach. The king could easily have avoided us. The
thought passed through my mind that he might object to my
having taken some pictures. My camera was clearly in sight, but
the king was apparently not bothered at all by it. The thought
also passed through my mind that this young man was extraordinarily brave. Had we been fanatics with weapons, he would
have been quite vulnerable. We must have appeared quite harmless because he continued up the beach to another shaded
chair and called for a soft drink.

King Hussein has been the victim of attempted assassination
so many times that I doubt he could give you the exact figure.
You may recall that when President Kennedy was killed, King
Hussein sent a telegram of condolence that included the phrase
"It was the will of God." This phrase comes from the king's
belief as a Muslim, and he subscribes to it regarding his own
fate and his ultimate death, violent or otherwise.

Our plan had been to leave Aqaba that morning and return
to the cool, cool evenings of Jerusalem. Now, encouraged by
the fact that the king was a guest in the hotel, we felt certain
that the air-conditioning system would be pressed into service
for the whole day. Not so. We stayed on and thoroughly enjoyed watching a king at play, but he did not ask for any
special attention. He sweltered through the heat of the day
along with the rest of us.

A Royal Incident

An unusual incident took place at Aqaba while the king was
in residence. Some American men had come to the Aqaba Hotel on business. One arose early in the morning for a quick
swim and then took a nap on the beach in the sun. Seeing
him sound asleep, one of his associates was tempted to become

playful. It was close to the Fourth of July and for some unaccountable reason, these grown men had with them a supply of firecrackers. What do you do with a firecracker? Naturally —you set it off near the sleeping man, stand back, and laugh when he jumps sky high. This prank went off as planned, except that the planner had not had the foresight to judge the effect of the explosion on the Jordanian soldiers who act as the king's bodyguard. They came on the run, guns drawn, to capture a possible assassin, but found instead a very sheepish and apologetic American. The soldiers, somehow, did not find the prank too amusing. Nor I assure you, did the gentleman who had perpetrated the trick for long.

Aqaba hopes to develop its resort as a center for deep-sea fishing. Certainly marvelous fishing should be found here in this relatively untouched area. The resort does have a glass-bottomed boat that takes tourists out over the multicolored reefs. Friends who took this water tour said it was thrilling.

Solomon's Seaport

The Gulf of Aqaba, quiet and restful today, once supported a teeming port, Ezion Geber. It is believed that the gold and silver, almug trees (sandalwood), and ivory, apes, and peacocks mentioned in I Kings 9:26–28, 10:11, 22, entered the Holy Land here. Likewise, as mentioned in I Kings 10:1–13, an even more precious cargo, the Queen of Sheba, landed here to continue her journey to Jerusalem. Ezion Geber was at its zenith during the reign of King Solomon.

Two miles north of the present-day ports of Aqaba and Elat (in Israel), Ezion Geber appears to have been heavily populated as early as 1200 B.C. It was an import and export center, a busy commercial city, and a storage center for grain. The excavated buildings and walls in Ezion Geber show such similarities to other Israelite cities known to have been built by King Solomon that most scholars feel that Ezion Geber can definitely be said to be Solomon's city.

Many of "King Solomon's mines," where copper was taken from the mountains and refined in open hearth installations, have been found north of Ezion Geber in the Wadi Arabah. The copper may then have been further refined and fashioned into ingots at Ezion Geber. At the time that the city was first excavated, archaeologists found that four cities had been built here, one on top of the other and that each had been destroyed by fire. Some of the buildings excavated showed possible air ducts or open channels, cut horizontally, or horizontally and vertically, in the walls. Archaeologists suspected that such channels might have been vents to channel the winds of the Arabah to serve the needs of a foundry. Ezion Geber became known as "Solomon's foundry."

Recently, archaeologists have changed their minds about the air channels and the purpose they served in Ezion Geber. Other structures in the Holy Land, known definitely not to be foundries, showed the same type of apertures in the walls. These open holes were proved to have been holes in mud brick walls left by wooden beams that had been burned or had decayed. Such beams added considerable strength to large mud brick buildings, as they do today in the adobe dwellings of our Pueblo Indians. Consequently, the buildings at Ezion Geber formerly thought to have been foundries are now considered granaries, or to use a term better known today, grain elevators.

The site of Ezion Geber, tell el Kheleifeh, is no longer accessible to scholars or tourists due to its location, very close to the Israeli-Jordanian truce line, but it can be seen on a clear day from Aqaba.

Also of interest to the biblical student is the theory, not yet proved, that Moses and the children of Israel traveled the length of the Arabah desert to arrive at the Jordan Valley. Moses, denied passage through the populous area of Edom, may have had to traverse this forbidding area with his motley band of disgruntled ex-patriates.

Seeing the ruggedness of the Sinai Peninsula and contemplating the barren wasteland of both the Negev and the Arabah, you have a new picture of Moses as a leader of men. It seems absolutely impossible that any man could persuade his fellow men—and so many of them—to accompany him for such a long period of time on this incredibly difficult journey. It could not have been accomplished—yet, it was! The time given by the Bible for this trip was forty years. It has been suggested that the Bible at times uses the number "forty" vaguely to denote a very, very long time. To this we must agree. The wandering of the Israelites must have seemed to the participants very, very long indeed.

X For Those Who Have Eyes...

In chapter 37 of his prophetic book, Ezekiel writes that he accompanied the Lord on a visit to a valley that was filled with bones. The Lord asked him, "Son of man, can these bones live?" Ezekiel answered, "O Lord God, thou knowest." The Lord then prodded Ezekiel to speak with the bones and as Ezekiel complied, he heard a noise and a shaking and the bones came together one by one, flesh and skin appeared on the bones, "the breath came into them, and they lived, and stood up upon their feet, an exceeding great army" (Ezek. 37:3, 10).

Every tourist in the Holy Land has the opportunity to share with Ezekiel this awe-inspiring spectacle. The Holy Land is a graveyard of hallowed bones. There are thousands of tourists who pass through this graveyard glancing at the remains only to see nothing but evidence of the dead. It is necessary to take time to speak with the remains of the past and, in turn, to give them time to speak to you.

The Holy Land does not yield her secrets to every peripatetic curiosity seeker. She sits in reserve, warming to you only as you warm to her. As you meditate with her and study her and let her take her time to reveal herself to you, only then will all her heroes and villains of the past ages return with breath in them, they will live and stand up on their feet—and they do comprise an EXCEEDING GREAT ARMY.

This very personal encounter with the men of faith of both Old and New Testament is not dependent on any clairvoyant or telepathic ability. It is dependent on the ability to release your mind and spirit from the present and to let yourself be-

come completely occupied for a time with the past. The rewards
are great.

To make a simple comparison: your own state has probably
preserved some historic shrine as a replica of a past culture,
such as Williamsburg, Virginia; Greenfield Village, Michigan;
Salem, Massachusetts; New Salem, Illinois; even the ghost towns
of the west. It is possible to visit any one of these places, walk
through it with your mind planning tomorrow's business con-
ference or tonight's menu and to leave the site without taking
away with you even a slight revelation from the past.

However, if you enter such a shrine, let it envelop you and
absorb you, you are transported for a time back into history so
completely that you actually live briefly in that distant age. You
gain understanding of the time, but more important, of the
people who lived at that time. This understanding, this feeling
of communion with the past makes a little home deep inside
you and it never leaves you.

Exactly this sense of communion with the past comes to the
pilgrim to the Holy Land, but there is one difference: in the
Holy Land the encounter is far more significant because it involves persons of the most impressive stature—Abraham, Moses,
Isaiah, and even Jesus, the Christ.

This adventure to try to communicate with the past could
start with Abraham. What can we know about the man other
than the fact that he left his homeland and traveled to Canaan
in response to a directive from a higher power?

If we reread the Bible, we learn that Abraham lived sometimes at Bethel, sometimes at Hebron. Now, if we visit these
two towns, we notice that the path between them (passing
through Tequ'a) follows the ridge that defines and separates
the hill country from the Jordan Valley. Why would Abraham
want to live here, on the fringe of the populated centers of
Canaan? Abraham was a sophisticated man. He had come from
the very cultivated city of Ur. He had traveled through Iraq,
Syria, Canaan, and Egypt. He had business contacts in the
large cities. He was a wealthy merchant prince and patriarch of

a large tribe. Yet the Bible seems to indicate that Abraham
lived simply, as do the nomads.

It is probable that Abraham's enormous holdings in livestock
dictated that he live in the manner of the nomad—in tents that
could be moved to allow for the seasonal migration of his flocks
and herds to provide fresh pasture.

Why would he have settled so far from the fertile and beautiful
Mediterranean coast? From what is known of the culture of the
day, Abraham needed to maintain his distance from the coastal
plains and the farmlands where the settled inhabitants looked
with disfavor on voracious sheep and cattle.

Abraham's "territory" should fit perfectly with what we know
of nomadic living. His area was large enough, (Bethel to Hebron,
Hebron to Bethel) to allow for regular seasonal migrations. It
was quite well watered, catching the rains that fell in the hill
country and channeling them down the hills to the edge of the
valley. That pasturage was a major consideration we can further
deduce from the fact that Abraham moved to Egypt in times
of drought.

Abraham's conduct seems to fit with what we know of a wise
and benevolent patriarch of a nomadic tribe. That he was kind
and generous was illustrated by his handling of a crisis at Bethel
when it became apparent that this encampment would not provide for the enormous flocks and herds of the tribe. Abraham
summoned Lot and suggested that perhaps the tribe should split
and that Lot could have his choice of the territory. Lot, looking
out over the valley and remembering where the best grazing
land lay, chose to move toward Sodom. This would have been
a move of approximately fifty miles from Bethel, a respectable
distance to ensure the separation of the livestock of each man.
Abraham willingly allowed Lot to take over the best land in the
territory.

In still another way, Abraham assumed the role of a nomadic
patriarch. Twice during the period that Lot dwelt in Sodom, he
found himself in trouble. First, he became trapped in a war
between neighboring kingdoms and those of Sodom and Gomor-

rah. He was taken prisoner. Abraham, fulfilling his duty as guardian of his tribe, rescued Lot along with Lot's family and his goods. Second, when Sodom and Gomorrah were to be destroyed, Abraham interceded with the Lord and Lot was warned to leave Sodom in time to save his life.

Previously in the book, incidents have been related in the life of Abraham that seem to parallel traditions in nomadic culture. Rather than labor through all the details of the Abraham narration, let's turn to one last incident that pictures Abraham as quite human in dealing with typical human beings in the Middle Eastern culture.

Sarah had died and Abraham was pressed to find a suitable family burial plot. He found what he wanted near Hebron. The detailed description of his acquiring the land is so characteristic of Oriental bargaining that it is amazing and amusing to find it so clearly represented in literature from so long ago.

Abraham presented himself to the landowners in the Hebron area and stated: "I come to you as a stranger who seeks a plot of land suitable for a family burial ground." The landowners replied, "It is *our* honor to have you among us. Take your choice of the best land of any one of us." Abraham continued, "Perhaps, then, I might choose the cave of Machpelah, owned by Ephron and I am prepared to pay whatever it is worth." Ephron now enters the conversation: "Take my field for nothing. I shall give it to you." Abraham repeated, "While I appreciate your kind offer, nonetheless, please accept my payment for the worth of the land." Ephron stated the heart of the matter, "Indeed the land is worth only four hundred shekels of silver, but what is such a small price between us. Take it for nothing" (Gen. 23:3–16, freely paraphrased).

In this short dialogue, the reader can observe that the customer was even then the honored guest, treated with the greatest courtesy. The customer started the negotiations by admiring what he hoped to purchase and was entreated to "take it for nothing." The quoted phrase, so often heard today in Middle Eastern lands, was never meant to be taken literally. It still means that

the merchant will quote a price which he will represent as so
ridiculously low that the purchaser might as well pay nothing.

Ephron, of course, accepted the purse of silver from Abraham,
whereupon Abraham very wisely took the precaution of precisely
defining the boundaries of the property, the trees and caves
included therein, before sealing the bargain.

While the Holy Land pilgrim discovers Abraham, the man,
and warms to him, he can also recall with pride that Abraham
was a spiritual man. He erected altars to honor his God in the
areas of Shechem, Bethel, and Hebron and he witnessed to his
God in conversation with Melchizedek, the king of Sodom, and
Abimelech.

In the same way, we can follow Jacob, the man who may have
been sufficiently infected with Middle Eastern cunning to have
convinced himself that it was no more than clever business procedure to outwit his brother and father in obtaining the birthright.
Certainly when Jacob was later outwitted by Laban in much the
same slick manner, Jacob submitted to the humiliation in good
grace as if he had been legitimately out-maneuvered.

Again we can meet Joshua at Shittim as he prepared his
invading forces for a holy war. We can sit with his army at the
foot of Mount Nebo as they break camp and prepare to line up
behind the Levitical priests who would spearhead the procession,
holding aloft the ark of the covenant. We can look over Joshua's
shoulder as he sends out spies to bring back intelligence reports,
plans his strategy whether to use force of arms or psychological
warfare. And we can be impressed by Joshua's rigid disciplining of
his troops according to the rules of the covenant, traditionally
spelled out by Moses.

Or we can stand in awe of David, the gifted, and his whirlwind
rise to power. David had about his person the aura of success
so appealing to the Oriental mind and such a necessary qualification for leadership. In this land of intrigue, filled with con-
niving would be supplanters, we admire David's ability to hold
the friendship of men, the loyalty of followers, the love of
women, and we grieve with him over his great failure, the

tragedy of his son, Absalom, whose adolescent rebellion goaded him to plan an insurrection against his father.

Once more, when we view the prophets against what we know of their times, we understand more clearly their messages and we feel with them the agonizing pleadings with the people to remember their covenant with the Lord. We sympathize as well with their frustrations as they clenched their teeth and shook their fists in outbursts of temper against indifference and apathy.

So it is that the pilgrim, by study of the Bible, the land, and the circumstances, becomes thoroughly acquainted with a group of men who formerly have been only shadows that glide through printed pages. The timeworn narratives of the Old Testament, read so dispassionately at home, spring from the page as fresh, vivid, and intensely interesting human documents. To state a fact, the Bible when viewed in its proper setting becomes such engrossing reading that the reader can't put it down, so anxious is he to find out which sentences on the pages will take on new meaning or provide a small clue that has been previously overlooked.

When the Holy Land pilgrim seeks to know more about Jesus, the most immediate evidence that Jesus was here comes from the familiar imagery used by Jesus in his teaching. Just about all of it is still here—the shepherd so alert to the needs of his flock, the greedy money changers, the lilies of the fields, the sower of the seed, the headdress from which a woman lost one of her precious dowry coins, the reeds shaken by the winds in the wilderness, the fig tree, the mustard plant. Jesus looms before your eyes often as the master teacher sitting on a hillside pointing out simple daily scenes and using them to teach religious truth.

The need for the healing ministry of Jesus is as apparent today as it must have been two thousand years ago. The streets are often hosts to the blind, the lame, the sorrowing who would reach out to Jesus in desperation.

When we reconstruct the Holy Land as it was under the military arm of the Romans, we might find some surprises. At the time that Jesus was born, Herod the Great had already accomplished structuring the country into a rather efficient "police state." Herod had used the entire country as a vast personal estate, with homes and fortresses (some within walking distance of each other) strung along the populous areas of his kingdom. With the legions of Rome at his disposal, he could have kept a very close watch on the political health of his regime. If, as the Bible states, Mary and Joseph were warned to take their child to Egypt to protect him from the king, the flight would have been most difficult, carried out successfully only by stealth and secrecy. You will recall, that it was only after Herod's death that the family felt it was safe to try to return to their homeland.

From the ruins so generously scattered through the land, we are forced to conclude that this tiny land was no quiet, sleepy, rural haven for fishermen, peasants, and shepherds. The Holy Land apparently supported at least two widely divergent societies —say, the "in" crowd and the "out" crowd. The difference in living standards between these two social groups at the time of Jesus was far greater than I had imagined.

The fashionable—and they were present in great numbers— lived rather grandly in the most elaborate and magnificent Greco-Roman cities. They strolled in the manner of superior men through columned streets, gathering in groups to discuss politics and business. They entertained themselves lavishly and leisurely, attending the theater and lolling in the Roman baths. Most likely, they were not repelled by temples to the mythological gods of Rome.

On the other hand, in the outlying areas of the kingdom, the poor lived the life of toilers on the land and the sea. They were peasants, serfs of the Romans. Jesus came out of the culture of the latter group. He selected most of his disciples from the same group.

How amazing it is then that Jesus arrived on the scene as a man who taught with authority, who did not flinch from debating with the sophisticates in the city. Jesus would have been considered, frankly, a "rube" from Galilee. No man in authority would have taken him seriously. Some of them may have tried

to bait him into showing a disloyalty to Rome, but Jesus was
clever enough to turn aside their barbs with an innocuous answer.
And it also seems apparent that he was not anxious to arouse
the suspicions of Roman soldiers with the evidence of his growing popularity among the common people. Often after he had
drawn large crowds of people, he quietly withdrew to a solitary
place.

In the Gospels, Jesus is such a central figure that it is easy
to forget that, set in the entire social structure of his day, he was
relatively unknown. At the time that Jesus fell into the hands
of the soldiers in the Garden of Gethsemane, his arrest by the
Romans was most likely just another of many such precautions
against disturbers of the peace, possible insurrectionists. Most
of the people of Jerusalem were sleeping, unaware that Jesus
had been arrested, nor would it have been of any consequence to
them had they known.

Jesus was taken before Pilate, who transferred the whole matter to Herod Antipas because of Jesus' Galilean background.
Pilate did not think he had uncovered a prize political prisoner.
Herod and his soldiers made fun of Jesus. Considering him of
no great importance to the Jewish community, they turned him
back to Pilate to handle the affair after the usual procedure of
the Romans. The trial, the sentence, the capital punishment
were Roman procedure for handling political criminals.

Jesus' disciples, after witnessing such a commonplace and un-
climactic end to their dreams of a kingdom of God, dispersed.
They were disillusioned and, as is obvious from the Gospel stories,
determined to act like human cowards to save their own skins
from like punishment.

Dead leaders are soon forgotten.

Then something happened. There was a complete revitalization
among the disciples. How did it come about? That is the per-
plexing question. Is it possible that among the disciples there
was left a leader of sufficient influence, courage, and conviction
to rally his group in the name of Jesus? If there were such a man,
the Bible does not name him. It has been suggested that the

disciples entered into a plot to secrete the body of Jesus and to
then pretend that Jesus had triumphed. Is it possible that the
disciples could delude themselves with such a hoax to such an
extent that they *martyred* themselves? That would be incredible.

If we remember that the disciples, even at the late date of
the Crucifixion, did not understand Jesus and his kingdom that
was not of this world, then there is only one person who could
have revealed to them the meaning of the mission, the message,
and the triumph over death. That person had to be Jesus, himself. There is no other sensible answer to the spectacle of the
flourishing, enthusiastic, and fearless body of Christians that greet
us in the Book of Acts. They are the witness.

There is another witness encountered in Jerusalem that cannot
be slighted. It is the stream of pilgrims of differing faiths to the
Holy City.

It is not far from the truth to say that most of us Westerners
are content to live and subscribe to "belief" within a very small
framework of religious understanding. You have seen a glass
globe paperweight that houses a country scene. If the weight is
shaken, it manufactures a little snowstorm. Just such a tiny storm
typifies the experience of most of us who have encased ourselves
in a little capsule of religion. Religion is what goes on, not
within one denomination, but within *one church*. The religious
philosophy as expounded from one pulpit, the ritual so routinely
practiced becomes almost a "god" in itself. It has become right
because it is that to which we have become accustomed. So
indoctrinated have we become we dismiss other teachings and
practices as odd and probably heretical.

In Jerusalem pilgrims from all countries in the world crowd
into the shrines. Those from the Western culture are usually
Christian, but their customs and traditions vary greatly. Those
who come to Jerusalem from the Middle East are in the majority
Muslim. They usually stop in the Holy Land on their way to or
from Mecca. If it were not precluded by the present unrest
between Israel and Jordan, there would be still a third group of
pilgrims—the Jews who wish to worship at the Wailing Wall.

The pilgrims have not come to Jerusalem to *see* the city, but to visit the shrines sacred to them from long tradition, and there to bow down and worship. To observe the devotion of the pilgrims as they prostrate themselves in attitudes of prayer—thanking, fearing, pleading, despairing, glorifying—is to have your heart opened and moved by genuine concern.

We, you and I, are not alone in our desperate need to seek help from a higher power. The need has been placed in every one of us. To complement that need, we have all been given the ability, if we choose to exercise it, to respond in love.

This again, is a witness. For those who have eyes to see, let them see.

XI   Tips for the Traveler

Earlier in the twentieth century, the tourist determined to explore the Holy Land needed to be fortified with a stout physical constitution, an indifference to where he might lay down his head to rest, and an attitude that accepted co-existence with creepy crawlers. Although Jerusalem had establishments which were described as "fairly comfortable" by Baedeker in his 1912 guidebook, the author felt compelled to add with German cautiousness that "the standard of cleanliness and punctuality is somewhat different from that of Europe."

Traveling through the land in those more virtuous days could only be accomplished with the help of a Bedouin guide and protector, who secured horses for the trip. At eventide, the Bedouin would seek shelter for his party in a *khan* (caravansary) or a peasant's hut. Baedeker warned his genteel travelers that the *khans* or huts

> "which are generally built of mud, should never be resorted to, except in cases of absolute necessity, as they swarm with fleas and other vermin. The traveller should see that the straw matting which covers the floor is taken up and thoroughly beaten and the whole place carefully swept and sprinkled with water. Every article of clothing and bedding belonging to the inmates should also be removed to another room. The tents of the Bedouins are free from these insects, but on the other hand are terribly infested with lice. Scorpions abound in Syria, but they seldom sting unless irritated. If the bed is slightly raised from the ground, the sleeper is quite safe from their attacks."

The Holy Land, anyone?

The Best Hotels

Since 1950, Jordan has made a truly amazing effort to house tourists in a manner to suit Western standards of cleanliness and convenience. The result of that effort is that the tiny country, still impoverished in large areas, now has de luxe hotels that compare favorably with fine accommodations anywhere. Since the country is small and the roads and taxi services are excellent, tourists can see the country in daily excursions and return to Jerusalem each night. In Jerusalem, the newest and best appointed hotels are the King George and the Intercontinental. Also first-class, but not quite so luxurious are the Ambassador and the National Palace. Of the many second-class hotels, the American Colony is a charming and storied old residence rich in atmosphere. The YMCA hotel is ultra modern Arabic in design and thoroughly comfortable. Other second-class hotels recommended as good, and easier on the budget, are the New Palace, Cliff, New Orient House, Shepherd, Ritz, and Capitol.

Outside Jerusalem, only two cities have satisfactory hotels. Ramallah has the Grand Hotel, second-class. Amman has the de luxe Al Urdon, the first-class Amman Palace, and the Philadelphia. At the Dead Sea, near Jericho, there is a first-class hotel and dining casino. On the Gulf of Aqaba, there is the Aqaba Hotel.

You Need a Visa

Most tourists enter Jordan through the Jerusalem (Kalandia) Airport, coming from either Beirut or Cairo. These tourists must have valid passports and an entry visa. The visa may be procured from the Jordanian Consulate in New York (this takes about three weeks) or it may be applied for at the Kalandia Airport where it would be issued almost immediately. Because of the tensions between Israel and Jordan, tourists should be aware of the fact that Jordanian officials may require them to show a letter or document proving church membership.

For persons entering Jordan by taxi, the same requirements apply except that the person without a visa would have to apply for one at the border crossing. The taxi, for instance, from Beirut to Jerusalem requires about eight hours (a very pleasant drive through Lebanon, Syria, and Jordan) and with five passengers in the taxi, it costs about $5 apiece.

Driving Your Own Car

Persons driving their own cars must have an international driving license, a *Carnet de Passage,* a document proving ownership of the car, both available at any AAA office or travel agency. Included in the *Carnet* are separate sheets on which customs officials in Middle Eastern countries will stamp the dates of the entries and exits of the car. Such information is required as proof that a tourist has not sold his car. Some tourists mistakenly believe that they may buy a car in Europe, tour in it, then sell it in the Middle East. Customs officials have placed such a high assessment on such a transaction that it is completely impractical to sell a car.

Vaccination

To enter Jordan it is necessary to have proof of a recent smallpox vaccination. For his own protection in the Middle East, the visitor should have as well immunization against typhoid, paratyphoid, typhus, and cholera. For the tourist on a short trip, it might be well to consult a doctor on the advisability of gamma globulin as a protection against infectious hepatitis.

Customs

Jordanian customs officials are most gracious to American tourists. Because automobiles are subject to heavy tax in Jordan, the officials will check quite carefully on the car itself, but they are not overly concerned with its contents. Tourists are allowed to bring into the country duty free all personal effects, two hundred cigarettes (or 200 grams of tobacco), sports equipment including firearms and ammunition, cameras, films, typewriters, binoculars, jewelry, animals if vaccinated, and one liter of wine or spirits.

Foreign and Jordanian Currency

Tourists are also allowed to bring into the country any amount of foreign currency, banknotes, or traveler's checks. Officials limit the amount of Jordanian money brought into the country at 100 Jordanian *dinars*, or $280. There are enough banks to handle exchanges of money, but most tourists find it more convenient to deal with a money changer recommended by their hotel. The money changers, while susceptible to some bargaining, usually give tourists a fair exchange and, very conveniently, will generally cash personal and traveler's checks on the spot.

The Jordanian monetary unit is the *dinar* (J.D.) which is comparable to the British pound. The *dinar* is composed of 1000 *fils* and worth approximately $2.80. If the natives would always quote prices to tourists in terms of *dinars* and *fils*, the monetary system would be quite simple to understand. In practice, however, Jordanians use the terms *dinar* and *pound* interchangeably. They most often quote prices in "piasters," a coin worth ten *fils*. Occasionally they will quote a price in shillings, which are comparable to 50 *fils*, or 5 *piasters*. As is true in so many countries, in Jordan the cautious tourist must become familiar with his money and take time to count his change carefully. There are always some merchants who enjoy handing back to the tourist a bunch of small change that does not add up to being quite correct.

The U. S. Consulate

The United States Consulate in Jerusalem is near the YMCA Hotel on the Nablus Road quite near the Mandelbaum Gate where tourists may cross over into Israel. Passageway into Israel must be cleared through the consulate, and in advance. Such an exit for four-day tourists in a tour party has usually been arranged in advance by travel agents. For the tourist who is planning his own trip, an arrangement for passageway should be cleared far prior to the date of his exit. Persons who have been in Jordan for a long stay may have to wait for a period of weeks before such passageway can be cleared.

How to Dress

Many persons believe that the temperature in the Holy Land remains warm throughout the year. This is not true. The Holy Land has seasonal weather. The winter season, from November through March, is cold. While the thermometer rarely dips to below freezing, winter is apt to be rainy, windy, and raw. In winter, archaeologists working outdoors wear sweaters, plus suit coats, plus sheepskin-lined jackets. Male tourists will need topcoats; women, three-piece suits. Women will also need hats that hug the head in spite of strong winds. Boots that can withstand a coating of mud are desirable. On winter days when the sun shines, the climate may be very pleasant and the topcoat will not be needed.

In April–May and September–October the Holy Land is warm (65–75° F. by day) and both men and women will be comfortable in suits. In June, July, and August tourists may encounter weather that is warm to extremely hot depending on what section of the Holy Land they visit. In the cities of Jerusalem, Hebron, or Ramallah, daytime temperatures might be quite warm but by three o'clock in the afternoon the air will start to cool. In these cities the tourist could use a wrap for late afternoon and

evenings. In summer, desert areas as well as the Jordan Valley
will be extremely hot. The area around the Dead Sea and
Qumran may be stifling. All summer tourists need hats that allow
for air circulation on top of the head and sun glasses (the
darkest you can find) are a necessity. Tourists can count on
not encountering rain in the Holy Land from the first of May
through the middle of October.

Electric current in the hotels is 220 volts, A.C., single phase.
Unless male tourists have an adapter plug, they will not be able
to use an electric razor.

Tourist Services

Taxi service to all areas of Jordan can be arranged through any
one of the dozens of Jerusalem travel agents. On an arranged
tour, all taxi services will have been contracted in advance.
For the independent tourist, a trip to the Tourism Authority in
Jerusalem will be advantageous. The office of tourism has good
literature about what is going on each week in Jordan, as well as
a large tourist map. The literature includes official maximum taxi
tariffs to all sites in the Holy Land.

Museums

Jordan has two excellent museums. The Palestine Museum in
Jerusalem is filled with archaeological artifacts and has a special
exhibit of some of the Dead Sea Scrolls. There is an entrance fee
for the regular museum and an additional fee for the exhibit.
Hours are 9 A.M. to 2 P.M. daily. The Jordan Museum at
Amman is free. While it is as yet operating in cramped quarters,
it is well filled with items of exceptional interest. It is open
from 7:30 A.M. to 1:30 P.M. Saturday through Thursday, closed
on Fridays.

Jerusalem has several small museums. In the Haram area there
is an exhibit of Islamic artifacts. Also in the Old City, on the
Via Dolorosa near St. Stephen's Gate, the Flagellation Museum

has a remarkable collection of pottery and coins, plus a special section devoted to the flora and fauna of Jordan. This museum is not open to the public except by appointment. Schmidt College has a museum similar to that of the Flagellation.

Repairs and Services

While the tourist will be able to buy almost any product he might need in Jerusalem, probably a word of caution might be said about using some of the services available in Jerusalem. Jordan is a young country and while it is catching up in "know how," it has not caught up all the way. The enthusiasm and assurance with which any Arab may tackle a job for you may foreshadow a mechanical disaster. Arabs are most accommodating and eager to please. They would consider it humiliating to admit that they did not know how to do a job well. They will do their very best, but their best might not be enough. If you have a car, a camera, a watch, or any appliance in need of repair, take care with whom you deal. Likewise, if you can manage it, do not take to the dry cleaners any material that will shrink if too much water is added to the cleaning fluid. If you need a doctor, call the United Nations.

Some Arabic Expressions

The gracious tourist will attempt to master a few words of Arabic. Language is not a problem in the Holy Land because all hotel employees and most merchants speak and understand English well. Nonetheless, here is a small Arabic vocabulary that might prove helpful. The words are spelled phonetically, the accented syllables printed in small capitals.

To greet the natives whom you encounter, you may use "*Sah bahl* CARE," "Good morning," or "*Mahr* HA *bah*," "Hello." "SHOOK *rahn*" is "Thank you." If you get to know one of the Jordanians well it would be permissible to follow a greeting with an inquiry about his health, say, "*Keef* HA *lek*," "How are you?" He would probably answer, "*Mab* SOOT," "I am well." It would be improper to ask a stranger about the state of his health.

The greeting most often extended to the tourist is "AH *lan wa* SAH *lan*." It means "welcome" and is often shortened to simply "AH *lan*." If the tourist wishes to make an inquiry, it would be polite to precede such a request with "*Min* FUD *lahk*," "If you please." There is a second term for "please" and it has a masculine and feminine form. This second term would be used by the tourist when he opened the door of a shop or an automobile door for another person whom he wished to precede him. He would say "FUD *ehl*" to a male, "FUD *ehlee*" to a female.

In a shop, the tourist might ask the shopkeeper, "*Kahm*," "How much?" If the tourist is not going to buy any merchandise despite pressure from the shopkeeper, he might tell the merchant "*Bah* DANE," "Later," indicating that he might return another time. "Boo *kra*" could also be used, indicating that he might return "Tomorrow." Perhaps the tourist would rather tell the merchant, "Boo *kra* MISH *mish*," a very strange idiom—literally "tomorrow apricots"—that means "Never."

On the highway, a tourist might find it helpful to tell the driver to slow down. "*Shway*" repeated frantically four times or so will do the trick. "Yes" is "I *wah*." "No" is "*Lah*." "No" is also commonly expressed all over the Middle East by giving the head a slight toss upward while clicking the tongue against the gum behind the two front teeth. If the tourist wished to say neither "Yes" nor "No" but wanted to suggest that he really didn't care one way or another, he would say, "*Mah* LESH," "It makes no difference to me."

If the tourist is wandering around the Holy Land on his own, he might be quite surprised when natives are puzzled when he asks them, "Where is Jerusalem?" Jerusalem is known to them as "*el* KOOTZ," the holy city. "WAYN *el* KOOTZ?" would bring a response. Similarly, the natives might be unfamiliar with the name "Jericho." "WAYN *er* REE *ha*?" would help a tourist find his way to Jericho. After the natives have given help, the tourist who wished to be polite would shake hands with them all and bid them "S<small>HOOK</small> *rahn*," "Thank you," and "K<small>HA</small> *trahk*," "Good-by." The natives would wave tourists on their way with a warm and heartfelt "M<small>AH</small> *sah* <small>LAM</small>*eh*." This last bit of Arabic furnishes the finest expression to close this Holy Land guide—"Go in peace."

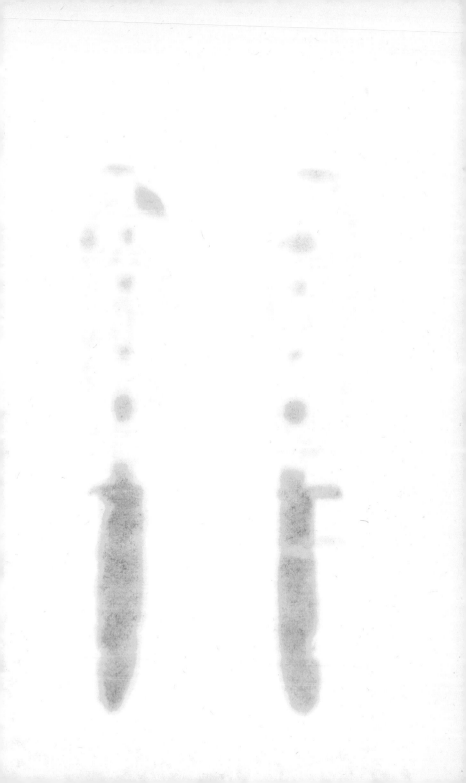

2/17/67

DATE DUE
